Her Own Business

Her Own Business

Success Secrets of Entrepreneurial Women

by Joanne Wilkens

McGraw-Hill Book Company

New York   St. Louis   San Francisco   Toronto   Hamburg   Mexico

The lyrics quoted from *My Fair Lady* in Chapter 3 are from the song ''A
Hymn to Him.'' Copyright © 1956 by Alan Jay Lerner and Frederick
Loewe. Chappell & Co., Inc., owner of publication and allied rights
throughout the world. International copyright secured. All rights reserved.
Used by permission.

ISBN 0-07-050854-2

1 2 3 4 5 6 7 8 9 DOC DOC 8 7

Library of Congress Cataloging-in-Publication Data

Wilkens, Joanne.
  Her own business.

  1. Women-owned business enterprises—United States—
Case studies.   2. Women in business—United States—Case
studies.   3. Success in business—United States—Case
studies.   I. Title.
HD2346.U5W548 1987   338.6′422′088042   86-27780
ISBN 0-07-050854-2

BOOK DESIGN BY M.R.P. DESIGN
EDITING SUPERVISOR: MARGERY LUHRS

For my
father, William B. Wilkens
and
mother, Laurose MacFadyen

Contents

PART 4   *Women Entrepreneurs at Work* / 95

PART 5   *Building Relationships That Work* / 153

Acknowledgments

When I first started writing this book, I knew I would spend many, many hours working alone. Yet, thanks to my family, friends, and colleagues, my job was never a lonely one. Support and assistance came in many forms and often from unexpected quarters. Norman Kurtin of Design Media in San Francisco generously offered me the use of word processing equipment just when I began the first complete draft of the book. His thoughtful gift changed my whole approach to writing and made me wonder how I ever committed a word to paper before a computer graced my desk.

A number of people read various chapters and drafts as this book passed from one version to another in search of its final form. My thanks to Wendy Wilkens, Surja Jessup, Karen Joffee, Paul Hennessey, Karen Day, and Ann Rankin for their comments and criticism. Back in 1981, when I first started my research, I had the good fortune to meet three fellow writers at the Berkeley Women's Center. We began meeting every other week to discuss each other's work and have continued these sessions for over five years. For their honesty, love, and endless patience as we worked through each draft, I thank Linda Blachman, Susan Rothbaum, and Ellen Ullman. Wanda Price provided magnificent assistance as she transcribed many hours of interviews.

I am also grateful to Michael Larsen, my agent, who believed in this project from the moment he first heard about it. He has supported my work from its first sketchy form through the final draft. My editor at McGraw-Hill, Leslie Meredith, read each of four drafts with great care and offered many helpful comments. I thank her for asking me the right questions and then giving me the time to answer them to our mutual satisfaction.

Several people were key resources, providing me with papers and other research material. I thank Professor Arnold Cooper of Purdue University, Professor Anne Peterson of The Pennsylvania State University, and Lynn Rosener for sending me unpublished papers. My special thanks to Lynn for several helpful conversations. Juanita Weaver, Assistant Director for Public Affairs at the Small Business Administration sent me several key publications. She was always available to answer my questions and help expedite the mail. I am also grateful to Joyce Ford of the University of California, Berkeley, Doe Library for granting me access to the library's vast stack collection. She and her fellow librarians were of invaluable assistance.

During my travels, three families offered me kind hospitality. My thanks to Clark and Peggie Robinson, John and Debbie Wilkens, and John and Mary Vaccaro for providing me with a room, fine food, and cheerful company when I was on the road. I am especially grateful to the many women's networks and professional groups who helped me find my study participants and to the new entrepreneurs themselves. Without their willingness to share their lives, I could not have even started this work.

My final thanks are reserved for my wonderful family. I can never fully express my gratitude to my father, William Wilkens, who himself is a successful entrepreneur, and to my mother, Laurose MacFadyen, a writer, teacher, and independent woman. They have never wavered in their support of my work nor in their belief in me. My sons, Nick and Dave, soon came to accept "the book" as they would a new family member, respecting its corner in our dining room where it was ever-present over the past five years. And Jim Vaccaro cheered me on with love and patience until I crossed over the finish line.

Introduction

The new woman entrepreneur: Who is she? What is her life like? Why did she choose independent enterprise, and what makes her successful? These are just a few of the questions I sought to answer six years ago when I first considered writing this book. At that time, I wanted to know more about women and entrepreneurship, so I set out for local libraries and bookstores in search of information. To my surprise, I found practically nothing. Even the nearby University of California yielded disappointing results. There were shelves of books and lists of scholarly papers on the development and personality of the entrepreneur, entrepreneurial psychology, the stages of business growth, and the problems and rewards of small business ownership. But this body of literature was written almost exclusively about men, from a male point of view. Where, I wondered, was comparable information about women?

At local bookstores, I fared little better, finding only *The Entrepreneurial Woman* by Sandra Winston. Although interesting, Winston's book left many of my questions unanswered, and no other source had the exact information that I needed. The only way to answer my questions was to write about the woman entrepreneur myself.

WOMAN AND ENTREPRENEURSHIP: A NEW PHENOMENON

As my research progressed, I discovered that women entrepreneurs are a fast-growing phenomenon throughout the United States. There are female-owned businesses in every area of the country, and Ohio, Illinois, California, Hawaii, and the industrial states of the Northeast boast the greatest numbers.[1]

To my surprise, I learned that between 1975 and 1985, the number of self-employed women in the United States increased by 76 percent.[2] By 1982, women constituted 31.8 percent of all self-employed people in this country, and that trend continues today.[3] Women are leaving secure jobs for the risk of independent enterprise five times faster than are their male counterparts.[4] These facts made me even more eager to seek out the woman entrepreneur to find out about her life.

BREAKING BARRIERS: THE ROAD TO ENTREPRENEURSHIP

This book provides what I was unable to obtain in any library or bookstore five years ago: the exciting life story of the woman business owner. You will learn about the problems she has faced and the barriers she has overcome to create the national phenomenon she presently leads. You will follow this woman through her academic and workplace careers until the moment she chooses business ownership. You will discover what she thinks about family and business, money and credit, networks and mentors, risk and success, and the failure of today's business community to use her strengths and meet her needs. And you will discover the barriers that every woman must break before she can succeed on her own.

On a practical level you will find advice and inspiration to help you succeed should you be, or hope to become, an entrepreneur. Each woman interviewed had to face certain realities as she decided to strike out on her own. Finding the money, taking the risk, leaving a secure job, hiring her first employee, and getting her first clients or customers were all problems that she had to handle. You will see what enabled her to succeed as she encountered these tasks one by one.

Once her business is established, the entrepreneurial woman then must guide its growth and development. In doing so she must consider other important points, such as when and how much to expand, what leadership style to pursue, how much structure to impose on her youthful enterprise, what personnel practices to follow, and why she may or may not be making the money that she wants. Following the stories of the women interviewed will show you the strategies they developed to handle these problems successfully.

In addition, although men and women alike must face these business dilemmas, the female entrepreneur faces other obstacles unique to her sex. These obstacles include economic, legal, and sexual harassment; harmful stereotypes that suggest that women "do not have a head for business" cannot understand economics and finance, and are too "soft" to succeed in the rough world of double-dealing; the opposing pulls of family life and business success;

the view of women as dabblers who are not serious about their work and therefore lack credibility; and the conflict between our cultural definition of femininity and the characteristics necessary to make money. These additional problems mean that women face complications in every step of the entrepreneurial process.

WHO ARE THE NEW ENTREPRENEURS?

Her Own Business is based on information collected from 117 women business owners around the United States. (For a detailed description of the sample and methodology, see Appendix A.) All the women were volunteers who wanted to participate in the study. Some responded to a letter that I sent to their local business and professional networks; others replied to a personal inquiry that described the project and sought their participation. After indicating her interest, each woman filled out and returned a 4-page questionnaire. Seventy women, representing different types of businesses and varied geographical locations, were contacted for in-depth personal interviews.

All these interviewees were proud and eager to share the results of their hard work and effort. I visited elegant showrooms, bustling warehouses; retail stores which reflected the personality of their particular owner; small, cramped offices which ran large, profitable construction or wholesale businesses; large suites of offices with sweeping views of Lake Michigan or Manhattan; three impressive and carefully designed educational centers; manufacturing locations where a woman's creative concept was translated into reality; and a myriad of offices— offices in suburban professional complexes, in small back-room locations, in restored historical buildings, and along quiet country roads. No matter where it was located, each business was the center of the daily entrepreneurial activity orchestrated and managed by its talented, independent owner.

After completing my analysis of the interviews and initial questionnaires, I sent each interviewee a follow-up questionnaire to determine how her life had changed since our first meeting. This final mailing took place three years after the initial interviews. I was gratified to learn that only three women, or a little more than 4 percent, had closed the doors to their businesses. The other sixty-seven enterprises were still in operation, and despite the recession of the early 1980s, most had grown larger and had become more successful.

From the very beginning, I decided not to reveal the identities of the women interviewed, and each participant was assured that all information was confidential. Although cases presented in the book are based on real information, they are not ''real'' women. Individual remarks and comments are quoted much as the women said them, but all names and details have been changed to protect the identity of the interviewees. Similarities in names or other characteristics between any subjects and their businesses in this book and other persons and businesses is purely coincidental.

PROFILES IN ENTREPRENEURSHIP

These pages will show you a profile of the woman entrepreneur in the United States today. I offer this portrait to assist you should you decide to undertake a journey similar to hers, but keep in mind that the experiences presented here are those of leaders in a new phenomenon. These experiences are not necessarily requisite for success in business ownership, rather they indicate what steps were followed by a group of pioneers.

Her Own Business is divided into five parts. Each part should help you understand a different aspect of the entrepreneurial woman, her business, and her life. Part 1 addresses three related topics: (1) how women choose, start up, and develop a particular business enterprise; (2) how the entrepreneurial personality affects a woman's ability to succeed; and (3) what particular strengths women bring to the entrepreneurial world. Sharing the experiences of the interviewees will give you new insight into what it takes to succeed on your own.

Part 2 takes you back to the childhood and adolescence of the new entrepreneurs. As you read their family histories, you will discover what conditions foster autonomy in women and what forces undermine the development of confidence and independence. The stories of these inspiring women will encourage you to identify and overcome the negative experiences in your own life that have kept you from reaching your goals. This part concludes with an analysis of the typical career patterns of the interviewees. This analysis will assist you in examining your work experience to assess whether you are ready to strike out on your own.

Part 3 formalizes the information presented earlier into a series of practical exercises and worksheets that will guide you through a process of self-analysis. You will assess your strengths and weaknesses, analyze your business ideas and plans, focus your ideas, and master the steps to starting and developing an independent enterprise. You will also examine your personal motivation and goals and will identify any ambivalence you have regarding financial success.

Part 4 moves into the everyday world of business ownership. You will learn about the joys and rewards, the problems and frustrations of running an independent enterprise—from a woman's point of view. Topics covered here include learning to make a profit, dealing with banks and bankers solving the most common business problems, and handling sexual harassment. In addition to inspiring stories to encourage you, these chapters also include worksheets to help you solve your day-to-day business problems.

Part 5 addresses the personal life of the woman entrepreneur. Balancing a business, a marriage, and perhaps children is not easy, and many entrepreneurs experienced painful problems in the attempt. Yet their stories offer hope that meaningful solutions to these problems can be found.

As a woman and potential business owner, you may share much in common with the new entrepreneurs. Certainly the barriers that you face are similar. I hope that as you begin your journey to independent enterprise you will find the experiences shared on these pages useful. The new entrepreneurs offer hope that all women can break both cultural and personal barriers to achieve the psychological and financial independence necessary to stand on their own.

PART 1

Becoming an Entrepreneur

CHAPTER 1

The Moment of Decision

Do you want to start a business? Or do you already have one? In either case, you are among a fast-growing group of women who are changing the face of U.S. enterprise. Perhaps you are an independent professional—a photographer, lawyer, accountant, or masseuse eager to succeed in your own practice. Maybe you have long worked for someone else as a bookkeeper, sales rep, marketing specialist, or office manager and are now ready to make your years of experience work for you. Or possibly you are nurturing an idea for a new and unique product or service that you are certain will make you money.

Now you ask yourself, "What does managing a business involve? How do other women find the strength to start up or keep going when obstacles stand in the way?" This chapter introduces some women who, with energy and determination, turned their ideas into money-making ventures.

LIZ G. MATERNITY FASHIONS— A MANUFACTURING CONCERN

Training for Entrepreneurship

When she was twenty-five and pregnant with her first child, Liz Gausted got out her sewing machine and started on a familiar path—designing and making some stylish clothes appropriate for her new stage in life. For Gausted, this was nothing special. "I was raised in downstate Illinois where my father was a farmer," she began, "and sewing was always part of my life. When I got bored, I made clothes for my Barbie doll. Then one day my best friend and I pooled our allowances, bought a lot of fabric, and made these cute cut-off jeans and other stuff for Barbie and sold them to our friends.''

Gausted credits her father with starting her down the road to business ownership: "When I was in high school, Dad capitalized on my knack for sewing. He told me, 'If you buy your clothes ready-made, I'll put you on a budget. But if you make them, you can spend as much as you want on materials.' I gladly took his offer, and soon I was deep into textiles, design, and pattern making. I always thought I was going to be a teacher and in fact did teach for several years, but my Dad really trained me for entrepreneurship even though I didn't know it at the time."

Like her two brothers, Gausted attended the University of Illinois in Urbana, where she majored in both education and design. "I spent most of my time designing and making clothes," she continued, "and my wardrobe really expanded. I lived in a sorority, and my sorority sisters used to come up to me and say, 'This is great. Can I borrow it?' After getting things back with cigarette holes or wine stains, I stopped lending and started selling. Some things I hardly ever wore and gladly sold them. I had a nice turnover in inventory right in my own closet but still never thought of having my own business."

Finding the Right Opportunity

After college, Gausted married and moved to Chicago, where she got a job teaching home economics in a large urban high school. "I enjoyed my work," she recalled, "and even started an after-school sewing club to encourage kids who had a special interest in design. When I got pregnant, the students used to analyze and criticize my maternity designs. Then I started getting compliments about my clothes from women I didn't even know.

"When two of my friends got pregnant, they asked if I would make clothes for them. One is an attorney and the other a personnel manager, and they couldn't find things in the stores with the same professional look that my clothes had. When I started looking carefully at what was available in the maternity shops, I realized that no one was catering to the pregnant professional woman and her needs. After my daughter was born, I decided that I would give it a try."

Liz Gausted saw a unique opportunity to turn her talents into a money-making venture. Making clothes for "Barbie" and for her sorority sisters had brought in spending money, but making maternity outfits for the professional woman could bring in a handsome income. The market was there, and she gambled on her ability to capture it. Like many women, Gausted was pulled into business ownership by a ready-made clientele.

Putting an Idea into Action

"There was only one problem," here Liz Gausted smiled, "I knew a lot about textiles and design but nothing about business! That was good in one way because I didn't have any old habits to break, but I had a lot to learn. When things went wrong, I would say, 'OK, that didn't work, so I won't try it again.' In spite of my mistakes, I feel very good about one thing: There are many great ideas in this world, but so few of them get executed. Too many people are afraid. I took my idea and made it into a reality, and that makes me special.''

When Gausted started her business, she did everything herself. By the end of her first year, she was exhausted. Although she farmed out most of the sewing to several helpers, that provided only temporary relief. "I knew I couldn't continue in the same way," Gausted remembered, "so I decided to sit back and look at the big picture. Before hiring anybody else, I first had to decide what my goals were. Did I want to design and sew clothes, or did I want to run a business? These were tough questions to answer, and it took me a while to decide.''

After Innovation, Organization

Liz Gausted had little trouble with one entrepreneurial function: innovation. Creating unusual designs and coming up with new ideas to make the business grow were easy for her. However, she had more problems with organizing her creative enterprise into an ongoing concern. To help herself do this, Gausted followed an unusual process. First, she made a list of everything that she did in the business. This included not only design work but also a myriad of other tasks that she hardly was aware of doing. After finishing her list, Gausted grouped similar activities together and found her business could easily be organized around specific activities: design, production, marketing and sales, personnel, finance, and overall coordination.

Gausted was then able to decide which jobs she wanted to do herself, which she wanted to delegate to others, and where new staff people could best be used. Consequently, instead of hiring someone simply to take over a job she was too busy to do, she put new people into an area where their skills were needed. The entire exercise helped Gausted understand her business better. She learned that Liz G. Maternity Fashions had a natural structure and that she could fit into that structure in any way that suited her own needs: "At that point," Gausted said, "I decided that I could make a lot of money with this as a business, and that helped me determine my role. I knew I wanted to keep creative control over the design concepts, but I could delegate the rest of the work to other people. I also wanted to stay involved with marketing. As far as the day-to-day operations are concerned, I now have a production manager to help me. I also have a financial person who takes care of the books and payroll. My focus is on guiding the business and making it grow as large as it can.''

Advice from an Expert

Last year Liz G. Maternity Fashions generated just over $5 million in sales, and Liz Gausted is justifiably proud of her success. When asked what it takes to succeed, she immediately replied, "Persistence, determination. If you really believe in your idea, don't give up. You'll make your share of mistakes, but that doesn't mean you've failed. Just step back, look at the problem, and then try a new approach. Stay flexible and keep an eye on your goals. Do your homework. And remember, you probably have more going for yourself than you think.''

What else about the entrepreneurial venture can we learn from Liz Gausted? At the outset, she was clear about what her business was. She had one product, maternity clothes, and her market was narrow and well-defined. ''You can't be all things to all people,'' she advised. ''Decide who you are and what makes you special. Focus is the key. If you define your market carefully, developing a marketing plan will be much easier. Remember, if you don't know where you're going, any road can take you there, and you won't know when you've arrived.''

Gausted believes that focus is also important when a business owner wants to expand her firm. Although she once considered opening retail outlets for her products, she eventually abandoned the idea. ''I am a manufacturing concern,'' she stated, ''and operating a retail chain would really be a different business. I decided to expand my product line to meet the needs of my present customers —sportswear, exercise clothes, loungewear. That made more sense than trying to get into a whole new type of operation. Having more things to manage doesn't necessarily mean that I'll make more money, and profit is always my bottom line.''

For Liz Gausted, the future holds endless possibilities. She wants to develop her new exercise and fitness line more fully, and she knows that she has barely tapped the national market. ''This business could get as big as I want it to,'' she smiled. ''And as far as I'm concerned, the sky's the limit.''

RITA VACARO— THE INDEPENDENT PROFESSIONAL

Struggle for Independence

To Rita Vacaro, the road to entrepreneurship was not always so clear as that taken by Liz Gausted. Both women were encouraged to be teachers during their youth, but otherwise their lives were very different. Vacaro grew up in Hartford, Connecticut, the only daughter of a widowed insurance clerk. ''I was raised to teach kindergarten,'' she began. ''My mother told me that was a good thing for a girl because I could have a family and then come back to it. I was the oldest child and something of a rebel. Teaching just didn't appeal to me, and I struggled a lot with my mother over issues of independence. I wanted to do my own thing, but she was overprotective.''

Unlike Liz Gausted, Vacaro had no outstanding interests in high school. She did, however, know that she wanted a job. Money meant independence, and that was more important to Vacaro than anything else. "My mother wanted me to finish high school," she continued, "before I started work, but I told her, 'Forget it!' High school was boring, and I wanted something better to keep me busy. When I went to college, things didn't improve. I lived in a dorm, which I hated, and found my schoolwork tedious. After dropping in and out several times and trying several majors, I started taking biology and loved it. Soon after, I met some people from the veterinary school and decided that this was the field for me."

The following semester found Vacaro enrolled in zoology, chemistry, and calculus. By the end of the year, she had been accepted into the veterinarian program at her university. "I couldn't believe how exciting the work was," she noted. "From the moment I walked in the door, it was like coming home."

Making Your Experience Count

Rita Vacaro finished her veterinary training ten years ago. Today, she is almost forty and has had her own clinic for two years. Unlike Liz Gausted, Vacaro worked with someone else for a long period before striking out on her own. "In school, I was well trained in diagnosis and treatment," she noted, "but they didn't teach me anything about bookkeeping, billing systems, setting up an office, or personnel management. Working as a junior associate was a wonderful experience. I not only developed professionally but got a look at the business problems firsthand. Helping my associate with the office was very good for my confidence. I quickly learned what can happen if you're not careful with how you set your business up. When I opened my own clinic, I was able to avoid quite a bit of headache."

What pushed Rita Vacaro to strike out on her own? "That same need for independence I always had," she said and smiled. "I wanted more control over everything. I guess I'm somewhat of a loudmouth and want things done my way. In my own office, I insist on a nurturing atmosphere. People get very involved with their animals, and it is important to be kind and supportive. And the animals respond better when they are treated with warmth and care. One day I decided I'd had enough of working for someone else. It was time for me to stand alone."

Understanding the Entrepreneurial Process

On the surface, Liz G. Maternity Fashions and Vacaro Pet Hospital are totally different businesses. One is a growing manufacturing concern, the other a small veterinarian service. However, in terms of the entrepreneurial process, Rita Vacaro and Liz Gausted followed a similar course. Once she decided to strike out on her own, each woman had to raise the necessary money. Gausted used some personal savings and put as much of her earnings as she could back into the business. Eventually, she obtained loans based on the size of her accounts receivable. Vacaro also used savings and borrowed from her family, carefully repaying the loan during her first year of operation.

Raising capital is only the first step in the entrepreneurial process. After finding the funds, both Vacaro and Gausted had to decide on the best location, order equipment and supplies, establish a billing and bookkeeping system, develop a marketing plan, and hire the necessary personnel. And, perhaps most important, each woman had to decide on her ultimate business goal.

Vacaro, no less than Gausted, had to determine where she would concentrate her focus: "When I opened my office," she recalled, "I did everything with the help of a receptionist and part-time technician. Soon I realized this wasn't a wise use of my time. When I could afford them, I got an office manager, a bookkeeper, and a full-time person to help with routine shots and lab work. Last year, another vet joined me as an associate, and about six months ago, I opened a pet shop in a building adjacent to this one. That venture has been really successful. Now I have the opportunity to hire a dog groomer and to offer obedience classes."

Vacaro constantly sees new possibilities for growth and expansion. "There are so many exciting things going on in my field," she stated, "that I'm constantly finding something interesting to work on. There is also some space behind the pet shop where I could start a whole animal training center, but I'm not sure that's what I want to do. It would mean a lot of marketing and coordinating and less time actually spent on practicing veterinary medicine. I already have enough managing to do, so at least for now I want to focus on doing diagnosis and treatment. What I do makes an immediate difference for both the animals and the people I see, and that is what's important to me."

Advantages of the Entrepreneurial Life

When asked what advantages entrepreneurship offered, Rita Vacaro laughed and quickly replied: "Independence. This clinic is something I've created, that exists apart from me, and I see that as something to be proud of. I do work that I love with people that I care about, and I don't have to answer to anybody. Of course the risk is all mine, but so is the reward. I may get tired, and sometimes I am discouraged, but I never feel bored. There are always new problems to solve or new possibilities to explore. As I meet each challenge, my confidence grows. I believe I can do anything I want with my life, and that's really exciting."

Vacaro advises other women to get as much experience as possible before starting a business. "Learn all you can about what running a business involves," she noted. "There are certain functions common to any enterprise, so skills you master in one setting can easily be transferred to another. If your business idea doesn't relate to anything you've ever done, try working for someone in a similar field. That will give you some sense of what's involved or of whether you even like the business. And most of all, remember that you have what it takes. Look at your strengths and capitalize on them. They are there just waiting to be used.''

VAN PELT ROOFING—TAKING OVER THE FAMILY BUSINESS

Entrepreneurship Through Life Crisis

At fifty-nine, Florence Van Pelt has been running Van Pelt Roofing Company for nearly twenty years. Unlike Rita Vacaro and Liz Gausted, Flo's business is in a strictly male domain. Hard hats, competitive bidding, structural engineering problems, and all-male crews are part of her daily routine. She has long been familiar with this world, which she entered as boss through an unexpected life crisis. When she was forty, Van Pelt's husband died in an automobile accident, and the business suddenly belonged to her.

"Necessity pushes you across life's bridges," said Van Pelt, who laughed as she remembered those terrifying days twenty years ago when all the responsibility fell on her shoulders. "We were in the middle of three major projects, and the bonding company pushed me hard to get those jobs done. I had no choice. But the real kicker came a year later when the work was finished. The head of the bonding company called me in, looked me in the eye, and said, 'Flo, as far as I'm concerned, when Norm died, Van Pelt Roofing died, and I wouldn't bond you for anything.' Of course without bonding, my company couldn't continue.''

With characteristic determination, Van Pelt fought back. Her husband had left her and their four children well provided for, but family pride was involved as well as family finances. "My husband's father started this business," Van Pelt continued, "and we had a really good reputation all around Milwaukee. I hated to see the business go under for no reason other than simple discrimination. And I knew I would lose my shirt if I let them get away with this, so I decided to fight back. I called everyone I knew—suppliers, other contractors, our insurance agent, guys from Rotary who were Norm's friends, my lawyer—and really put the pressure on the bonding people. When other contractors threatened to go elsewhere, they relented.''

For Florence Van Pelt, persistence has long been a part of her character. During her teenage years, she worked hard to save enough money to put herself through secretarial school. Her father, an independent plumber, was hard hit by the Depression, but the family survived thanks to her mother, who worked cleaning office buildings in downtown Milwaukee. "I am a very positive person

and have faith that things will work out. I am also very, very persistent,'' she
noted. ''My mother was the same way. If you keep trying and don't give up,
you can reach your goals and make your business succeed.''

New Roles, New Goals

Taking over Van Pelt Roofing meant a big change in roles for Florence Van
Pelt. ''I always worked for my husband,'' she stated, ''but I was really his
assistant. I did all the typing, bookkeeping, phone calls, and payroll and quarterly
taxes. When Norm got too busy, I started going over all the bids and learned
how to bid on a job. I guess I knew a lot about the way the business was run,
but I never really made any financial and business decisions. Norm would consult
with me, and then he'd make the final choice.

''Now I make all the business decisions alone and have been doing so for
almost twenty years. It was hard at first for people to accept me as the boss.
But I sat everybody down and told them, 'I'm all you've got, and we all have
the same goal—to keep this business going as best as we can.' Even the kids
were supportive. My oldest had already started college, and she helped me in
the office part time. I brought my two teenage sons in, and they both became
apprentices. My youngest still works in the business with me.''

Over the years, Van Pelt proved to be a strong leader and adeptly led the
company through two expansion cycles. ''I work on marketing the business and
keeping our profile high. My philosophy is bid to win and operate to make
money. Bob, the project manager, oversees all the roofing crews, and each job
has a superintendent on site. My role is to set financial goals and keep an eye
on the growth and development of the company. We have a good management
team here, and that helps keep the smaller problems away from me.''

Although nearly sixty, Flo Van Pelt doesn't plan to retire just yet. Running
Van Pelt Roofing is a challenge that keeps her young. Her advice to the aspiring
entrepreneur? ''Learn to develop your employees and get people involved with
your company goals. That will make you a better leader. And keep up on trends
that affect your industry. If something occurs that will affect your business,
you'd better know about it. Keep an eye on demographics, too. Your client base
may be growing or shrinking or demanding a different kind of product. These
things may not seem important to you now, but they will affect the success of
your business later.''

TAMARA ARNOLD— PUSHED INTO ENTREPRENEURSHIP

Out of a Job, into a Business

Tamara Arnold was pushed through the door of her own business by the most
traumatic event of her life. Raised in the ''typical American family,'' Arnold
described her childhood as happy and uneventful. She was a good daughter who

achieved well in school, held various part-time jobs, attended a state college, and married right after graduation. Her father was a middle manager with a *Fortune*-500 company based in Los Angeles, where she was raised. Little in Arnold's background suggested a career in independent enterprise.

When asked why she decided to become an entrepreneur, Tamara Arnold answered with a tinge of anger still in her voice: "You know, my parents taught me that if you worked hard and did everything right, life would treat you well. I found out that's wrong! It was such a blow to have lived by that belief all my life and suddenly have the rug pulled out from under me, but that's what happened on my last job."

Arnold described herself as a loyal and energetic person, who was dedicated to her work. Originally a high school teacher, she eventually moved into the training department of a major corporation, where she remained for thirteen years. "I was gradually given bigger and bigger projects to manage," she continued, "and three years ago was made assistant to the director. Then last year he retired, and I was appointed to his position on a temporary basis. I was ecstatic. Before they could hire me permanently, I knew they would advertise the job, and I applied along with everyone else. At the time, I thought it was just a formality. Then they hired a young man who was still wet behind the ears and asked me to train him. I was furious!"

In effect, Tamara Arnold had been demoted, and she faced a painful choice. "I had had a ton of responsibility," she declared emphatically, "and had carried it all really well. Then they wanted me to go back to being a trainer and someone's assistant. But first they expected me to show this guy everything I knew. He would get the high salary and all the prestige, and I would get nothing but my old job back. I went through a real trauma over this, but I was determined not to let them get me down. Instead I decided to beat them at their own game, and started a training business of my own. That's how Management Training Systems was born, and in the end it was the best thing that could have happened to me."

For Tamara Arnold, entrepreneurship offered a positive route out of a negative situation: "You know," she continued, "I thought, if I could do it for them, I could do it for myself. I knew I wouldn't work any harder than I already was, and the rewards would be much greater. After the initial shock, I decided it was time to stop complaining and start acting. It's important for women to remember that we don't have to be anybody's victim if we don't want to be. We can take charge of our own lives and and don't need to put up with the kind of treatment I got."

Two's Company: Entrepreneurial Partnership

When the incident in the training department occurred, Arnold coincidentally reestablished contact with an old friend, and the two decided to form a partnership. "I belong to the American Society for Training and Development," she explained, "where I met Darlene about eight years ago. We worked on several ASTD projects together, and I thought we had very complementary skills. Darlene left the Los Angeles area, where I was based, and moved to San Francisco for a while, but she returned just about the time that I decided to quit my job. One day I called her and told her what had happened, and she asked me if I wanted a partner. I decided that working with her would give me a boost, and I've never regretted that choice.''

What makes a successful partnership work? Arnold had some specific ideas about that. ''We have totally different talents,'' she declared, ''and totally different personalities. Together we equal a really terrific person. We both have tremendous respect for one another's work and accept the differences in our style. Each one of us lets the other alone to do her job. We also have similar goals and ideas about what we want. And we've never had a disagreement that's lasted more than two days. Eventually we talk everything out and resolve our differences. Learning to work with Darlene has helped me in my personal relationships as well. I've become more open about discussing problems. My husband says we have a remarkable synergy that we shouldn't take for granted.''

Having a partner has some business advantages as well. ''We can have the input of two people on a given problem,'' Arnold continued, ''and that is especially helpful with difficult clients. We've also developed a twosome strategy which works really well. When we have a critical meeting, both of us will attend but with different goals in mind. Sometimes Darlene will be the 'tough guy,' and I'll be the 'softie.' If clients get mad at her, they can turn to me for a sympathetic smile. Of course we always decide on our bottom line before going in there, and we both know what result we want. But our strategy is very helpful for deflecting bad feelings. People may get angry with her, but they keep good feelings about the company.''

BECOMING AN ENTREPRENEUR

The Moment of Decision

Liz Gausted, Rita Vacaro, and Tamara Arnold gladly left the security of a regular job for the risks and responsibilities of independent enterprise. Florence Van Pelt chose to keep the family business after her husband died. Each of these woman arrived at the moment of decision in her own way. There is no ''right'' time to start a business, no formula that will enable the propsective business owner to know if this is indeed her moment.

However, the new entrepreneurs' stories show that certain negative and positive factors may push or pull a woman into an independent venture. Missed promotions that went to outsiders or male colleagues, low pay and lack of advancement, conflict with company policy or bosses, and simple boredom and lack of creative challenge were the most frequently mentioned negative reasons for change. Often, a woman described more than one of these as contributing to her decision.

Those interviewees who experienced a positive pull were usually at some critical life juncture. Change in marital status, moving to a new city, a husband's career change, and readiness to resume work after children were born or entered school were some of the most common transition points. A number of women were approached by a partner with an intriguing business plan. Others were urged by clients to develop a product or service on their own, and this natural market was too great to ignore. Still others were given the chance to purchase the business for which they worked.

When these incidents occurred, the interviewees realized that the time was right for them to strike out on their own. They experienced some sense of awakening, a feeling of "Why not?" and a belief that they had nothing to lose. At that point, their previous experiences came together and pointed in one direction: Business ownership was the logical next step in their lives.

No matter what the precipitating factor, the interviewees drew on all their professional and personal resources to become entrepreneurs. Regardless of their background, all the women believed that business enterprise was a natural out-growth of their particular set of circumstances. They saw education, travel, jobs, and even personal setbacks as contributing to their moment of decision. This belief was best expressed by Bonnie Baker, owner of a large advertising agency, when she made the following comment: "In order to start this business, I've had to draw on every experience I've ever had. I've done everything that's legal and worked for some companies that don't even exist anymore. And whatever it was, I've used something from that experience."

At the moment of decision, the women interviewed also chose to take active responsibility for their lives. If they were dissatisfied with their situation, they stopped complaining and began formulating a new direction. If they were wandering or in a time of transition, they sought opportunities that would help set them on course. Like Tamara Arnold, they decided to stop waiting and start acting; at that point, they realized that they didn't have to depend on anyone to make their lives happen. They were more than capable of setting their own course.

Minding Your Own Business

Once the decision was made, all the interviewees then faced a single problem: learning how to manage their new business enterprise. At some point during the first phase of entrepreneurship, each woman had to decide on her focus. Narrowing her business concept and pinpointing her market were two of the most important steps she had to make. She then had to determine her goals and develop an action plan to reach them.

As an actual or potential entrepreneur, you, too, must take these same steps.

Chapter 7 includes a series of self-assessment exercises designed to help you focus your ideas and analyze your business plans. Upon completing the self-assessment process, you will understand more clearly what business you are in, who your market is, how you can reach that market, and what people you will need to assist you.

Chapter 10 observes the new entrepreneurs at work and shows how they handled some of the most common business problems. Through their stories, you will learn about the four entrepreneurial functions and how to avoid the pitfalls that trap the aspiring entrepreneur. Chapter 10 also offers valuable worksheets to help you analyze your own business situation. But now let us turn to the key ingredient that pushes a woman to strike out on her own: the entrepreneurial personality.

CHAPTER 2

The Entrepreneurial Personality

What kind of woman decides to become an entrepreneur? What characteristics typify her personality, and what motivates her to succeed? According to the myths surrounding this ever-popular figure, the entrepreneur is an independent soul, a creative risk taker who, through her own force of will, turns an idea into a money-making venture. The true entrepreneur finds starting new ventures almost irresistible and thrives on bringing her ideas to life. However, creativity, imagination, and a penchant for action compose only one side of her character; she may be autocratic, rigid, and controlling as well. The typical entrepreneur often views "her way" as the only way to get something done. Understanding the entrepreneurial personality involves separating the myth from the reality and determining what motivates an individual business owner to succeed.

UNDERSTANDING YOUR NEED FOR ACHIEVEMENT

Psychologist David McClelland believes that entrepreneurs have a high need for achievement and that fulfilling this need impels them toward independent enterprise. A professor at Harvard University for the past twenty-five years, McClelland has extensively studied the behavior of high achievers. As a result of his work, he developed a profile of the achievement-oriented person and identified certain needs that such a person has to fulfill. Included in McClelland's profile are the following five behavior patterns:

1. Achievement-oriented people like working on their own. They seek out situations in which they are able to take personal responsibility for solving problems.

2. Achievement-oriented people dislike petty, routine work. They avoid situations that demand repeating the same task over and over. Once they solve a problem they are off to the next one.

3. Achievement-oriented people seek experts over friends as working partners. When they have problems or need assistance, they don't hesitate to call someone with the expertise they lack.

4. Achievement-oriented people want some concrete measure of how well they are doing. Such people work hard to earn a lot of money not simply because they want money but because financial reward is a measure of their achievement and success.

5. Achievement-oriented people set moderate goals and take calculated risks. By setting goals which they can meet, they maximize their feeling of achievement. By contrast, people who set unrealistic goals are always striving or always failing and rarely reach the point of actual achievement.

McClelland concludes that people who have some of or all these traits will be most successful in an entrepreneurial setting. Running a business allows them to use their talents and fulfill their personality needs far better than other work situations.[1]

THE CREATIVE ACHIEVER

At forty-one, Sandra Miles is the president of a successful marketing firm. She has been her own boss for the past three years. Vivacious and outspoken, Miles thrives on the responsibility and creativity that running a business demands. Her previous two jobs, each in the marketing department of a major corporation, did not bring her nearly the same satisfaction. "I had more than fifteen years' experience before I started my own business," Miles recalled in the large suite of offices that her twenty-two person firm now occupies, "and not one of them was as exciting as my first year here.

"In this business, there is always something new for me to do. I am an idea person and constantly see new ways I can make money. But the best part is taking my ideas and turning them into reality. This business offers me a lot of opportunity to do that. At the beginning, setting up the day to day operations was a challenge. Then, once I got everything going, I hired someone else to manage the details so I could move on to something else. I have the feeling that after my business gets really big and organized it won't be so exciting. But then I will be free to sell it or to branch out into something different."

Making lots of money also appeals to Sandra Miles. Although she was reasonably well paid in her previous job, she never felt that her efforts were properly rewarded. "I would like to be a millionaire by the time I'm forty-five," she laughed, "and that was never a possibility for me before. My salary and promotions always depended on what someone else thought of my work, whereas now my income depends on how clever I am to think through my problems alone."

As an independent business owner, Miles has full responsibility for her life. Of all the benefits that entrepreneurship offered, it was this one that excited her the most. "When I started, I was very ready to go it alone," she noted with enthusiasism. "I no longer wanted to be somebody's assistant and part of a bureaucratic team. I don't mind if the buck stops here. I think it's fun. Before, I always had a boss checking on me, a bunch of regulations telling me what to do, a legal department to back me up, and a supervisor to edit me. Now I don't have anybody, and I love it!

"If I have a problem, I can always call a colleague," she continued. "I also developed an informal board of advisors—my banker, attorney, and accountant; a woman who has a similar business; and a former professor I had in business school who has been like a mentor to me. But otherwise, I'm in control of what I'm doing. It's wonderful to wake up in the morning and know that my success depends entirely on me. I love the feeling of independence and achievement that this brings."

According to McClelland's profile, Miles has a high need for achievement, and running a business allows her to fulfill that need. It offers her the opportunity to develop new ideas and undertake new projects, to increase her income, to work with people of her choosing, and to control the decisions that affect her work. Business ownership also requires that she take full responsibility for her life.

SUCCESS: A PERSONAL DEFINITION

Denise Rosenthal is almost the same age as Sandra Miles. She, too, had nearly fifteen years' experience when she started her business. However, the similarity between the two women seems to end there. Miles's vivacious manner and fast-growing marketing company stand in sharp contrast to Rosenthal's quiet voice and tiny two-person industrial design firm. In business six years already, Rosenthal is quite happy with the size and prospects of her small but well-respected company.

"I'm not a very flamboyant person," Rosenthal noted at the beginning of our interview. "In fact I don't fit most people's idea of the entrepreneurial type. Two years ago, I reached a point where I had to decide whether I was going to expand. Was I going to hire more people, train them to do what I do, and develop a big business? The opportunity was there, but I decided not to take it. I am as successful as I want to be and feel very fulfilled."

Yet as Rosenthal continued talking, it became apparent that she and Sandra

Miles had much in common. Both women wanted to earn more money, but Rosenthal held a more modest long-term goal. "Even without hiring more people," she continued, "I have regularly increased my income. As the jobs have become larger and more complex, I've expanded my fees. I like knowing that I'm worth more each year, but as long as I'm comfortable I don't need to be a millionaire."

No less than Miles, Rosenthal enjoys the sense of accomplishment that independent enterprise offers. "To me," she exclaimed, "the greatest reward in the world is knowing that I'm responsible for my own success. I feel a wonderful sense of accomplishment when I pay my taxes knowing that nobody told me to get up each day and work. I set my own goals, and then it's totally up to me to reach them. I either make it or break it all by my own effort.

"In most cases, people come to me with problems," she declared. "I get tremendous satisfaction in working with them to find good solutions and then in following through to see that implementation occurs. After I finish one project, a whole new problem-solving cycle begins, and I'm faced with something entirely different. I have a secretary who provides plenty of support and a part-time bookkeeper. Sometimes when things get too hectic, I contract the overflow out. Otherwise, the work rests on my shoulders, and I like it that way."

SEPARATING MYTH FROM REALITY

Not every entrepreneur wants to build an empire, nor does every one seek to become a millionaire. Entrepreneurial styles also differ, yet the basic needs of most business owners do not. Independence and the desire to take personal responsibility for one's work are indeed strong motivation for most entrepreneurs. Sandra Miles and Denise Rosenthal sought a situation where these needs could be met, and for both women that situation involved an independent venture. As the leader of her own firm, each woman can delegate the routine work that she dislikes and concentrate on new projects and problem-solving cycles. For Miles and Rosenthal, entrepreneurship offered the best outlet for their creative energy.

ENTREPRENEURSHIP AND RISK-TAKING BEHAVIOR

Meet the Mythological Gambler

To a casual observer, entrepreneurship is indeed a risky business. Entrepreneurs put money, assets, and energy in situations where the first two could be lost and the third depleted. Most people don't consider business ownership an option because the stakes seem so high. Entrepreneurship, they believe, requires the ability to take bold risks, and the entrepreneur is a wild gambler who without hesitation risks everything to make a business succeed.

Owning a business certainly involves some risk, but the typical entrepreneur is much less a gambler than popular belief suggests. In his profile of achievement-oriented people, David McClelland describes such people as moderate risk takers. Rather than setting impossible goals and then gambling everything they have, achievement-oriented people set objectives which they can achieve and then work to minimize the risk of failure. This behavior characterizes the entrepreneurial personality far more accurately than does the myth of the flamboyant gambler. The story of Yvonne Fletcher clearly illustrates this point.

An experienced conference planner, Yvonne Fletcher decided to open her own meeting planning service fifteen months ago. She correctly sensed a strong demand for such a service in the growing southern city where she lives, and today Conference Planning Associates is rapidly expanding. Fletcher was forty-five when she took this step, and her youngest child had just graduated from high school. When asked how she handled the risks involved in starting a business, Fletcher laughed and replied, "Risk? What risk? When people say to me, 'How can you take such a big risk?' I'm surprised. I didn't perceive going into business as a risk, or I wouldn't have done it. I don't do things if I think I'm going to fail."

Having survived that critical first year, Yvonne Fletcher feels justifiably confident and proud. As she looked back on her progress, she gladly shared her formula for successful risk-taking behavior. "Assessing a risk takes common sense and experience," she began. "Before I take a step, I research things pretty carefully. Instead of just impulsively running out and doing something, I base my decisions on as much knowledge as I can. I also operate on an intuitive level of what is right from a business point of view. All of this helps me minimize the risks involved.

"At the beginning," she continued, "I moved step by step. I'm not a foolhardy person, especially when my money is at stake. I never considered taking out a huge loan or doing something radical. It's very hard to get in over your head if you start small, work, gain confidence, and then expand your business little by little. That's a natural process."

Fletcher also emphasized flexibility as a key element to minimizing risk. "If something doesn't work, you have to be willing to change it," she declared. "I don't involve my ego in any particular idea, and this makes it a lot easier to toss something out if it's not working. So what if I make a mistake? One mistake isn't a lifetime failure. As long as I'm still alive, I can try something else."

Yvonne Fletcher's story was echoed again and again by all the interviewees. When something didn't work, they only tried harder. If one path did not lead to the desired place, then they tried another. Persistent and determined, these women clearly believed they controlled their own show. However, they were quick to acknowledge that unforeseen obstacles did arise and that a well-planned course of action could go awry. When events failed to go as planned, they did not feel swept along by forces beyond their control. Instead, they worked hard and tried new approaches until they found the best way to succeed.

Their advice to other women was best expressed by Yvonne Fletcher when she said: "Spend time directing those things you can control and forget about the rest. Things turn out a lot better that way. I keep saying that I'm really lucky, and I am, but part of it isn't luck. We make our own luck in many ways."

Without exception, the interviewees believed that if all else failed, they could rely on themselves to survive. In remembering her decision to strike out on her own, Fletcher smiled and said: "You know, at that point I had nothing to lose. I thought to myself, 'My kids are all grown, I'm tired of working for someone else, and I'm just going to do it.' If you want to start a business but are a little afraid, just ask yourself 'What's the worst thing that could happen?' In my case, I could lose my business, but then I could always work for somebody else. I have enough skills to know I'll never starve, and no one's going to take my life away. So what if I lose? It's better than never trying."

Women and Risk: Do They Mix?

The image of the bold, risk-taking entrepreneur is not the only myth that may hold a woman back. Popular stereotypes suggest that women are more timid than men, are less adventurous, and have a stronger need for security, so "naturally" they are also less willing to take risks. As little girls grow up, they internalize these stereotypes, which then become part of their self-images. The degree to which this occurs depends on each person's individual upbringing, but most women absorb to some extent the belief that women and risk don't mix. This belief may then arise as an internal barrier, which inhibits them from undertaking something new.

When discussing these issues, Angela Warshawski, owner of AW Electrical Contractors, attacked the prevailing viewpoint. "I think it's a myth that women don't take risks," she declared. "Women do take risks. Not just entrepreneurial women, but I mean all women. We bear children, and that's one of the greatest risks in the world. We uproot our whole families and move thousands of miles with no cocoon to go into. While the spouse has a ready-made set of friends in the office, we have no one. We pioneer. We're much more earth-bound than men are, and that means we take more risks. We're tied to the pragmatics of life and death in our lives, so we take risks more consistently. But our risks are the ones that no one sees."

Warshawski's point of view is substantiated by two little-known but important studies. Psychologists Nathan Kogan and Michael Wallach have written many books and articles on risk-taking behavior among both sexes. They agree that the issue of women and risk is highly colored by sex role stereotypes.

In one experiment, Kogan presented his students with a group of scenarios that involved difficult choices. For example, in one story the central character was playing a game of chess. Suddenly he was confronted with a dilemma: He could make a certain move that, if successful, would win the game. If the move were unsuccessful, he would probably lose. Another option was to make a clearly safe move that would bring neither victory nor defeat. After making their own choices, the students then described which course they believed their male and female peers would follow. The results were very interesting.

Kogan discovered that women do not avoid risk even though everyone believes that they do. Regardless of their own sex or the sex of the character in the story, all students in the experiment indicated that women would make more cautious choices than their own. However, in reality, both male and female participants usually chose the riskier course for themselves. Kogan concluded that ''[t]here is a discrepancy between what females actually do in respect to the riskiness of their choices and what their peers, male and female, think that they do. Females are believed to be more cautious than, in fact, they are.''[2]

In another experiment, Kogan and Wallach discovered that ambiguity more than anything else caused conservative behavior in women. When they are on uncertain ground, women are less likely to take risks than when they are on their own territory and surrounded by familiar circumstances. Then the opposite occurred. Kogan and Wallach conclude: ''When women are very certain, they are more willing to go out on a limb about it.''[3]

As wives and mothers, women take greater risks in the world of home, family, and personal relationships, where they understand the stakes better and have some control over the outcome. This may be perceived by other women, such as Angela Warshawski, but it is not well understood by men. The Kogan studies are among the first to acknowledge that women not only take risks but take large risks when they are on familiar ground. Women are fairly new to the corporate world and to many of the professions. If they are not out there visibly risking high stakes, it should not be surprising. They may be wisely proceeding with some caution until they are as familiar with this new environment as they are with the old.

The new entrepreneurs worked in the business world for an average of twelve years before stepping out on their own. Moreover, three-fourths had a parent, grandparent, or close relative who owned a business. Thus both family background and later life work enabled them to develop the confidence, insight, and knowledge necessary for risk-taking behavior. Their upbringing and experience helped to diminish the ambiguity that most women feel in a business setting and prepared them to pioneer on an exciting new frontier.

Assess Your Capacity for Risk

For some women, opening a business may still feel like a very risky step. You may be one of these women. Perhaps you want to start a business and hesitate because it seems too risky. Or maybe you want to expand your present business but consider the gamble too great. In either case, it is important to separate myths which might be holding you back from the reality of your situation. To evaluate your capacity for risk-taking behavior, turn to Part 3's two self-assessment exercises.

THE ENTREPRENEURIAL PERSONALITY: A CONTRADICTION IN TERMS

Entrepreneurs are well-known to have imagination, creativity, and a flair for making money. They are equally notorious for their tendency toward rigid, autocratic behavior. Flexible in their ability to generate ideas, they are simultaneously rigid in insisting that "their way" is the only way that something can be done.[4] Few of these innovative people, either male or female, understand how their conflicting needs to create and control may interfere with the success of their business. For Christine Stewart, this was a painful lesson.

The Innovative Autocrat

Now thirty-three, Christine Stewart was born in England and moved to the United States when she was eight. At that time, her parents were divorced, and her American mother came home and resettled in Connecticut. Stewart returned to England for college but dropped out after two years. She subsequently found a job with British Airways as a reservation clerk and enjoyed the travel benefits that her position offered.

When she was twenty-five, a family friend contacted her about working for his small travel agency in New York City, and she decided at once to accept the job. A year later, the friend decided to retire, and, to her surprise, wanted to sell her the tiny three-person firm. She didn't hesitate to take the offer, especially when he included financing as part of the package.

Now, seven years later, Stewart is on the verge of a breakdown. Her "first baby," as she calls Stewart Travel, is making lots of money but has grown beyond her control. Exhausted and nervous, she is a victim of her own creative ability. When I visited Stewart in her elegant Manhattan office, she was discussing her problems with the consultants she had in desperation called in to help her. She moved from that interview directly into conversation with me, all the time keeping one eye on her two-year-old daughter, Sally, who played noisily nearby. It was already apparent that Stewart was dividing her energy and attention among too many places: Baby, business, and new projects were competing for her time.

Stewart started our conversation with a difficult confession. "I had a very high turnover rate," she began, "so I called in these consultants to help find out why. They discovered that most of the problem was me! This has been very painful for me to accept, yet I know it is true. I'm not very tolerant of people who are not like I am. I get real snappy with them if they don't demand the kind of perfection that I expect, either from themselves or their work."

As Stewart continued her self-description, she honestly assessed the negative side of her personality. "I don't really trust other people either," she declared. "When there is a lot of work to be done, I know I can do the job. If I hire someone, that person is an unknown quantity, and I have to count on her or him. The stress comes in realizing that someone is not doing the job right, something is late, and the customer is irate. I tend to fume about these things, then my bad attitude starts showing, and finally it comes down to a confrontation. Instead of handling things constructively, I let the situation become destructive. I have a lot of great ideas, but I am not a very good manager."

When our conversation turned to the growth and development of her business, Stewart's entrepreneurial flair became apparent. However, too many good ideas coupled with controlling management policies resulted in problems.

"This business is my first baby," she smiled. "I gave birth to it, and I've helped it grow. When I took over from Don, my parents' friend, there were only three of us here, and we did the usual travel things for people in the neighborhood. Now I have a reputation for arranging really unusual as well as routine travel packages. I also added a visa service when I noticed that customers were having problems getting the information they needed, especially for quick or unexpected trips. That involves a lot of detail work, but it has resulted in our getting more United Nations trade.

"Now I have an opportunity to open a branch out on Long Island, and people have asked me about franchising my business operation. And I have notes for some little how-to books on running a business like this. I used to be a great writer, but I'm not sure I can even write sentences any more. You know, things have happened so fast that I never took the time to ask myself, 'Where am I going? What am I doing?' I just keep hiring new people to get the job done."

At this point, Stewart's daughter, Sally, began marching around the room wearing her mother's large blue shoes. Barely able to keep her balance, she grabbed the table, then a nearby chair, smiling triumphantly as she made a path across the room without stumbling. The connection between mother and daughter was clear: Christine Stewart was floundering around in a business grown too large for her to manage alone. Like Sally, she was trying to assume a role that was impossible for her to fill without support to steady her steps.

Stewart's problems were threefold: First, she was unclear about her role and her primary responsibility in the business; second, she supervised her staff too closely instead of training them to work on their own; and third, she refused to relinquish the day-to-day operations to anyone. Typical of the entrepreneur, she had conflicting needs both to create and control. Unable to share the reins, she was not guiding a team so much as riding several horses at once. The result was confusion for the business and exhaustion for its owner.

The Flexible Leader

Christine Stewart's story stands in sharp contrast to that of Jackie Edwards, another interviewee. Jackie Edwards is an outgoing black woman now in her early thirties. She was raised in Seattle, where her father was a purchasing agent for the city and her mother ran a small day-care center. Edwards's vivacious personality and open manner are ideally suited to her chosen field—advertising and public relations. In addition, she has strong writing and organizational skills.

Edwards attended Reed College in Oregon, majored in English, and, upon graduation, found a job with a large development company in Portland. This company specialized in planning real estate projects, such as shopping centers and professional complexes in suburban areas. Starting as a copywriter, Edwards was responsible for preparing brochures, press releases, and other promotional materials for the new developments. After three years, she was offered a supervisory position that required working with company designers, printers, and distributors as well as performing some writing duties. She continued in this capacity for another three years.

During this period, Jackie Edwards made a lot of contacts and friends in the development industry. She noticed that colleagues often needed the services of a small firm to help them with a new logo or brochure, or even to assist them with a major promotional campaign. Edwards quickly realized that there was indeed a market for the enterprising individual—contrary to what she had expected, major advertising agencies did not fill the needs of everyone. Teaming up with a graphic designer whose work she respected, Edwards started her two-person firm while working full-time. Within six months she left her job, and four years later she was running a business with eleven employees and a gross of over $1 million yearly.

Today, her company is a smooth-running organization, but that wasn't always the case. Like Chris Stewart, Jackie Edwards was once an innovative autocrat, but she quickly learned that making herself indispensable was not the best formula for success. "When I first started," she remembered ruefully, "I became totally attached to the business. In fact, I was the business, and I tried to do and be everything. If the business didn't succeed, I felt I would be a total failure. And that's ridiculous! A year later, I saw it wasn't working: I was exhausted, my staff was resentful, and the firm wasn't making any money."

Edwards soon realized that unless she delegated work to other people, her company would never grow. "Gradually I structured my company along two functional lines," she continued, "design and production. Suzanne is my art director and Tom, my production manager, and I finally learned to delegate the authority to them to do the job. Delegation is very important, but it is hard to do, particularly if doing the work yourself is easier. Now Tom and Sue have a lot of authority to see that the work gets done, and that keeps the everyday problems from getting to me."

As she gained experience, Edwards slowly developed policies that helped her become a better leader: "When I'm gone," she noted, "I expect people to make decisions about problems that come up. If you make a mistake, I'm not going to get you in front of a hundred people and curse you out. I'm going to sit down with you and say, 'Your idea was good, you did your best, but it was wrong for this reason.' And then it's a closed issue. I also realized that my role is to generate new business, to plan where the company is going, to set the financial and marketing goals, and then to guide others so we can fulfill those goals. One of my most important tasks is to create an environment in which my staff can come alive and do the best work possible. Then I can be free to identify problems, develop new ideas, and pursue opportunities when they arise. I think Edwards Enterprises will be incredibly big some day unless I choose to stop it. Our capability to do new things is unlimited.''

Edwards and Stewart: A Comparison

Both Jackie Edwards and Christine Stewart have an obvious entrepreneurial flair. Thanks to the imagination of their respective owners, Edwards Enterprises and Stewart Travel have grown from single-function operations to multifaceted businesses offering a wide range of services. Yet the atmosphere in the two businesses is totally different. One, unstable and chaotic, continues to make money but is on the verge of disaster despite increasing profits. The other has grown in an orderly, structured manner, gradually fulfilling the creative vision of its owner.

Both women are strong innovators who instinctively reach out for new opportunities to make money. Stewart, however, did not recognize that entrepreneurial success involves establishing some workable business structure. Instead, she allowed the firm to grow in a haphazard fashion, expanding in whatever direction her next idea took her. Although she continued to make money, she was almost strangled by her own creativity. An innovative autocrat, Stewart also maintained tight rein over every detail of her business operation. As long as the controlling side of her character dominated, she tried to do every job, make every decision, and fill every function. As a result, there was insufficient job definition, a lack of delegation, and considerable staff resentment.

Jackie Edwards, however, better understood how her personality interfered with the growth of her business. Once she recognized and understood her need to control, she was then able to let some of the responsibility go. This in turn enabled her to establish a workable structure for her business and then to hire people to manage it. At that point, she realized that her primary job was to continue generating new ideas for the business, not to manage every detail of its operation.

Once Edwards became more flexible in her approach, she developed better management techniques. She began taking her art director and her production manager to important client meetings and then listened to their opinions about the job. When clients called, these coworkers could handle their problems, leaving Edwards free to investigate new plans and projects. She also encouraged employees at every level to make decisions and helped them understand mistakes as they arose. She wanted to develop her staff and see them grow right along with the business. By giving part of her work to others, she realized that she would increase her effectiveness as a leader.

By contrast, Christine Stewart failed either to organize or to delegate. As the years passed, her needs to create and to control became increasingly deadlocked, resulting in erratic growth, frustration, and exhaustion. Unable to separate her own needs from those of the business, Stewart remained caught in a web of innovation and routine management tasks and could not untangle the situation until she obtained outside advice.

If you have or hope to have an independent enterprise, you undoubtedly share some of the characteristics that we have described. To assess your entrepreneurial strengths and weakness, turn to Chapter 7, where you will find an exercise to help you.

Understanding yourself as an entrepreneur is an important step along the road to business success. As we have seen, certain characteristics are typical of the entrepreneurial personality. Some of these are positive and contribute to effective business management, and others are negative and must be diminished or controlled. The characteristics and situations that we have described here are common to both men and women. People of either sex who hope to be successful entrepreneurs will recognize themselves in the profiles we have drawn. However, women entrepreneurs bring special strengths and weaknesses to a business setting. Understanding yourself as a woman is thus the next critical step you must take on your journey to independent enterprise.

C H A P T E R 3

Choosing Independence:
Why Is It So Hard?

Linda Ullenberg was born and raised in Cincinnati, Ohio, where she worked for years at the side of a well-known real estate mogul. When he started his firm, he hired Linda as his secretary and general assistant. Loyal, efficient, and hard-working, Linda remained with this company as it grew from just the two of them to over 100 people. The business eventually dominated Cincinnati's real estate industry, but Ullenberg's career did not match that of her employer. Instead, she remained in the lower echelons of the company, where her accomplishments were not widely recognized.

During our interview, Linda looked back on her life and talked about why the disparity between the two careers existed: "I used to see myself as a dependent sort," Ullenberg remembered, "more of a follower than a leader, so I wasn't aware that I was practically running the company. I was doing so much and was so poorly rewarded that I should have left years ago. One day my boss hired another woman as vice president and gave her a big salary and a bright corner office with windows. That jolted me out of my dream world. There I was in my dark, rinky-dink space with all the responsibility and none of the rewards. I finally realized that I could have easily started my own firm, but I had never even thought of that. The whole experience made me ask, 'Choosing independence—why is it so hard?' "

Remembering her transition from follower to leader caused Ullenberg to remember her childhood as well. "My parents owned and ran a restaurant," she recalled, "and they worked hard to provide for us children. My mother in particular was a wonderful role model. She worked full-time, cleaned, shopped, entertained, and made all our clothes without ever complaining. She also encouraged me to go out and find new opportunities. When I wanted to take piano lessons, she told me, 'Linda, get a job and earn yourself some money.'

"Well, I did," Ullenberg continued. "Even though we lived several miles outside of town, I was determined to get a paper route. I thought I could earn more than I would baby-sitting. Every day I jumped on my bike and delivered those papers, and I got more than enough to pay for my lessons. In a way, it was like having a business. If I worked harder, I could get more customers and earn more money. But somewhere along the way, I lost sight of this side of my life. When I got older, being independent didn't mesh with my self-image."

Linda Ullenberg eventually reconnected with the spirit of independence that kindled her early entrepreneurial drives. She quit her job in disgust, became a licensed broker, and started her own real estate company. With her contacts and experience, she was destined to succeed. However, she never fully answered her original question: Why is independence such a difficult choice for women?

SUGAR 'N SPICE ISN'T SO NICE

The answer to Linda Ullenberg's question lies in cultural stereotypes that discourage independence in women, thereby causing some of the conflicts that Ullenberg experienced. Although we are almost in the twenty-first century, our feminine ideal still reflects a picture of women that reached its peak during the Victorian era over a 100 years ago. Women's roles may be slowly changing, but there have been few accompanying changes in our basic definition of femininity.

In 1969 psychologist Inge Broverman conducted a now-famous study entitled "Sex Role Stereotypes and Clinical Judgments of Mental Health." As part of her research, Broverman asked a group of mental health professionals of both sexes to outline their portrait of the healthy, mature woman. Her survey revealed that even today the "normal," "feminine" woman is viewed as "very submissive, not at all aggressive, very easily influenced, not at all skilled in business, very dependent, very emotional, very illogical, not at all confident, very home oriented, very tactful, very gentle, and very aware of feelings of others."[1] The picture presented in Broverman's study hardly differs from that drawn by nineteenth-century poet William Wordsworth in his famous "Lucy" poems, where he describes the ideal woman as, "A violet by a mossy stone/Half hidden from the eye!"[2]

A woman who wants to open a business may be inhibited by these cultural stereotypes even though she may be unaware of their influence. Linda Ullenberg offers an interesting example. Verbally encouraged by her mother to be independent, Linda simultaneously picked up other cues that too much independence was not good. The extent to which she internalized this belief is evident in her self-image. As a youngster, she had willingly delivered papers, eventually organizing her route into a little entrepreneurial venture. Yet as an adult she saw herself as dependent, destined to follow others rather than to lead. How did this happen?

In earliest infancy, parents treat sons and daughters differently. Boy babies are bounced and tossed high in the air, but girls are coddled and petted. As children grow older, fathers in particular encourage their sons to be competitive, independent, and oriented toward achievement but praise their daughters for sweet, ladylike behavior. Girls also face greater parental restrictions and are more closely supervised than boys.[3] When children start school, teachers in turn reinforce sex-role stereotypes by rewarding girls who are compliant and docile and disapproving of those who are independent and assertive.[4]

The world of business, no less than that of home and school, helps perpetuate stereotypes. In 1978 researchers Benson Rosen and Thomas Jerdee, then at the University of North Carolina, surveyed a large and diverse national sample of people in business. Their goal was twofold: to find out if sex role stereotypes were still pervasive and, if so, to discover to what extent they influenced a woman's ability to succeed. When their sample was analyzed according to job, industry, organizational size, and region, Rosen and Jerdee found no significant variations in response. The U.S. business world still views the average woman as:

- Good at detail work as opposed to understanding the "big picture" in business
- Emotional and sensitive to criticism rather than rational and steady when under fire
- Sensitive to others' feelings instead of assertive about her own
- Timid and quick to cry as opposed to confident and self-sufficient
- Home-oriented rather than oriented toward the world of business, finance, science, or math[5]

LEGALIZING DEPENDENCY

Our legal system joins family, school, and business in encouraging dependency for women. In fact, for many years independence was practically illegal for the fairer sex—dependency was built right into U.S. family law. Concerning the rights of married women, nineteenth-century lawyer William Blackstone wrote, "By marriage, the husband and wife are one person in law: that is, the very being or legal existence of the woman is suspended during the marriage, or at least is incorporated and consolidated into that of the husband: under whose wing, protection, and cover, she performs everything."[6]

In Blackstone's day, women were unable to own or control property, to make contracts, to incur debts, or to be sued. Classified with infants and lunatics, they were deemed not only incompetent to manage their own affairs but also unworthy of individual existence apart from their husbands. Although the majority of women, then as now, were married, their single sisters fared little better. The affairs of single women were usually handled by a father, brother, uncle, or son, and the effect was to render these women economically dependent, legally invisible, and therefore almost totally powerless. The legal situation thus reinforced the cultural image of women as shy violets and further strengthened the feminine ideal.

Since the passage of the first Married Women's Property Act in 1839 up to the enactment of the 1974 Equal Credit Opportunity Act, women have fought to eradicate legal obstacles to their independence. Nevertheless, laws have changed slowly, and attitudes have changed with equal delay. Attorneys John Johnston and Charles Knapp note that "male-dominated legislatures and courts have historically exhibited the belief that women generally are, and ought to be, confined to the social role of homemaker, wife, and mother. Opinions continue to appear in which both the result and the reasoning are virtually indistinguishable from those issued nearly a century ago."[7]

In addition, vestiges of the old laws remain, making the entrepreneur's quest for both economic and psychological independence even more difficult. As late as 1969, several states (Michigan, Alabama, Arizona, California, Florida, Georgia, Idaho, Kentucky, Nevada, North Carolina, Utah, and Maryland) still had laws that limited the capacity of a married woman to act independently of her husband.[8] These limitations apply primarily to her ability to convey real property and to cosign a loan with another person without her husband's consent.

For the potential entrepreneur, the problems such restrictions could cause are obvious. Furthermore, in 1970, five states (California, Nevada, Texas, Florida, and Pennsylvania) had "sole trader" laws that require a married woman to "set forth her character, habits, education, and mental capacity for business and to explain why she should be allowed. . . to open a business of her own." These laws typically require a woman to serve her husband with a copy of her petition to obtain his signed consent.[9]

Even where such laws are not strictly enforced, their very existence reinforces harmful stereotypes about women. For the woman entrepreneur, the legal situation brings both physical and psychological harassment. When outmoded laws are enforced, she must spend valuable energy responding to unreasonable demands. For example, Nell Smith, owner of a popular Los Angeles coffee shop and wine bar, was required to have her estranged husband sign her application for a liquor license transfer. Although she was legally separated from him and sole owner of the establishment, when she filed her papers the California Alcoholic Beverage Control Department was unyielding. This stance finds precedent in the famous *Goesaert* v. *Cleary* case of 1948, in which the U.S. Supreme Court decided that a woman could not be a bartender unless her father or husband owned the bar. In 1971 the California Supreme Court presented a different opinion regarding this issue in the judgment of the *Sail' er Inn* case. At that time, a group of bartenders sought assistance from the court to prevent the California Alcoholic Beverage Control from revoking their liquor licenses because they employed women as bartenders. In this ground-breaking opinion, the court made the following observation:

> The claim of unwholesomeness [in environment] is contradicted by statutes which permit women to work as cocktail waitresses, serve beer and wine from behind a bar, or tend bar if they or their husbands hold a liquor license. The objections appear to be based upon notions of what is a ''ladylike'' or proper pursuit for a woman in our society rather than any ascertainable evil effects of permitting women behind those ''permanently affixed features'' known as bars.[10]

Problems occurred in other areas as well. In 1972, Hannah Joffrey was refused tuition-free business courses at a local state college on the grounds that her husband, then serving in Viet Nam, held legal residence in another state. Since she was married, she no longer was able to establish her own residency but was required to take his. Several other women reported that landlords refused them long-term leases without their husband's signature, and banks still routinely and illegally demand a husband's cosignature on his wife's loan application.

The legal system has helped rigidify stereotypic roles by casting women as dependent, weak figures in need of male protection. No less than our educational institutions or business communities, the courts inhibit the development of independence in women and demand conformity to an outmoded feminine ideal. Such overt pressure makes it difficult for the woman determined to break barriers and develop new modes of behavior. Instead of helping her resolve internal conflicts, our social structures do just the reverse.

TRAPPED IN A HALL OF MIRRORS

From infancy right into adulthood, women are pressured to conform to a feminine ideal that has both positive and negative sides. However, a woman who chooses business or another nontraditional field will soon discover that neither side of the ideal will serve her well. In contrast to teaching, nursing, social work, or child care, where the so-called feminine touch is highly valued, the business community views a woman's assets as liabilities that will hinder her success. An aspiring business woman is thus trapped in a hall of mirrors—wherever she looks, her image is distorted.

The first mirror reflects negative characteristics that will clearly hold her back: dependence, timidity, submissiveness, lack of confidence. Should she try to modify her behavior and become more independent, assertive, dominant, and confident, the next mirror will reflect a woman in a man's clothing. And if she relies on the more positive qualities of the ideal, such as empathy, tact, adaptability, and nurturing, she may see a charming wife and mother rather than the successful executive she hopes to become. The worst part of all this stereotyping is that she will find little encouragement or aid should she despair at the images around her. Instead, society will blame her and ask, "Why did you enter the hall (of mirrors) in the first place?" Trapped in this situation, it is no wonder that, for most women, choosing independence is so hard.

ESCAPE INTO ENTREPRENEURSHIP

Back in 1979, when I first thought of writing this book, I was trapped in my own hall of mirrors. Recently divorced, I was struggling with issues of independence and femininity, and my mirror images weren't too encouraging. At that time, seminars to help women like me gain confidence and succeed in the business world were very popular. The theory behind these seminars was that if women were only more assertive and independent they would function much better in a business setting. Learning to "play the game like a man" would ensure their progress up the corporate ladder. However, for me such seminars only reinforced the distorted images that I perceived in the hall of mirrors. So I quit my classes and struck out on an entirely new course. I had met a number of women who started and managed their own businesses. To me, these women were a model of independence. How, I wondered, had they escaped the hall of mirrors? By writing a book about their lives, I would discover their secret exit.

At the outset, I had few expectations, and as my investigation moved forward, I encountered lots of surprises. The first one came in reply to my question, What are the advantages of being in business for yourself? Many women prefaced their answers with the advantages of being a woman in business. Still confused by the old mirror images, I did not understand the significance of these replies. I was far more attuned to responses that explained why being a woman generated so many barriers. I never thought being a woman in business had any advantages. The stories of three women clarified this point for me.

Megan Kelly is the owner of a growing public relations firm. Before opening her business, she had worked as a copywriter for a major ad agency, as public information officer for a junior college, and as an account executive for a large public relations firm. Well-trained and highly professional, Kelly was sure of her business-related skills before she struck out on her own. She was confident of her personal skills also, but she recognized that her male peers did not understand the worth of these personal skills. Kelly laughed as she remembered the perception that many of her clients initially had: "I was in a meeting with one of my most important clients," she noted, "and he made some joke about women being too soft and kindhearted. He must have thought that I would feel so sorry for him that I wouldn't charge him what I was worth. What he didn't know was how important my feelings about people really are. I was able to read between the lines and find out what his problem was, even though he couldn't come right out and say it. And instead of charging him less for doing this, I charged him a little more.''

Kelly's story shows that the popular view of women as empathetic, tactful, and understanding contributes to the belief that they cannot succeed in the business world. Her client thought that she would be unable to compete effectively because she could be easily exploited. Concern for other people's feelings would keep her from protecting the interests of her business. Clearly he viewed empathy, tact, and understanding as business liabilities, but Megan realized that these qualities were really assets. Her ability to understand people enabled her to look below the surface problems and to find out what the real issues were. To Kelly, this personal radar was a strength on which she consistently relied.

When compared to the masculine model, other strengths identified as feminine fare little better. A woman who is able to adapt and shift course when necessary becomes the "fickle female" who can't make up her mind. This popular image obscures the benefits that flexibility genuinely provides.

Tommie Roth, a successful landscape contractor, encountered such stereotypes soon after starting her business. As she remembered her early experiences, she, too, laughed good-naturedly and said, "I always kept a positive attitude even in the face of strong male resistance. At first, the building contractors were very hostile. When I walked onto a site, I could just see them thinking, 'Oh my God! We have thousands of cubic yards of earth to move, and this woman is going to change her mind every few seconds. She's probably going to have us move it an inch to the left, then an inch to the right, and then back again until she can decide what she wants.' I understood where this image came from, and I never took a hard line. Once they realized that I knew what I was doing, then everything changed. My ability to stay flexible and bend in face of such resistance was a real asset."

"Woman's wiles" and the intuitive approach to problem solving are other popular targets. The usual stereotype is expressed well by Henry Higgins, hero of the musical *My Fair Lady*, who plaintively tells a friend, "Women are irrational, that's all there is to that. Their heads are full of cotton, hay, and rags." Befuddled by women's behavior, Higgins goes on to ask a question still posed in the business community: "Why can't a woman be more like a man?"[11]

Unlike Henry Higgins, software consultant Amanda Johnston does not view her approach to problem solving as "irrational." By contrast, she described her intuitive decision-making style in positive terms. "I've found that if I allow something to develop," she stated with conviction, "and just guide it in a certain direction it works much better than planning too carefully. I used to go banging and plugging away trying to make things happen, and that process just didn't work. Now I find it much easier to let things take their course, but I keep a grip on them just like I would on the steering wheel of a car. I let the car follow the road even when the way is circular and indirect. It's important to hold onto the wheel, to slow down going around a curve, and to keep the car on track. Otherwise I keep moving ahead and everything turns out ok.''

Our contemporary feminine ideal includes the same traits as those described by Kelly, Roth, and Johnston: empathy, tact, adaptability, and intuitive thinking. However, though intrinsically positive, these traits are not so admired as the stereotypic male's qualities of logic, constancy, straightforwardness, and objectivity. The two groups of characteristics are polarized along gender lines, and the male pole is regarded as positive and the female pole as negative.[12]

This polarization is particularly destructive for women, because it devalues all female-associated traits, including the positive ones. Individual women internalize this devaluation and consequently do not recognize their strengths for what they really are. As psychiatrist Jean Baker Miller notes, "women's major difficulty lies more in admitting the strengths that they already have and in allowing themselves to use their resources."[13] For many women, less sure of their personal capabilities than Megan Kelly, Tommie Roth, or Amanda Johnston, it is understandable that independence is such a difficult choice.

CHOOSING INDEPENDENCE—IT'S NOT SO HARD

By the time I finished my research, I had learned an important lesson from all the interviewees. Choosing independence is not so difficult once we have accepted who we are and can capitalize on our individual strengths. For women, this means accepting our female-associated strengths and acknowledging that they provide a strong base on which to develop ourselves as whole human beings. Such acceptance is the first step to building the confidence necessary for true independent and assertive behavior. As I learned back in the seminars, simply trying to be more like men is not a meaningful answer.

Spreading so-called good male qualities over "bad" female ones will not solve women's problems nor make us more independent. An externally defined model of strength is no substitute for one developed from within. Accepting such a model will only reinforce, not eliminate, feelings of low self-worth, because this process requires rejecting our inner core. Developing a strong internal model is particularly difficult for women because mirror messages lock them in—no matter which way they turn, their reflections tell them that they cannot succeed. Working in the business world only reinforces these messages, but running an independent enterprise does not.

By allowing a woman to explore her particular strengths, entrepreneurship offers her a direct escape from the hall of mirrors. Because she owns the business, she creates the particular environment that she wants. As a result, she can be who she is as a full human being and can use all her personal resources when and where they are appropriate. Instead of hearing that what she has doesn't "count," she learns that what she has not only counts but also is essential for her success. As Megan Kelly noted: "Confidence in myself and credibility for myself have been two of the hardest things for me to develop, and I've gained them in very strange ways. Running this business has helped me realize that what I have holds up anywhere and that I don't have to be anything other than who I am in order to succeed."

For any prospective entrepreneur, Megan Kelly's words hold particular significance. Many women who want to start an independent enterprise may hesitate to make the final step, frequently held back by an inner belief that who they are is not good enough to bring them success. This belief is based on mirror images that they have been viewing for many years, and becoming an entrepreneur involves shifting those images and seeing them in a new light.

If you are such a woman, realize that strengths you may not associate with business success will in fact be useful to you as an entrepreneur. The first step to building confidence is self-acceptance, including understanding and accepting who you are as a woman. Instead of viewing your female-associated strengths as weaknesses and blaming yourself for lacking independence, look again at how your personal qualities will enable you to succeed. The self-assessment exercises in Chapter 7 will guide you in this process.

PART 2

Entrepreneurial Roots

CHAPTER 4

Childhood and Adolescence: Breaking the First Barriers

What conditions best foster a young girl's nascent autonomy and growing interests? What barriers stand in her way? Our examination of these issues discusses the typical story of Anne Munsey. Her story not only captures the spirit of her particular childhood but also highlights elements common to the lives of all the new entrepreneurs.

Munsey was born in Boulder, Colorado, where her father was a history professor at the university. When she was four, he died unexpectedly, and her mother moved Munsey and her younger brother back to Denver, the Munsey hometown. The young family lived near Munsey's maternal grandfather, a well-respected local business owner and avid backpacker. The Munsey children were surrounded by cousins and numerous other members of the family. At that point, Munsey's mother started teaching elementary school.

Munsey remembers her childhood and her large, extended family with much affection. She was an independent girl whose behavior delighted her grandfather but often left her mother and aunts in silent despair: "I really liked my grandfather, and he liked me," Munsey began, smiling at the recollection of this spirited man. "He was my favorite member of the family and always encouraged my interests. My aunts were very different. They were always telling me that if I didn't do this or that I'd never get into college. All the women in my family were teachers, and they wanted me to go into education, too. So the only goal I remember having was not to be a teacher.

"We lived right near the Rocky Mountains," she continued, "and I used to backpack with my grandfather. When I was about thirteen, I took rock-climbing lessons and paid for them myself with money I earned baby-sitting. As soon as I was old enough, I got a job in Rocky Mountain Park with a rock-climbing school there. I always loved the mountains. To me there was nothing more rewarding than setting out alone into the backwoods knowing that I could be my own company and guide.''

As she grew older, Munsey maintained her interests in face of strong pressure to conform to a different standard. ''I stayed with the rock-climbing school even when my friends couldn't understand it,'' she noted. ''They were all waitresses or sales clerks and thought mountain climbing was too dangerous. My mother was the same way. She was not a climber and would be delighted if I didn't kill myself or disgrace her. She was usually holding her breath hoping I'd behave. We simply didn't march to the beat of the same drum.''

Anne Munsey remembered liking school and being a good student. However, even in the classroom her independent behavior stood out. ''By senior year,'' she remembered, ''I was one of the only girls in my trigonometry class. Most of the other girls dropped out after taking geometry or second-year algebra. I was interested in majoring in math or science in college, but my counselor told me to go into education. I could get a scholarship for that, and it would be a good career for me.''

As a youth, Munsey certainly was adventuresome and perhaps in her choice of activities more daring than most. Yet, except in its details, the pattern of her life is not so different from that followed by the other women interviewed. Although many did not literally climb mountains, they nonetheless broke other barriers in an effort to pursue what interested them. Many described themselves as ''tomboys,'' a description that suggests their pursuits were more appropriate for little boys than little girls. Nevertheless, these women ignored gender-related restrictions, pushed beyond stereotypic limits, and successfully followed their own paths.

The first barriers that Anne Munsey broke involved narrow, limited definitions of appropriate feminine behavior. Because of sex-role pressures, she was pushed to drop what challenged and interested her. Rock climbing is not intrinsically better than baby-sitting, nor is math more worthwhile than history. The critical factor is that girls are channeled into certain activities and out of others simply because they are girls, consequently limiting their options and their ability to make meaningful choices. Instead of choosing what they want to do, girls start following what they believe they should do. Such a course inhibits their ability to make independent decisions and to carry out those decisions effectively.

When they were girls, the new entrepreneurs were able to bypass such restrictions and take up activities that challenged their abilities and piqued their interest. Throughout childhood, they maintained a surprisingly independent course. They saw the world as wide open, full of fascinating promise and unlimited possibilities.

The story of Anne Munsey illustrates six critical factors that influenced these women and helped shape their world views:

1. A large majority of the new entrepreneurs enjoyed a special position in the family. Half were first-born children; some were the only female sibling, determined to keep up with their brothers; still others came from all-girl families where they became their fathers' "sons." In these special roles, the new entrepreneurs were allowed unusual independence and responsibility.

2. These women came from basically stable families that provided an economically secure and psychologically safe base from which to experiment. Even those whose families experienced times of stress, such as death, illness, or unemployment, did not recall a sense of desperation because of such events; instead, their parents communicated a sense of underlying security, teaching their daughters that no matter what happened, the daughters need not be overwhelmed by forces beyond their control.

3. These future business owners had families who established firm guidelines but then allowed their daughters to set their own goals and make their own decisions. Most women remember parents who encouraged independence, responsibility, and excellence— three themes that surface again and again in their stories.

4. Almost every woman had a strong, positive role model who affected her life choices. For the majority, this model was the subject's mother, described variously as "incredible," "very strong," and "the dominant person in my life."

5. In general, these women remembered their fathers as surprisingly distant, absent, or weak figures who hardly compared to the "incredible" mothers in influence and strength. Daughters were separated from their fathers by death or divorce, perceived their fathers as passive and unsuccessful, or felt estranged from fatherly affection right in the home.

6. Three-fourths of the new entrepreneurs had a parent, grandparent, or other close relative who was an entrepreneur, independent professional, farmer, or contractor. Many women mentioned how important this familial example had been to them on their own later journeys to entrepreneurship—even when the parent or grandparent involved was the distant or absent father. A number of interviewees strove to establish a relationship with this remote figure through following a career in entrepreneurship similar to his. In some cases, business ownership eventually provided a new basis for communication between father and daughter.

During adolescence, the new enterpreneurs heard one message above all others: "Find a husband to take care of you. Once married, you will be happily secure for life." However, as adults, they followed a different path. Although almost all married, none remained in a position of dependency. On the contrary, these entrepreneurs emerged as leaders of an unexpected national phenomenon —the rise of the woman business owner—and, as such, chose an unusually independent course.

LEARNING A LESSON FROM MOTHER

The Incredible Mothers

Almost every woman had a positive parental role model who affected her later in life. Many of the new entrepreneurs openly admired their mothers and were grateful for the models they had provided. The story of car dealer Susan Clemons clearly illustrates this point. As she shared her story, Clemons's voice became choked with emotion and her eyes clouded over with tears.

Susan Clemons grew up in North Carolina, where both her parents worked in local factories. One of six children, she recently looked over some old family pictures with her younger sister. The photos brought back memories of hard times but also of strength, determination, and challenge. Clemons described her mother as the backbone of the family, the driving force that kept them all together. Although she has since moved far from the town of her birth, Clemons still remembers those days with much admiration.

"My father and mother were both factory workers," she stated, as she leaned back in her beautiful mahogany office chair, "and their jobs were tiring and difficult. There was a lot of work at home, too, but I don't remember any sexual bias in the house. We lived in a big, old place, and my parents were always tearing down walls, digging out the cellar, and fixing the roof. My mother did those things right along with my dad. She planted flowers, took care of the garden, and worked in the factory. I never heard my mother say, 'I can't do that.' "

When she was about six, Clemons's father became very ill, and full responsibility for the family fell to her mother. "My father spent a lot of time in the hospital," she continued, "and was unable to work a whole lot after that. He really had a hard time of it for a few years, and during that time my mother kept the family together and put food on the table. In fact, my dad was still sick when I got married. Looking back, I guess there must have been some hard times, though I never was aware of it."

Clemons also recalled her mother as a wonderful role model: "She encouraged all of us to be independent," she declared. "If we wanted to use the family car, we had to demonstrate how to change the oil and fix a flat tire. And by the time we were in high school, we all had to buy our own clothes. I got a job cleaning house for a woman with a fabulous library. She let me borrow books and encouraged me to read whatever I wanted. Our whole family was raised like that. We had lots of good people in our lives and a mother saying, 'You can do it.' "

Susan Clemons's story is echoed again and again throughout the interviews. A strong mother takes care of the family financially and/or emotionally while the typical father is unable to fulfill his role as provider. This situation occurred for several reasons—death, illness, divorce, unemployment, or the personal characteristics of the man involved. However, no matter what the cause, the results were the same: The mother overcame hardship with independence, strength, and determination.

So outstanding was this feminine influence that a number of women talked at length about their grandmothers and great-grandmothers as well. Whether they had moved westward to the frontier, kept the family together after the Civil War, emigrated from foreign lands, or built businesses of their own, this older generation of women represented persistence and courage to younger family members. They had in fact become family legends, noted for their ability to take charge under difficult circumstances.

Two-thirds of the new entrepreneurs had mothers who worked outside the home. As young girls, these future business owners were aware of the importance of the mother's earnings to the family's economic well-being. However, only one woman reported that her mother, a physician, worked in a nontraditional field. The other mothers included farm wives whose work was perceived as necessary to the family's survival, owners of nursery schools and dress shops who managed their own economic affairs successfully, teachers and librarians, phone operators and factory workers, domestics and food service workers, writers, secretaries, and clerks. Several helped their husbands run the family business and were often described as the driving force behind its success. Those who did not work outside the home were usually active volunteers involved in youth organizations and community service.

The outstanding factor here is the mother's independent character rather than the type of work she did. Since most were employed in traditionally feminine occupations, they did not provide role models of women pioneering in new occupational areas. However, they did offer examples of strength, of women succeeding in risky situations, winning against the odds, and discharging necessary responsibility in a calm, capable manner. Confident of themselves as people, they passed this same confidence on to their daughters.

The Dependent Victims

A small group of women perceived their mothers as dependent victims, unable or unwilling to exert any real control over their lives. In general, these mothers denied their own needs in order to accommodate the wishes of husband, family, or boss. They believed themselves unable to influence the course of their lives, and many were resigned to an existence of frustration and dissatisfaction. In most cases dependency contributed to keeping these mothers from taking action: Some were dependent on a boss to keep them employed, others relied on their husbands to provide for their needs.

For Margaret Schulz, president of Round Hill Gifts, starting her own business was the best way to avoid what happened to her mother. As head of a prosperous mail-order firm, she depends on no one for her money and her success. Her present situation is very different from the one her mother experienced. "My mother was always a hard-working career woman," Schulz recalled, "but she came home from work destroyed every day. She got no money, no recognition, and no good treatment. Every night, she came home worn out and cried because her boss abused her. When I was very young, I decided I'd never be in a situation where anybody could make me feel like that."

Gail Monteux, head of TechnoCrat Computers, also decided at an early age that independence was vital to her survival. Like Margaret Schulz, she observed the destructive effect of dependency on her mother's life. "My mother was enormously intelligent," she stated emphatically, "and a great charmer. When I was very little, I saw the effect she had on men. She always got her own way when she wanted it by being charming, but she was not responsible for her own life. She had to live through others to a certain extent and ask, 'May I have this? May I have that?' That was horrifying to me, and I didn't want my life to be like hers."

Although Schulz's mother worked outside the home and Monteux's did not, both women were trapped in the position of depending on a man for their survival. To her daughter, each woman was a victim, unable to direct her own life either at home or at work. Schulz and Monteux learned at an early age that being independent and in control of your life is far better than depending on someone to take care of you.

WHAT ABOUT DAD?

On Permanent Leave

Although the typical entrepreneur remembered her mother as "incredible," she described her father in different terms. "Lovable mouse," "conservative," "withdrawn," or simply "not there" are only a few of the phrases applied to dad. A small number of women pictured their fathers as outstanding, powerful figures who were more influential than their mothers. But the majority found the most important male in their early life to be either distant and removed or lacking in some other major way.

Diana Epstein, now owner of a well-known art gallery, shared a particularly poignant tale. Epstein's father was a successful attorney and founder of a large corporate law firm. She grew up in Manhattan, the apparently adored daughter and only child of this accomplished man. Her description of her father and their relationship reflects a situation that many other interviewees experienced: "I was an only child," she recalled, "and my father was very enamored of me, but he didn't undertand the first thing in the world about children. To him, children were just short adults, and the way that my dad relates to adults is through business. His personal relationships always suffer for it, and his relationship with me was no exception."

Although she lacked a close personal relationship with her father, Epstein relished her role of "Daddy's little helper." Even when she was a small child, he treated her almost as an equal, encouraging her interest in his work. "My father had his routine," she continued with pride, "and it was absolutely standard and unbreakable. Every Saturday, he went down to his office and organized and planned his agenda for the following week. I usually went down with him, and he would sit and explain his cases to me. When he was at home in the evenings, he frequently had calls from clients. I can remember very vividly sitting at the bottom of the stairway where the telephone was located and listening to Dad by the hour. Sometimes he'd write me little notes while he was talking, and afterward I would ask him questions about what he said. It was real adult-to-adult talk."

After nearly nine years as his sidekick and protégé, Diana Epstein was abruptly separated from her father. Her memories at this point were tinged with bitterness as she recalled his sudden disappearance. "When I was eight," she stated, "my parents got divorced. My dad moved away, and I was cut off from any meaningful contact with him. Our visits amounted to two or three weeks a year, and my correspondence with him consisted of clippings about his accomplishments with little 4-by-6 notes saying, 'Hi, thought you'd enjoy these.' I went through a time of feeling very bitter about that. It was his way of telling me what he was doing, but I was angry because it wasn't personal. I guess it was no different when my parents were still together. He was always more interested in what he could teach me than in who I am."

For another group of women, abandonment was more figurative: Their fathers were absent without leaving. Although these men were present in the home, they remained distant from their children because of illness or the inability to relate on an emotional basis. Barbara Entwistle, publisher of a successful businesswomen's magazine, experienced a painful separation from her father even though he was physically present. "I don't think my father ever really considered me," she stated with conviction. "I don't think he even knew who I was. He went to work at 7:00, came home at 7:00, ate dinner, and then worked until 2:00. He spent no time with the family. The only good time I can remember having with him is when he took me for my college interview."

These future entrepreneurs lacked a close relationship with their fathers and felt disappointed and rejected. The physically abandoned women experienced a greater sense of loss and bitterness than did those women whose fathers were figuratively absent, but both groups remembered feeling deprived of the affection that they wanted. Early in life, these women learned to function independently and without close male support. If they could not count on their fathers to take care of them, why should they rely on any other man?

A third group of women did not feel abandoned or let down by their fathers, nor did they view their fathers in a particularly positive light. The theme here is less that of financial or emotional failure than of failure to live up to their daughters' expectations of masculinity. Women such as Nicole Petris, head of Petris Communication Group, viewed their fathers as lovable and sweet but passive, conservative, unambitious, and weak:."I loved my father," Nicole smiled, "and he would do anything for me. Still, I think he was a quiet, mousy man, not independent at all but sweet and lovable. I remember him as being very stable and conservative, never willing to take any risks. He worked for the post office and had the same job for forty-five years."

As "lovable mouse," Petris's father did not provide the same inspiring model as did her mother. Instead of patterning her behavior after her father's, Nicole looked to the dominant figure in the household for an example. For Petris, as for most of the study participants, that figure was her mother.

The Powerful Fathers: Larger Than Life

A small minority of interviewees described their fathers as forceful figures who exerted a dominant influence on their daughters' lives. To these daughters, their fathers were "domineering," "powerful, "fantastic," "inquisitive," "energetic," and "overpowering." These men took a special interest in their daughters' development and presented powerful models with whom the daughters identified. Maria Santori, a well-known designer and manufacturer of jewelry, expressed great admiration for this larger-than-life figure: "My dad had enormous energy," she said as she smiled, spreading her hands in an expansive gesture. "He just bowled his way through life. He had so much . . . oomph. When he was seventeen, he left Italy and came to this country without knowing a word of English. By the time he died, he had built up a big construction company. He was the original self-made man, and I always wanted to be like him. It was his basic teaching that instilled the drive that I have."

Amy Rosenthal, president of E-Z Clean-Up, also remembered her father and their relationship in very positive terms. "My father was ambitious," she noted, "and had very high standards. He was very demanding, and he always encouraged learning. We used to read books together, he taught me to dance as a kid, and he was a very domineering, powerful person. When I started working, it was with the company that he founded. I had a different relationship with my father than most girls did."

PARENTAL MODELS AND THE DEVELOPMENT OF INDEPENDENCE

The stories shared by the new entrepreneurs suggest the importance of parental example to the development of independence in women. As children, these women had at least one very strong, independent role model in their immediate family, and, in the majority of cases, that model was the mother. For a minority of study participants, a powerful, dominant father exerted a similar positive influence on his daughter's life.

Both independent mothers and powerful fathers offered more than a good example. Their unusual behavior accompanied equally unusual messages. From their mothers, one group of women learned that acceptable feminine behavior did not exclude independence and self-control, and a second group learned a similar lesson from their fathers. In addition, the first group also discovered the sad untruths hidden beneath popular stereotypes—marriage does not mean security, and successful women are not weak, dependent, shy creatures. Life often brings unexpected events that require the ability to act independently of male support, and their mothers showed them that a woman can handle such events successfully and can do so alone.

The distant, absent, or passive fathers also exerted a significant influence on their daughters' development, but this influence arose from what they did not do rather than from what they did. Psychologist Henry Biller, an expert on the role of the father in child development, notes in his writing about the father-daughter relationship that fathers, more than mothers, encourage stereotypic, "girlish" behavior. In assessing paternal influence, he makes the following observation: "Fathers often have unfortunately rigid sex role stereotypes, and in their zeal to feminize their daughters, they actively discourage the development of intellectual and physical competence within their daughters."[1]

The typical father hopes his daughter will be pretty, affectionate, well-behaved, and popular and will treat her in a such a way as to encourage this type of behavior. He is likely to criticize her less than her brother and expect less for her than he does for her brother. In fact, to most fathers, a "successful" daughter is one who marries young and has a family. Psychologists believe such "feminizing" behavior encourages passivity and dependency in women and discourages the development of independence and self-control.[2]

How does this theory apply to the new entrepreneurs? Those fathers who were absent, passive, or distant had less opportunity or inclination to exert a "feminizing" influence on their daughters. These women were then freer to develop along less stereotypic lines and to model their behavior after that of their mothers.

In addition, yet another aspect of their lives helped push the new entrepreneurs toward independent enterprise: Three-fourths of our sample had a close relative who was also an entrepreneur. This familial model proved highly influential on their later career choice. Research shows that a tradition of business in the family is one of the most outstanding motivators in prompting individuals to start their own enterprises.

CHOOSING ENTREPRENEURSHIP: IT'S ALL IN THE FAMILY

In the early 1970s Candace Borlund studied a group of students at the University of Texas in Austin. She hoped to isolate certain personality traits that would help psychologists and educators predict which students would be most likely to open a business at some point in their lives. After identifying such students, the university could provide them with the best preparation possible to encourage their potential. Borlund found that the most important variable for predicting whether students would start a business was whether their father had also started a business.[3]

Borlund's study indicates that, by their example, both fathers and mothers help children learn that certain options are clearly possible. This was the case for the new entrepreneurs—75 percent mentioned that a parent, grandparent, or other close relative owned a business or farm or was an independent professional.

Diana Epstein's story offers a particularly good example of how the family business influences a child's development. From an early age, Epstein enjoyed accompanying her father to his office. Sitting on his lap or near him when he talked on the phone, she was his "little assistant" and best student. Although Diana's father did not directly encourage her to pursue a career in business, she inevitably absorbed the belief that it was appropriate for her to do so. As she said, it was a lesson learned "by osmosis." Her father talked to her as an equal, discussing his problems and ideas and testing her ability to grasp business concepts. By implication, she learned that business ownership was not only a continual challenge but also an appropriate pursuit for a woman.

Other women looked back on the family business as simply a familiar part of their lives. "I was down at the plumbing business quite frequently to see what they were doing," one woman recalled, and another stated, "I often stopped in at Dad's store after school." These women watched their parents or relatives achieve success over the years and observed the respect they enjoyed in the community. The shop, with phones ringing and customers talking, was an exciting, stimulating place. They remembered it as a world where people not only worked and earned money but did so in an independent and challenging fashion.

The new entrepreneurs recalled helping out at the workplace as well as learning about the family enterprise at home. As children, they remembered joining in business conversations, meeting business associates, and being challenged by questions related to business practice. Becky Thompson, owner of West Side Deli and Sandwich Shop, described the situation in her family with obvious enthusiasm: "My father owned an import-export firm," she said, "and frequently had business friends over to dinner. I listened to the conversations and learned all the business terms. When my parents started talking about the latest problems, I loved to get involved. I got the impression that being in business was a good thing. If you were successful at it, you had a lot of freedom and financial security."

Like many of the new entrepreneurs, Thompson watched some close family member start with nothing and end up with a money-making enterprise—all by his or her own efforts. This was a process every woman remembered when she later established her own business. "I started with nothing and look what I have now" was a commonly expressed feeling. Since they regarded business ownership as a challenging and respectable endeavor, it is not surprising that they, as grown women, eventually chose the same alternative. Like Becky Thompson, they were well aware at an early age of the responsibility involved in running a business and of the independence that it allowed.

Their parents, too, were proud of this family tradition and eagerly offered their support in the form of advice, loans, encouragement, and the simple transference of confidence—a "You can do it" attitude. When these women doubted their own abilities, the example which their parents or relatives had set often kept them going. Sarah Winston, an importer of antiques, summed it up this way: "Whenever I have a real tough time, I call my Aunt Ethel. We chitchat for awhile, and I tell her about all my problems. And she always reminds me, 'Well, your Uncle Jack had problems, too, and he made it. You're that same blood and you can do it, too.' I'd get off that phone and start again, thinking, 'By golly, if Uncle Jack can do it, I can, too.' "

Those women who lacked such familial models were not deterred. Although helpful, such models are not prerequisite to entrepreneurial success. Confidence, independence, and persistence, traits shared by all the new entrepreneurs, can be acquired through a variety of life experiences. A tradition of business in the family is only one of six important factors that influenced the development of the women in this study.

INDEPENDENT ENTERPRISE: INSECURITY AND SELF-CONTROL

Throughout this chapter, we have examined early influences on the development of the new entrepreneurs. Focusing on parental models, we noted that many of the women interviewed perceived at least one of their parents in a negative light. The largest group had fathers who were missing from their lives. A smaller group had weak, vulnerable mothers who depended on males to take care of them. By contrast, almost every interviewee described one parent as a dominant, forceful figure who encouraged her to be independent. A tradition of business in the family further emphasized this message.

From their particular familial circumstances, the new entrepreneurs learned that real security was tied to independence and the ability to take care of themselves and that business ownership was one possible path for achieving this goal. Entrepreneurship, however, does not provide complete security but rather offers a peculiar combination of insecurity and self-control. Success in business ownership is never assured, although the risks can be minimized. The life of an entrepreneur rests on a fundamentally precarious foundation because the business can be lost at any moment. At the same time, the success or failure of an enterprise lies with its owner, who essentially controls the course that it will follow. In later life, the new entrepreneurs thus seemed to replicate a situation established during their childhood.

later life, the new entrepreneurs thus seemed to replicate a situation established during their childhood.

As an entrepreneur, each woman is in a position where she can be abandoned, this time by her business, but the insecurity is more tolerable because she now exerts some control over whether abandonment will occur. As a child she could not influence the actions of her parents, but as an entrepreneur she very much directs the course of the business. Business ownership thus provides a means through which she can chart the course of her own life and avoid a damaging pattern she experienced in her youth: either the abandonment and disappointment offered by her father or the dependency and frustration exhibited by her mother.[4]

Through independent enterprise, many new entrepreneurs came to terms also with their earlier father-daughter relationships. Some openly reconciled with their distant father and thoroughly enjoyed their newfound connection. For these women, their fathers became an important source of guidance and inspiration. Others, like Diana Epstein, did not achieve the desired closeness but rather grew to understand and accept their fathers for who they were: "It took me a long time to figure this out," Epstein noted with a smile, "but in the past few years I've begun to understand the value which my father placed on hard work. He is successful because he demands the best from himself, and that is an admirable characteristic. Business is still the basis for our communication, but that's OK. I am alot like my dad, and I'm proud of what he's done. And I know he feels the same way about me."

ADOLESCENCE AND THE DILEMMA OF CHOICE

As little girls, the new entrepreneurs were unusually independent; many broke social barriers, determined to pursue the interests of their choice. However, as adolescents these women squarely confronted a barrier that was not easily broken: the feminine ideal. For most, this encounter was their first experience in the so-called hall of mirrors.

This dilemma was tellingly described by Sara Tetreau, now thirty and owner of Green Mountain Graphics. Tetreau was born in Montpelier, Vermont, where her father ran a prosperous lumber mill and her mother was a secretary with the Department of Motor Vehicles. The youngest of three daughters, Tetreau remembered herself as an unusual child—dinosaurs and army men were her favorite toys, and she hoped to be an archeologist when she grew up. Searching for fossils in faraway countries was her dream.

When she went to high school, Tetreau found that her interests were too unusual to bring success in the areas that counted most—dating and social activities. As a result, she made some important changes. "When I was in ninth grade," she began, "I took earth science as an elective. On the first test, I got the highest mark in the class. Everyone made fun of me and called me the teacher's pet, and I remember feeling real embarrassed. I also joined the Geology Club, and was pretty excited about the field trips. It made me feel like I was getting closer to fulfilling my dream. But I was surprised that there was only one other girl in the club, and I felt a little out of place. Midway through tenth grade, I decided to quit.

"During my sophomore year," she continued, "I met this bubbly, blonde girl who really bowled me over. Here I was, this little mouse who wanted to be an archeologist, and she shook me out of my shell. I got a job working in a nursery school, and started going out with this guy who had ten brothers and sisters. In those days, I wanted to be a teacher because I loved the kids at the nursery school. But then I wanted to marry this guy and have eleven kids just like his mother had. I decided to work after high school so he could go to college, and we could get married."

At the age of fifteen, Sara Tetreau unknowingly entered the "hall of mirrors" and encountered her first image. Reflected in the glass was a painful lesson: The world is divided into two spheres, male and female, and she could not be successful in both. As a child, Tetreau believed she could do anything she wanted. She pictured an active life for herself in which she would travel to faraway places and make new discoveries. In high school, all this changed, and social pressure to conform to a different ideal became very strong.

In Sara Tetreau's case, success during adolescence meant fulfilling a socially prescribed role rather than pursuing her own interests. Succeeding in this role required that she become less independent and more accommodating. Although earlier she had set her own standard of behavior, at this point she stopped doing so. No longer able to resist pressure to do what other girls did, Tetreau embraced an externally defined model that severely limited her options, but she faced a difficult choice: She could drop her goals and change her standards and thereby succeed as a woman, or she could maintain her course and risk failing in "femininity."

For Sara Tetreau, the choice was clear. Within a year, she was transformed from a "mouse" to an outgoing, popular adolescent, and part of that transformation involved giving up her unusual dreams. At least temporarily, she abandoned her career plans and chose a more traditional course. At this point, the life path that stretched before her split and diverged in two directions. One path led to marriage and family, the other to active outreach and independent achievement, and following both seemed impossible.

CONFRONTING THE SPLIT PATH

When they started high school, the new entrepreneurs could not avoid the hall of mirrors. However, the women reacted to the mirror images in different ways. Some, like Anne Munsey, continued to pursue what interested them despite pressure to follow a different path. Some, like Sara Tetreau, gave up their unusual interests and conformed to the expected ideal. The majority took paths that fell somewhere between these two. Yet as they remembered their adolescence, even these women qualified independent achievement with a description of role-related success. The following are typical comments: "I was the smartest girl in my high school class—and the prettiest," or "I was part of a group known as 'The Workers.' We were also the prettiest girls in town and the most popular."[5]

In general, by the time they had reached their middle teens, the new entrepreneurs were uncertain about what course their lives would follow. Some interviewees were set on careers in teaching or nursing, and a small minority hoped to enter a nontraditional field. Only two women remembered wanting to have their own business some day. Education was usually tied to finding a husband, and, for most of the study participants, marriage and family started overshadowing all other goals.

This situation was best described by Nina Anderson, now a successful attorney with her own practice. When asked what goals she envisioned for her life during her teen years, Anderson threw up her hands and said, "Goals? What goals? I didn't have any goals. I knew I wanted to do something special with my life, but I just didn't know what it was. I knew it wasn't nurse, teacher, or secretary, but I couldn't quite get a handle on it. Although I graduated in the top 10 percent of my high school class, I somehow felt there was nothing out there for me. After college, marriage seemed the most obvious solution."

A majority of the new entrepreneurs responded to my question in similar terms. As adolescents, they remembered being unable to envision a future in which they were actively engaged at anything specific. Although all them wanted to "do something," many couldn't picture that "something" as distinct from marriage and family. At this point, they defined their lives in terms of the relationships they hoped to have rather than the achievements they hoped to accomplish. Although not necessarily negative, defining one's future through projected relationships does have some inherent danger. For example, some women experience difficulty in distinguishing their own boundaries from those of other people. Others may develop an excessive dependency that renders them unable to take control of their own lives.[6]

During this period, the new entrepreneurs also heard mixed messages at home. Nina Anderson spoke for the majority when she described the goals that her family urged. "My parents thought nothing would be more fulfilling for me than to marry a doctor and have children. Then I would be secure." By pushing marriage and family as the best goal, Anderson's parents reinforced broader social pressures to follow a certain path. Yet they simultaneously demanded independence, responsibility, and excellence from their daughter. This was true for a majority of the new entrepreneurs. Two-thirds of these women had jobs and managed their own money; many were required to pay for their clothes or other expenses. Such demands carried with them an implied expectation of individual autonomy and strength that stood in direct contrast to overt expectations of future dependency.

The new entrepreneurs thus confronted a dichotomy in life course that was to last well into their adult years. On one hand, they were told to marry and depend on someone else for their security; on the other, they were urged to be independent and take care of themselves. These contradictory messages further reinforced the split path and helped to confuse their future vision.

As young adults, the new entrepreneurs set out on a divided life path with few clear goals to guide them. Their stories reveal continued attempts to bridge the chasm between each side of the divide, but few women experienced full success in this endeavor. Instead, most were pulled from path to path as they attempted to propel their lives forward.

TRYING TO BRIDGE THE GAP

Colleen McClary's story illustrates how many women reacted to the dilemma of bridging the gap. McClary grew up in Austin, Texas, where her father worked in the state's Department of Education, and her mother owned a successful dress shop. The oldest of three children, McClary was always a hard worker. She started helping out in her mother's store when she was twelve and worked there until her high school graduation. At that point, she headed west to college, eager to leave home and test herself in the world beyond the Lone Star State. She described those years: "I just flowed along through college and wandered through a lot of different majors. At first, I was going to be an art teacher, and then I tried science. I even thought of teaching physical education. I had no idea what I was going to do, but I must have had some goal in mind, knowing I would eventually get a degree. I read the catalog and knew what I had to do to graduate, but that's the only thing I planned. I ended up with a major in English.

"I was always very interested in getting away from my family and into the big-time city. That's why I went west to Stanford University in California. I worked pretty hard and ended up on the dean's list all four years. After that, I felt like I could do just about anything. You know, I'd come to the big time and made it OK. Then I knew I could make it anywhere.

"At the end of my junior year," she continued, "I decided to explore the possibility of working at Lake Tahoe. I headed off on the bus with no job or place to stay but confident that I would find something. There are a lot of resorts around the lake, and I found a job as a waitress. The place even provided me with a room, and I met lots of nice people there. I stayed up at Tahoe all summer, made good money, and had a lot of fun.

"After I graduated I worked for another summer, and then I went to Europe and traveled around by myself for several months. I was only twenty-two, and now when I look back on it, I say, 'My God! How did I ever have the nerve to do that?' After I came home, I hoped to settle into a career but wasn't sure what I wanted to do. I had a fine education and some interesting experiences but no real life goal.''

McClary's story conveys a sense of reaching out, of exploration, and of meeting challenges in a world of unknowns. Yet, despite her intelligence, energy, and capability, McClary lacked a sense of direction. Although she continued to reach outward day by day, she could not envision her whole life in active, goal-oriented terms. Instead, she ''flowed'' and ''wandered,'' unsure of which way to go. A pattern similar to Colleen McClary's is evident in the stories of many other interviewees. After high school, these women set forth with energy and determination. Highly independent, they were eager to test themselves and find out what they could do. Moving to faraway cities, working at different jobs, making new contacts, and traveling alone are just some of the experiences that they described. For most, young adulthood was a time of active outreach and new achievement.

However, at the same time that they appeared active and goal-oriented, these women experienced periods of intermittent wandering and waiting. Some, like Colleen McClary, were unable to choose a college major; some dropped in and out of school, unsure of what they wanted to do; still others chose a course of study simply because it was easy. Many drifted into college because their friends were going or because they were unsure of what else to do. Even those who married young were unable to define their life path clearly. Such wandering can in part be ascribed to youth, but for many this pattern continued up to their late twenties, early thirties, or beyond.

Although three-fourths of the new entrepreneurs eventually finished their degree and started working, their plans for the future were vague. Whether married or single, a sense of wandering continued to permeate their lives; themes of waiting and uncertainty surface again and again in their stories. Single women waited to marry, married women waited to have a family, working women waited to find the ''right'' job, and many women waited for someone or something to make their lives happen.

Most of the new entrepreneurs had to resolve this dilemma before they could take full charge of their lives. Somewhere during her work years, the typical new entrepreneur experienced a pivotal incident that enabled her to reevaluate her situation and then to set a clear direction for her life. From that moment on, she stopped waiting and started making her life happen in the way that she actively chose. It is to these important years that we will now turn.

CHAPTER 5

The Work Years: Passages to Entrepreneurship

After finishing school, the new entrepreneurs set out on the road to entrepreneurship. Their stories show that no single way leads to independent enterprise. Many different experiences may prepare a woman to strike out on her own. However, each interviewee did pass certain milestones as she moved along the way. Her education provided a strong foundation on which to build her subsequent life, and the world of work helped her to develop necessary business and professional skills.

Throughout their years of employment, all the women in our study grew and developed. Professionally, they gained the knowledge and skills that they would eventually transfer to their own businesses. As the years passed, they continued building confidence and a sense of what they could do. On a practical level, they learned how to close a sale, order inventory, manage people, market a product, and coordinate the diverse elements of the organizational process. They acquired their understanding of what makes a business succeed or fail. During their work years, many women also developed a relationship with a mentor or guide who helped them grow and develop.

On a personal level, the new entrepreneurs learned to stand up for themselves and to assert their independence even when it was not welcome. Despite negative mirror images and self-doubts, they continued to reach out and learn. Because of their strength and persistence, even the painful lessons that they encountered helped them move ahead on the road to entrepreneurship.

Although the new entrepreneurs are a diverse and complex group of women, their career patterns fell into one of four broad categories: job-keepers, job-hoppers, career-changers, and homemakers. Half the interviewees were *job-keepers*. They worked for at least five consecutive years at one job and usually opened a business in a field related to their previous work experience. Even if they occasionally changed positions, the job-keepers did not change their field of expertise. Instead, they pursued their career in a more or less linear fashion, developing confidence and building skills as they moved ahead. This finding is somewhat different from what we might expect—the usual stereotype portrays entrepreneurs as restless and easily bored, hopping from one job to another until they finally settle down with their own firms.[1]

About one-fourth of the new entrepreneurs changed jobs more frequently than every five years or held several substantial jobs in very different fields. Unable to find their vocational niche, these women were clearly *job-hoppers* who had many varied and seemingly unrelated work experiences before they chose a particular business enterprise. For example, one woman worked with a neighborhood legal aid program, with the Department of Labor as a research assistant, with the welfare department as an intake counselor, and with the YWCA as program director. Finally she opened a fitness and health center for women.

Although her case appears extreme, such a history was not unusual among the job-hoppers. Although their work experiences were diverse, these women felt that their skills and talents were developed in an orderly fashion, even though the "order" may not have been readily apparent. This orderly skill development became evident only when a specific business opportunity arose, at which point everything "came together," and their life paths appeared to make more sense.

The remainder of the women were either *homemakers*, who took time out to raise their children, or *career-changers*, who worked in the traditionally "feminine" fields of social work, teaching, or nursing before making a radical change and becoming entrepreneurs.

On the following pages, we will meet women from all four groups and observe their passages to entrepreneurship. Their example will illustrate what life experiences best prepare a woman to undertake the demands of independent enterprise.

JOB KEEPERS: THE STORY OF MARILYN CARRANZA

The younger of two daughters, Marilyn Carranza was raised in suburban Cleveland, where her mother was a school librarian and her father was a traveling salesman who frequently was away from home. An economics major with a minor in marketing, Carranza graduated from Ohio State University. Soon after graduation, she was hired as assistant to the marketing director of a small Cleveland training firm that specialized in designing training programs for hospitals and clinics.

Marilyn remembered her first job as a time to learn: "My first boss was a wonderful man," she noted with much pleasure, "and he gave me all kinds of opportunities. Fifteen years ago, there weren't too many woman in marketing, especially in the medical field, but he was very supportive and taught me everything he knew. The first time I had to make a cold call, I wanted to die. We worked on sales techniques, and he helped me write a little opening. Now I laugh about that, but I sure needed it at the time."

Although Carranza loved her job and appreciated her boss, she eventually realized that her position was not going to change. This prompted her to make a difficult decision. "After four years I started to see that I would always be his assistant and protégé. The job didn't really offer me much more room to grow. At the time, I was active in my professional association, and, while attending a national meeting, I met a man who owned a firm that ran large medical conferences all over the United States. We hit it off, and he offered me a better job. It involved relocating to Philadelphia, but there was some real potential there for me, so I didn't mind. Once again I started out as an assistant, but eventually he put me in charge of our accounts for the whole mid-Atlantic region. Within three years I doubled our client base, and was promoted to director of marketing."

A couple of years later, Carranza saw yet another opportunity for advancement. "My company purchased a smaller company in Baltimore," she declared, "and sent me to evaluate what was going on there. I stayed for about six months, looked around, and could see that Baltimore was ready to change. A lot of things were happening in town. Well, this smaller company was very old-fashioned, and they had some management problems. I wanted to stay in Baltimore and help develop the new company, so I went to my boss and told him what I saw and made some suggestions on how to build things up."

Confident that she could handle the situation, Carranza was unprepared for her supervisor's reaction. "I'm not sure why he turned me down," she noted with dismay. "I guess he thought I was too assertive or would jeopardize his relationship with the new firm if he let me in there, so he said no. This was my big chance, so I argued with him, but he still refused. I wanted desperately to succeed at everything I did but felt like I was a real failure with this. So I went back and told him I would like to move to Baltimore and would work under the established management there if only he would back me and give me some responsibility. He told me that he had interviewed all the people in the new company, and they said they couldn't work with me because I was too aggressive."

Stunned by his assertion, Carranza temporarily withdrew, but withdrawal did not resolve the situation: "It was a really traumatic experience," she declared emphatically. "My job meant so much to me, and I was terribly hurt. I took a few days off, and then when I went back my boss accused me of being truant. I told him that I had cleared my leave with the personnel department and to call up to confirm it. He started yelling, and then we engaged in a shouting match, and I was fired. After that, I went through a breakdown and was in the hospital for a while. But then I bounced back because I never give up. I just wasn't going to let them get me down. Later I thought that maybe I was too aggressive, and maybe I was going to leave some day anyhow, but it was awful to have it happen like that.''

Several important lessons can be drawn from Marilyn Carranza's story. Like many of the new entrepreneurs, she developed a strong relationship with someone who could answer her questions and guide her development. Whether a valued teacher, a direct boss, or a professional colleague, these mentors were important sources of information and support. This was especially true for Carranza on her first job. A willing student, she learned all she could from the people around her. She also took whatever opportunities her boss offered and did not allow her initial nervousness to keep her from trying new things. Such active outreach and desire for professional growth characterized all the new entrepreneurs.

Another important component of Marilyn Carranza's professional development was her participation in her trade association. By taking part in meetings and serving on committees, she expanded her knowledge and her network. This participation in turn enabled her to meet new people and brought a better job offer. Carranza was willing to reach out on two levels: She sought to develop her skills on the job and simultaneously looked beyond her firm for other opportunities to expand her professional expertise.

Marilyn Carranza didn't allow attachment to her mentor or her firm to obscure what was best for her. She recognized when the time had come to move on and did so. Although grateful to her boss, she realized that remaining his protégé would not allow her to continue developing her talents. In short, she needed to find a new, more challenging position that would offer her more potential. Recognizing the right time to move, and moving, were important steps along the road to independent enterprise.

At each stage of her development, Carranza expanded her professional abilities as fully as possible. She started by reaching for a level that she could handle, and, after developing skills and confidence, then sought a more challenging position. For example, on her first job, she accompanied her boss on sales calls until she felt ready to do them herself. Then, after relocating in Philadelphia, she moved from handling individual clients to managing an entire sales region. Her success in this position further increased her sense of what she could do. Consequently, when she was offered a promotion to director of marketing, she had the confidence to accept it without hesitation.

For nine years, Marilyn Carranza's progress was steady. Throughout this period, she continued the kind of active outreach that was typical of all the new entrepreneurs. Her ability to learn on the job, to seek and meet new challenges, and to move on when necessary brought about continued advancement. But then she suffered a serious setback—instead of being rewarded for her achievements, she felt as though her initiative had been punished. What caused this setback?

Although Carranza had developed considerable expertise in her field, she was nonetheless young and still somewhat inexperienced. Rarely involved with major corporate reorganizations, she lacked the managerial experience to handle such arrangements with the required tact. She perceived the acquisition of a new subsidiary as a personal opportunity and was unable to see the threat that her many suggestions posed. With their jobs endangered by her company's takeover, the Baltimore management team was understandably on guard to protect themselves and their way of running the business. They would hardly welcome an assertive young woman full of new ideas.

When it became apparent that she wanted to run their company herself, relations deteriorated, and the old team reportedly refused to work with her at all. In short, her mistake was to push so unrelentingly for her point of view. At that point, Marilyn Carranza's boss made a clear choice. He decided that alienating her temporarily was better than losing an entire management team during a period of transition, and he refused her request.

Although her boss's perception of the situation was not entirely inaccurate, it was distorted by sex-role stereotypes. Because she was outspoken and direct in her approach, Carranza did not reflect a stereotypic feminine mirror image. Instead, she exhibited considerable initiative and persistence in pushing for herself and her ideas. Although such characteristics were necessary if she were to advance, the risks were high. Marilyn's failure rested in part on others' perceptions of her behavior as "unfeminine."

Carranza's request and the Baltimore company's reaction offered her boss a chance to examine his own biases. He did not recognize that his response to her behavior was colored by expectations of how a woman should behave, and he thus failed to learn an important lesson regarding the influence of sex-role stereotypes on his ability to manage people. He could have helped Carranza understand the situation better from a managerial point of view. However, instead of offering helpful criticism, he engaged in a shouting match, accusing her of being so aggressive that no one could work with her. Seeing beyond the stereotype to the real problem was impossible for him. As a result, he lost a valuable employee, Marilyn Carranza lost her job, and both experienced frustration and an increased sense of polarization.

Carranza described herself as a fighter, and this quality helped her bounce back from a traumatic experience. The ability to keep going and not give up characterized all the new entrepreneurs. Yet part of Carranza's struggle was wearing and unnecessary. In retrospect, she blamed herself, saying that perhaps she had been too aggressive in her approach; unable to evaluate the situation clearly, she accepted her boss's point of view. Instead of learning exactly what aspect of her behavior was unwarranted, Carranza labeled all her actions as negative, in part because she measured herself by a stereotypic yardstick that did not allow for independent, assertive action.

Assertive, so-called unfeminine behavior brought problems to other interviewees as well. One woman echoed Marilyn Carranza's story with this observation: "The preeminent problem in my business career was my lack of deference and humility. It's how I walk into a room—some men just don't like it. I do not walk into their inner sanctums like a secretary, with my body saying, 'May I get you a cup of coffee.' I walk in normally, rationally, and sit down. They're used to deference, and I treat them normally. I don't hesitate and say, 'Excuse me, uh, my name is Jane Goodson.' I just don't understand it. If I work well, it is to their honor, but they are uncomfortable with that. So even though I reached a very good position, I had to work twice as hard to get the same job as a man, and I could only get so far."

Jane Goodson recently became an entrepreneur after many years of working for a major corporation. Another job-keeper, she followed much the same pattern as Marilyn Carranza did. Her comment further illustrates how the male-dominated business world does not reward independence or initiative in women but perpetuates distorted images of femininity that keep women trapped. For both Goodson and Carranza, starting a business was the most effective way to escape the situation. Capitalizing on her strengths and skills, each woman struck out on her own to find greater success in the field for which she had been trained.

JOB-HOPPERS: LEARNING TO TAKE CHARGE

The story of Louise McFadden stands in sharp contrast to those of Marilyn Carranza and Jane Goodson. Carranza and Goodson worked for one firm or in one field for many years before starting a business, but McFadden jumped from job to job before settling down. Her experiences raise important issues that may surface for any woman on the road to entrepreneurship.

McFadden grew up in the suburbs west of Philadelphia. Her father owned a sporting goods store where the entire family pitched in and worked. An average student, McFadden attended Brandywine Junior College, dropping out several times before completing her associate's degree. Even while in school, she established a pattern of wandering that continued for fourteen years as she restlessly searched for the right path.

McFadden noted with some chagrin, "I began my career bouncing around from one job to another. After leaving college, I moved to Manhattan and worked as an assistant publicist for the United Way. Then I moved on to a top private school where I served as public information officer. After a couple years with the school, I started working for the United Nations compiling a directory of all their overseas programs. From there I went to a big international law firm and was trained as a paralegal."

By this time, McFadden's youthful wandering had become an established life pattern. Unable to settle into a career, she continued moving from position to position. "I was living from weekend to weekend," she recalled, "just waiting for life to come along. You know, all my life I'd heard, 'Boys go to college, they go to law school, they have careers.' But for girls, it's 'When you get married . . .' and 'When you have kids. . . .' For years, I wandered around unsure of what I should do. I moved from job to job while my parents waited for me to get married and I waited for my life to happen.''

At thirty, McFadden married a young attorney, but marriage did not solve her problem. She continued wandering for four more years before giving birth to a child. At that time, she quit her latest job and settled in to a period of reevaluation. She was thirty-four years old, had lots of experience, but was headed in no particular direction. ''One day,'' she recalled, ''a friend and I decided to make candles, and for some reason that became symbolic of my life. I had never tried making candles before, but they turned out beautifully. So I started thinking, 'Well if I can make candles, I can do other things, too.'

''At that point,'' she continued, ''it suddenly dawned on me that nothing was going to happen in my life if I just sat there and waited. After that, I stopped saying, 'Wouldn't it be neat if this or that happened,' and said to myself, 'Damn it, stop waiting. If you want to do something, *go do it*.' That was the moment when I began taking charge of my life.''

This was a pivotal incident for Louise MacFadden. Soon after, an old friend approached her with a business offer, and McFadden did not hesitate to accept. The two women pooled their resources and started an import-export firm. However, McFadden's willingness to confront her life and take responsibility for herself preceded this step. Without such an internal shift, she might have bypassed this opportunity and continued wandering. Instead, she took charge, setting her own goals and then working hard to make them happen. It was from this position that she was able to strike out and then succeed on her own.

What advice does Louise McFadden offer other women who feel adrift? ''If you just sit there and wait,'' she cautions, ''nothing will ever happen. Think about what you've always wanted to do and then go for it. You can accomplish anything you want if you just will yourself to try. Maybe you'll have to wait until some opportunities come along, but once opportunity knocks, make up your mind to open the door and answer. Otherwise you may find yourself sixty years old and nothing much will have happened in your life.''

Many of the interviewees described similar experiences of awakening. Irene Samuelson, manufacturer of a successful line of belts and handbags, shared her story: ''I started out teaching art in high school, moved into educational planning, then quit the field altogether. After that, I was unable to settle into one job, and never really earned the money I knew I was capable of earning.

''One day I was driving through a beautiful residential neighborhood on my way to the hairdresser's. I looked at all the large homes and started feeling sorry for myself. 'I'll never have the money to live like that,' I thought, 'unless I marry a wealthy man.' Then suddenly a thought came to me: 'I don't have to marry money, I can go out there and get it by myself.' It was a shocking experience to realize that I didn't have to be like Cinderella and wait for someone else to take care of me. I could be my own Prince Charming and make my life happen all by myself.''

For Louise McFadden, Irene Samuelson, and many other interviewees, taking full responsibility for their lives was a difficult step. Although as children these women were encouraged to be independent, as adults they still experienced conflict around issues of autonomy and self-control—even though almost all worked and were financially self-sufficient. Their stories show that economic independence does not equal psychological independence. Although important, a job alone does not always enable a woman to believe that she can and should set her own course. By pursuing a career, she may appear independent on the outside while feeling confused and dependent within. True independence requires a major internal shift and a new mirror image of appropriate feminine behavior. For McFadden and Samuelson, such a shift was necessary before they could truly stand on their own.

Once they crossed this psychological barrier, both McFadden and Samuelson could capitalize on the skills they had developed during their work years. In retrospect, each woman viewed her varied experiences as a real asset. "Every job I've had," Louise McFadden noted, "helped prepare me to run this business. Writing that overseas directory for the UN involved an incredible amount of detail work, and I learned to be very meticulous and careful. It was also a lesson in memory, and that is absolutely key to anything you do in business. If you don't have a good memory, you must train yourself and develop some system to help you remember what goes on. Otherwise you will be at a real disadvantage.

"My legal training has also been invaluable," she continued. "Since I'm familiar with key terms and procedures, I am not at all intimidated by the rules we have to deal with. Sometimes things get pretty complicated, but I understand the system well. Of course we have a good attorney, and I frequently call the Customs Service or the International Trade Commission for clarification. But none of it mystifies me. I have a good foundation, so at least I know what I'm talking about.

"When I look at everything I've done," she concluded, "I feel I'm ideally suited to this type of business. I've had lots of exposure to things that count, and have developed the flexibility necessary to succeed as an entrepreneur. I have to handle many different types of problems on a daily basis, and I believe that my particular background was the best training I could have had."

THE TRADITIONAL CAREER WOMAN: MAKING A CHANGE

A third group of women—the *career-changers*, worked in the traditionally "feminine" fields of teaching, social work, nursing, dental hygiene, or medical technology before making a dramatic switch into entrepreneurship. A few interviewees entered such professions with the goal of making a career; some even obtained postgraduate degrees in their field. However, after working hard for a number of years, they became tired, "burned out," or disillusioned. When an opportunity to change came along, these women were ready to take it and move in a different direction. In general, such a decision required the evaluation of abilities and interests and then a transfer of skills from one occupational setting to another.

For Alicia Markham this evaluation and transfer process took two full years. Markham was born and raised in Salt Lake City, where her widowed mother worked as a medical secretary. After graduating from Brigham Young University, Markham moved to San Francisco where she eventually completed a master's degree in social work. Soon after, she married a young businessman and settled down in Los Angeles. In the years that followed, Markham had a very successful career in her chosen field, eventually running an adolescent counseling center at a large Los Angeles hospital.

After fifteen years, her marriage ended in divorce, and she returned to San Francisco with her two children. She describes her life after this point: "After my divorce," she began, "I asked myself, 'What am I going to do now?' I knew a change was coming, but it took a lot of soul-searching before I decided what I should do. I started by taking an inventory of my life and figuring out what was really important to me. Part of my motivation also came from money. Social work would never give me the kind of income I wanted, and I had two children to support. So I went to a counselor, took psychological tests to find out my interests and skills, and analyzed how I could take all those intangibles I had and put them together. It took me two years to get the confidence in myself to make a change."

This period of evaluation set Markham on the road to self-discovery, and the results were surprising. "I found out that I had good leadership skills," she continued with pride, "that I could motivate people and guide them to do what I wanted. That came from running the counseling center, where there was a tremendous amound of pressure. My tests showed I would be really good in sales, and I said, 'Sales? Me? I never sold a single thing in my life!' "

Once they decided to make a change, all the traditional career women went through a process similar to Markham's. After some period of self-evaluation, they identified particular skills that could be transferred to a business setting. The important point here is that these career-changers derived confidence from what they had already accomplished, recognizing certain strengths with which to build the second stage of their lives.

The results of Alicia Markham's counseling persuaded her to try an entirely new course: "I thought medical sales would be the right thing," she declared, "but nobody would take me. I went from interview to interview, and everybody said, 'Lady, come back in four years when you've sold something.' Finally I found a tiny little company which was just starting out with computers. I knew nothing about computers, but I saw it as my big chance to get out and meet the public. So I went home every night and put in three hours of work learning the business. I read the *Wall Street Journal* and carefully observed what other people did and said. There were three salespeople in the office, and I sold the most each month. In a year, I almost doubled my social worker's salary."

Alicia Markham eventually moved into medical sales as she had earlier planned, working for a large company that supplied equipment to hospitals and physicians. When an opportunity arose for her to split off from the parent company and form her own business, she gladly took the step. Accustomed to dealing with doctors, she finds medical supply an ideal field for her skills and experience.

Throughout the transition from one field to another, Markham developed confidence by carefully analyzing what skills she had acquired. She discovered that she was an effective leader and coordinator, worked well under pressure, and understood how to make people do what she wanted. This analysis was a key step in the transition. Instead of devaluing or discounting skills she had developed over the years, she found strength and pride in what she had accomplished, which enabled her to take the first step toward changing careers. Once she decided to make the change, she persisted until someone finally hired her. At that point, she felt ready to prove herself and did so in an outstanding fashion. Drawing on experience, she moved out into a new world and learned all she could.

Once the decision was made, the career-changers followed a path similar to Alicia Markham's, working hard to learn the details of a new field and to establish themselves in a different business. This work involved doing extra reading, attending seminars, and, as Markham put it, keeping "your mouth shut, your nose to the ground, and your eyes and ears open." To their surprise, these women found that experience in the traditionally feminine fields had prepared them well, especially to deal with people. Over and over, they stressed that "people" skills developed earlier were an important contributor to their later business success.

FROM HOMEMAKER TO BUSINESS OWNER

The last group of women were *homemakers* who took time out to raise their children and help with school and community affairs. Although their path skirted the world of paid employment, these women also developed important skills.

Carmen Martinez is typical of the homemaker group. Martinez grew up in Ft. Lauderdale, Florida, raised by her mother, a Cuban immigrant. After graduating from high school, Martinez attended a local business college, where she studied bookkeeping and accounting. Martinez then moved to Atlanta and worked in her chosen field for several years before marrying a young police officer and settling down to have a family.

Martinez remembered that period as one of vitality and growth for both her husband and herself: "When we first were married," she began, "Jack and I decided to have three or four children. We both loved kids and wanted a big family. Our first child was born a couple of years later, and I soon found myself involved with a nearby cooperative nursery school. Jack had been a Big Brother for a long time, and he continued his work with fatherless boys even after we had our own kids. Our life was centered around the family and activities that concerned children.''

"When my oldest daughter was seven," she continued, "I helped organize a Brownie troop and eventually became president of our local Girl Scout Council. I also was treasurer of the PTA for several years and organized the most successful fund-raising drive that the school ever had. Eventually I was invited to join the board of a local children's welfare agency. I always liked figures, and my schooling came in handy with all these activities. Jack was really proud of my work. He used to tell me I could probably run the country more efficiently than the President!''

Carmen Martinez believed that her chosen path brought several advantages. "As I look back on it," she remarked with a smile, "I grew and developed more than many women who are actually out there working for money. After I completed one project, I always had the opportunity to move on to something bigger. I also could choose the jobs that I liked and wanted to do, and reject those that didn't feel right. At the same time, I met lots of different people and developed useful contacts throughout the community.''

The Martinezes had four children within an eight-year span. Throughout this period, she had one child or another in the same cooperative nursery. "One day," she noted, "the director asked me if I would be interested in doing the books—for money, not as a volunteer—and I quickly agreed. I thought it would be a one-time thing that would easily fit around my other activities. Well, the regular bookkeeper never returned from her maternity leave, and the next thing I knew I had a part-time job. My youngest was almost in kindergarten, so I decided to stay with the school as long as I could.''

Now, four years later, Martinez has her own business providing clerical and bookkeeping services to local companies. "When I got married," she said with a smile, "I never dreamt that I would end up with my own business. What I am doing now just evolved from all my past experience. Community service allowed me to develop strong organizational and leadership skills even while I was giving my children the attention that I wanted them to have. And my volunteer work always stayed related to my two most important interests: taking care of kids and managing money. When the right opportunity came along, I took it. My life is in a different phase now, but it is no less rewarding.''

Martinez is proud that she has never had to make an unsolicited marketing call. Highly visible and respected in her community, she obtained lucrative contracts by word of mouth. People who had worked with her on various projects knew that she was dependable and thorough. By the time she became an entrepreneur, she already had an outstanding reputation. Community service, she believes, enabled her to build a solid foundation for her later entrepreneurial venture.

Carmen Martinez has no regrets about staying home with her children. "For me," she smiled, "it was the right thing to do. Being a homemaker didn't mean withdrawing from the world and forgetting about my own development. It meant expanding my life in the way that was best for me. Wonderful opportunities for growth and development can appear in many different forms. The important thing is to recognize them when they come along.''

CONCLUSION

No matter what path she followed—job-keeper, job-hopper, career-changer, or homemaker—each woman in my study believed that her background had prepared her well for the rigors of entrepreneurship. Although some wished that they had had more formal business training, all emphasized the importance of gaining practical experience in the field. After starting their businesses, the new entrepreneurs still had a lot to learn. However, these women were able to transfer important skills from one setting to another—the management of an independent enterprise. Chapter 6 provides an opportunity to assess your skills and abilities and discover how you, too, can turn your experience into a money-making venture.

PART 3

Steps to Entrepreneurship

C H A P T E R 6

Assess Yourself

You have now shared the experiences of many entrepreneurial women. Up to this point, the focus has been on the new entrepreneurs and their lives, but in Part 3 you will examine your own situation. The exercises here will help you interpret your experiences in light of what you have learned from the women in this study. As you progress through Chapters 6 and 7, look closely at yourself, your business or business idea, and your attitudes toward making money. Completing these worksheets will give you greater understanding of your own strengths and weaknesses and of what starting and managing an independent enterprise require.

CAPITALIZE ON YOUR "FEMININE" SIDE

This exercise has three steps: (1) you will identify and define some positive characteristics that you associate with women; (2) you will determine how those strengths are useful in operating your business; and (3) you will learn how these strengths are often distorted into weaknesses, thereby undermining a woman's confidence and the ability to succeed. This exercise will help you develop a model for success that capitalizes on your particular female-associated strengths.

  STEP 1: In the table provided, list some positive characteristics that you associate with women. For example, you might start your list with "empathetic," "nurturing," and "intuitive." If you think of more than eight terms, continue on a blank sheet of paper.

Positive Characteristics Associated with Women	*Your Definition*
1.	
2.	
3.	
4.	
5.	
6.	
7.	
8.	

STEP 2: Write a brief definition for each term you have listed. For example, for *nurturing* you might have "helps things grow," "is persistent in caring," and "takes care of things really well." *Empathetic* might suggest "sensitive to other people's needs," "in rapport with others," and "understanding." Do not write any negative associations, only positive ones.

STEP 3: Answer the questions listed below. Be as specific as you can. For example, if nurturing is one of your outstanding qualities, you might answer the second question in the following manner: "Because I am good at nurturing, I will be skilled at developing and training my employees. I also will be good at guiding the growth of my business. I won't give up as easily as someone unaccustomed to nourishing growth. I also will be patient in developing my clients, giving them the consistent attention they need. This in turn will help me get repeat business."

1. What are my outanding strengths as a woman?

2. How will these strengths help me succeed in my business?

3. How can I capitalize further on these strengths?

STEP 4: Copy your list of positive characteristics onto the worksheet that follows. Now define each term in the most stereotypic manner possible. For example after *nurturing* you might write: "Is suited to child care, teaching, or nursing; would make a good wife and mother; worries too much, acts like a mother hen."

Positive Characteristics Associated with Women	*Stereotypic Definition*
1.	
2.	
3.	
4.	
5.	
6.	
7.	
8.	

FINAL ANALYSIS: In our culture, as in most others, masculinity and femininity suggest different constellations of characteristics. Over time, these gender-linked characteristics become rigidified into stereotypic pictures, and both men and women have difficulty adopting behavior associated with the opposite sex. Traits usually linked with women are viewed as especially useful in raising a family and taking care of the home. By contrast, such female-associated traits as nurturing and empathy have typically been seen as a liability for a woman hoping to succeed in the male-dominated business world.

The experience of the new entrepreneurs indicates that many female-associated characteristics are of positive value to the woman who owns a business (see Chapter 3). However, many potential entrepreneurs have internalized the cultural message that their female-linked strengths are not useful in a business setting. Such women may be discouraged from striking out on their own because they believe they lack the "right" qualities for entrepreneurial success. In this exercise, you have developed your own model of female-associated strengths. You then analyzed how that model forms the foundation for successful entrepreneurial behavior. By identifying and then capitalizing on your individual strengths, you have established a strong foundation on which to build your future entrepreneurial success.

ASSESS YOUR CAPACITY FOR RISK

In Chapter 2 we learned that popular stereotypes portray women as afraid to take risks. We also noted that such stereotypes have little basis in fact. Research shows that women take far more risks than is widely believed. Many women, however, have internalized a negative self-image where risk taking is concerned. They do not perceive themselves as risk takers even though they may have successfully handled many risky situations.

This exercise will help you evaluate your capacity for risk-taking behavior. In step 1, you will examine your self-perception where risk taking is concerned. After establishing your self-image, you will then analyze your life experiences carefully and assess how often you have really taken risks. You will examine what kinds of risks you have undertaken and how much credit you have given yourself for those that you have successfully managed. Finally, you will compare your self-image at the start of the exercise with your actual life experiences.

STEP 1: Choose the phrase that best describes you:

- A real gambler
- Unafraid to take risks
- Willing to take some risks
- Somewhat cautious
- Very conservative where risk is concerned
- Not willing to take any risks

Now answer this question: Overall, how do you view your own ability to take risks?

STEP 2: For purposes of self-analysis, answer the following questions:

1. In my personal life, what risks have I taken?

2. How well did I handle these risky situations?

3. What was the outcome of each risk I took?

4. How did I feel about the outcome?

5. What risks have I been unable to take? Why?

6. What has this exercise helped me learn about my own capacity for risk?

STEP 3: Answer the above questions again, this time regarding your work life.

STEP 4: When you finish Steps 2 and 3, compare the two sets of answers and then complete these questions:

1. In which sphere have you taken the most risks—personal or work?

2. Which risks were the easiest for you to handle?

3. Which were the most difficult? Why?

4. What would have made the difficult situations more manageable?

5. Overall, in your life how willing have you *really* been to take risks?

ASSESS YOUR ENTREPRENEURIAL TRAITS

Chapter 2 introduced two women, Chris Stewart and Jackie Edwards, whose stories illustrated the most common entrepreneurial traits and how these traits both help and hinder the woman business owner. To succeed in independent enterprise, you must understand how your entrepreneurial traits may interfere with your management of the business. Chris Stewart's conflicting needs to create and control kept her from delegating work even when her business was growing and she desperately needed good people to assist her. Her creative, innovative tendencies also prompted her to spin out new ideas without developing the structure necessary to carry them out effectively. The following exercise will assist you in identifying and analyzing your own entrepreneurial characteristics.

STEP 1: Start your self-assessment by reading through the groups of traits listed below. On a scale of 1 to 5, rate the extent to which each trait describes you (1 = ''very little,'' and 5 = ''a lot'').

Positive Entrepreneurial Traits	*Rating*
Intuitive	
Persistent	
Flexible	
Creative	
Confident	
Action oriented	
Innovative	
Independent	

Negative Entrepreneurial Traits	*Rating*
Autocratic	
Rigid	
Controlling	
Mistrustful	
Dictatorial	

STEP 2: Look at your *positive* traits and answer these questions:

1. Which of your positive traits are strongest?

2. How do these traits help you in managing your business?

3. Which of your positive traits might interfere with your ability to succeed? How?

4. Which of your positive traits are least developed?

5. How does this lack of development affect your ability to succeed?

6. How can you develop these traits more fully?

STEP 3: Look at your *negative* traits and answer these questions:

1. Which of your negative traits are most prevalent?

2. How do they interfere with your success?

3. How can you reduce or eliminate these traits?

4. Can you turn any of your negative traits into positive ones? How?

5. Can you turn tasks over to someone else when your negative traits interfere with accomplishing those tasks?

STEP 4: Overall, how much do you conform to the *positive* entrepreneurial profile (top score is 40 points)? How much do you conform to the negative entrepreneurial profile (top score is 25 points)?

ASSESS YOUR SKILLS

Throughout your work life, you have developed many skills which can help you succeed as an entrepreneur. This exercise will help you evaluate your particular strengths and weaknesses.

STEP 1: *Identify your skills and abilities.* In the left column of the table below, list all the jobs, both paid and volunteer, that you have held. In the center column, write next to each job the tasks you performed. In the right column, write the skills and abilities required.

Job	Tasks	Skills and Abilities Required
1.		
2.		
3.		
4.		

STEP 2: *Organize your skills and abilities.* This next step will help you assess your skills and abilities in terms of the specific functions necessary to operate a business successfully. Entrepreneurship requires some strength in each skill area listed in the chart that follows. However, like most people, you will not be strong in every area. It is critical that you understand where your strengths and weaknesses lie. Otherwise you may neglect or avoid important tasks, thereby undermining your success. Once you clarify your weak areas, you can then either obtain more training to develop skills that you do not have or hire someone else to do tasks that you are unable to do.

On the work sheet below, list each of your skills and abilities under one of the following nine categories.

Management	Leadership	Planning

Training	*Marketing and Sales*	*Entrepreneurship*
Finance	*Innovation*	*Professional and Technical Skills*

STEP 3: *Evaluate your skills and abilities.* Answer the following questions:

1. In which categories are your skills and abilities particularly strong?

2. In which categories are your skills and abilities particularly weak?

3. Which skills have you avoided developing? Why?

4. How essential are these skills in helping you reach your long-term goals?

5. Which skills do you want to improve first?

6. How can you improve these skills? With seminars and other short-term training? With further formal education? With the help of a mentor? With different work experience?

STEP 4: If you already have a business, look at those categories in Step 2 where your skills and abilities are strong and answer these questions:

1. To what extent are you using the skills that you already have?

2. Could you use particular skills to better advantage? If so, how?

3. To what extent do you avoid tasks that require skills you lack?

4. Which tasks do you avoid?

5. Who does the tasks you avoid? If no one else does them, when can you hire someone to take them over?

6. Overall, how do your strengths help you with the management of your business?

7. Overall, how do your weaknesses interfere with the successful management of your business?

If you do not have a business, look at those categories in step 2 where your skills and abilities are strong and answer these questions:

1. How can you draw your skills and abilities into a business venture?

2. What would this venture be?

3. Which, if any, skills do you need to develop or improve before making the step into entrepreneurship?

4. Which skills do you already have that would help you make this step right now?

5. Overall, in terms of skills and abilities, how ready are you to become an entrepreneur?

ASSESS YOUR ATTITUDES ABOUT MONEY

The final exercise in this chapter will help you analyze your attitudes toward making money. Although you may have a good business idea and lots of energy to carry it out, if you are ambivalent about making money you may actually undermine your own success. (In Chapter 8, you will see how this happened to a number of the participants in this study.)

STEP 1: Answer each question in the table by checking the appropriate box.

How Do You Feel About:	*Good*	*Neutral*	*Uncomfortable*
1. Charging highly for your product or service?			

How Do You Feel About:	Good	Neutral	Uncomfortable
2. Requesting payment when it is due?			
3. Demanding payment when it is overdue?			
4. Firing people who are costing you money?			
5. Facing male "authority" at the bank or negotiating table?			
6. Turning down unprofitable business—even if you need the work?			
7. Being responsible for other people's wages and livelihood?			
8. Making lots of money—all by your own effort?			
9. Making more money than your husband, mate, other friends, parents?			
10. Being perceived as financially grasping or "out there only to make money?"			
11. The financial risks involved in this venture?			

STEP 2: Go back over your answers. Outline each box checked in the "Good" column and congratulate yourself on your strength in this area. Now look at each box where you checked "Uncomfortable." Answer the following questions for each box:

1. What in particular makes you uncomfortable in this area?

2. How does this discomfort interfere with your ability to make money?

3. What would make you feel more comfortable?

STEP 3: The following suggestions will help you reduce your discomfort with money-related matters:

• Remember that you are not alone in your discomfort. Many women experience some of or all these feelings during the life of their business.

• Join a women's business, networking, or support group. Such groups provide encouragement as well as practical strategies for dealing with money-related problems.

• Focus on your business, not on your self. Separate your business goals from your personal goals—you are not your business. If you want your business to survive, you must put its financial welfare above your personal feelings and do whatever is necessary to make a profit.

• Set clear financial goals that allow for the growth and development of your business. Remember, if there is no profit, there will be no growth and, eventually, no business.

• Balance business and personal concerns where your employees are concerned. You need not be ruthless, but you must keep the financial standing of your business in mind at all times.

• Discuss your financial goals with the people closest to you. This may be your husband, mate, or extended family. Make clear what you hope to achieve and ask for feedback.

• Acknowledge any uncomfortable feelings that your husband or mate may express about your financial success. Get him to discuss these feelings as much as he can. He may have fears that are totally unfounded, which you can acknowledge and then dispel.

• Acknowledge your ambivalence about making money. Ask yourself: "What am I afraid of? How realistic is this fear? What will happen if I allow myself to be ruled by these feelings? How can I diminish my fear?"

• Remember that owning a business is no different from any other job. You work hard, and you should be paid for your efforts.

• When negotiating a contract, always determine your bottom line in advance so that you can compromise without giving away what is essential to your survival.

• When collecting overdue accounts, remember that you *earned* the money. It is owed you for services rendered.

• Read Chapter 8 to discover how the new entrepreneurs handled similar problems related to making money.

CHAPTER 7

Assess Your Business

In Chapter 6, you identified your strengths, weaknesses, skills, abilities, and attitudes about making money. In Chapter 7 you will move from assessing yourself to assessing your business venture. The exercises in this chapter will help you to analyze the nature of your business, establish some clear goals and objectives, and assess the risks involved in striking out on your own.

THE MOST PROFITABLE BUSINESS ENTERPRISES

For those who are looking for a business idea, I have supplied a list of the most profitable businesses. If you have the necessary training and the interest, you might consider choosing one of these ventures. This list is based on the 1985 edition of *Business Profitability Data*, by John B. Watson, available from Weybridge Publishing Company, 16911 Brushfield Drive, Dallas, Texas 75248. (Watson analyzes 287 different businesses—if you are interested in the complete data, write him at the above address or check your local library or bookstore for his book.) I selected businesses from his list that seem to be particularly interesting to potential female entrepreneurs. I also added from Watson's list a few businesses that I thought had outstanding potential. The number to the left indicates what rank Watson assigned that particular business.

1. Legal services
2. Accounting, auditing, bookkeeping
5. Management consulting and public relations

6. Employment agencies

7. Hair stylists

9. Engineering and architectural services

10. Computers and software (retail stores)

12. Auto repair and body shop

13. Computer programming and software services

14. Insurance agents and brokers

15. Advertising

18. Extermination services

19. Janitorial services

20. Travel agencies

22. Detective agencies, protective services

23. Direct-mail advertising

30. Cut flowers and plants (retail)

49. Fish and seafoods (wholesale)

51. Miscellaneous home furnishings

52. Women's dresses (manufacturing)

65. Books and stationery

66. Restaurants

69. Shoes (retail)

85. Fast-food restaurant

84. Fresh fruit and vegetables (wholesale)

96. Bread and other bakery products (manufacturing)

97. Jewelry (retail)

135. Toys and hobby equipment (wholesale)

140. Women's dresses (retail)

148. Grocery and meat (retail)

157. Women's and children's clothes (wholesale)

STEP 2: Keep this list in mind and answer the following questions:

1. Which businesses most interest you?

2. How much experience have you had working in these, or similar, businesses?

3. If you have not had much experience in the field that interests you, where can you find more information about running a business in that field? Through courses or seminars? Through working for someone in the field? Through books and pamphlets? Through talking to someone with a similar business?

4. List four steps you can take to get the information you need.

One source of information about any of the businesses listed here is the appropriate trade group for a particular industry. The names and addresses of such groups are listed in the *Encyclopedia of Associations*, available at your local library. This useful three-volume set lists all the professional and trade associations in the United States. In general, such groups provide statistics, guidelines, and practical tips for prospective business owners interested in a specific industry.

For example, if you want to start a florist shop (item 30 in the above list), you would look in the *Encyclopedia of Associations* under *florists* or *floral*. There, you would find the address for the Florists' Transworld Delivery Association (FTD) in Southfield, Michigan. FTD provides many valuable publications, statistics, and guidelines for people involved in the floral industry.

Most libraries have a business section containing useful references on a wide variety of business ventures. If you are interested in a particular industry, ask your librarian what publications are available to help you. In addition, university extension programs, community colleges, local adult schools, and the Small Business Administration all offer introductory courses in different business fields.

DETERMINE YOUR PERSONAL GOALS

Whether you own a business or hope to start one, you must clearly understand your personal goals. Some women become entrepreneurs because they want to achieve independence in their work life; some hope to find an outlet for their ideas. For example, a talented jeweler wants the opportunity to make money from her creative abilities. So she sets up a workshop, designs and makes jewelry, and sells her work as she produces it. At some point, this woman will have to make a decision regarding her long-term goals: Does she want to design and make jewelry or build up and run a business? If her business is to grow and prosper, she must guide its development. As she becomes more involved in managerial and entrepreneurial tasks, she will have less time for artistic and creative endeavors. To use her time and talents most productively, it is critical that she clarify her goals. This process will in turn help her to determine her role in the business and the role of her staff. Filling out the following *personal motivation inventory* is the first step in the clarification process.

1. My goal in starting/running this business is to
    a. Practice a profession or craft
    b. Build and manage a small business
    c. Build as big a business as I can
    d. Sell this business and eventually start another one
2. My financial goal is to
    a. Supplement family income
    b. Contribute 50 percent or more to family income
    c. Support myself and/or my family
    d. Make as much money as I can
3. To succeed, I will have to be

    a. Hardworking   *g.* Competitive
    b. Persistent   *h.* Driven
    c. Dedicated   *i.* Ruthless
    d. Energetic   *j.* Single-minded
    e. Ambitious   *k.* Self-sacrificing
    f. Organized   *l.* Other
4. At this point, how prepared am I to do what is necessary to achieve my goals?

DETERMINE YOUR BUSINESS GOALS

Your next step in the clarification process is to define the focus of your business as narrowly and specifically as you can. Management consultant Peter Drucker believes that the most difficult question any business owner or corporate leader can answer is, "What business am I in?" This question appears simple but is frequently difficult for business people to answer in specific terms.

At some point during the first phase of entrepreneurship, you must decide on your focus. Narrowing your business concept and pinpointing your market are two of the most important steps you will make. You must know *what* you are doing before you can determine *who* you are doing it for and *how* you will accomplish it.

After establishing the "what" and "who" of your business, you must develop a specific action plan. The *business-focus work sheet* below will help you narrow your ideas and clarify your goals. Complete each sentence in as much detail as you can. Avoid generalities, and be as specific as possible. You will see that these sentences are not as easy to complete as they first appear.

1. My product or service is:

2. This product or service is unique because:

3. My primary market is:

4. I can best reach this primary market by:

5. My role in the business is:

6. My key staff members and their duties are:

7. My sales goals for the next year are:

8. My marketing goals for the next year are:

9. My staffing goals for the next year are:

10. My training goals for the next year are:

11. My research and development goals for the next year are:

Now go back and check your answers on the work sheet—have you completed each item as *specifically as possible*? You may have to review and refine your answers several times before you have developed the necessary details. For example, the first time she worked on this exercise, one of my seminar students filled in the first statement as follows: "My product or service is a café serving coffee, pastries, sandwiches, and soft drinks." In the third entry, she put down, "My market is everyone."

When we discussed her answers, I suggested that she better focus her ideas. Did "coffee" mean espresso? "Regular" coffee? What about tea and hot chocolate? Were "soft drinks" Coke and 7-Up, or would she offer Italian sodas? "Natural" fruit sodas? Mineral water? Pastries could mean donuts and Danish, Greek baklava, French eclairs, or brownies. Sandwiches include hamburgers, sprouts and avocadoes, natural grain breads and gourmet cheeses, corn beef and pickle deli-style items, and old time favorites such as grilled cheese.

As we worked together, she realized that the type of food she offered was directly related to the image of her business and therefore to the type of clientele she would attract. She began to think about what type of cafés her city already had, what image she wanted to foster, how her ideas differed from those of already established business owners, and what customers she wanted to attract. Different food products require different suppliers, so before she could proceed with her plans, she had to rethink her business concept and narrow her focus. This process was the primary step on which all the others were based.

Now look at item 5. As you review your "role in the business," consider the goals that you established when completing the personal motivation inventory. When you start your business, you may have to fill many roles. However, your primary function will ultimately be determined by your long-range plans and by your ambitions as an entrepreneur. How specifically have you identified your role? How realistic is your answer? Are you trying to fill too many roles? If so, what can you do about this situation?

In items 7 through 11, have you established specific goals, using specific numbers you hope to achieve where appropriate? If not, go back and work on these items until you have entered number amounts wherever possible. For example, sales goals would be dollar figures; staffing goals, the number of new people you hope to add; training goals, how many seminars you hope to attend or how many you will provide your staff members. Remember, if you don't have a specific goal, you cannot plan how to reach one.

STEPS TO STARTING A BUSINESS

Following certain steps in starting a business will improve your chances of success. The exercise below will help you gather data, organize the information that you have collected, and develop a plan to move you nearer to your goals.

The business I hope to start is: _____

STEP 1: Complete the necessary research by answering the following:

1. What is the market potential of my business?

2. Where will I locate my business?

3. What are the advantages and drawbacks of this location?

4. What are the financial requirements to start a business like mine?

5. What is the typical amount of capital needed?

6. For retail, how much inventory is necessary?

7. For a product, how will I manufacture my product?

8. What legal form will I choose?

9. How will I deliver my product or service?

10. What is the competition?

11. What pricing structure will I use?

12. What bookkeeping system will I use?

STEP 2: Locate resources to help you (see Appendixes C and D); then fill in the appropriate information for your community:

1. Local libraries that can help me are:

2. The city or county economic development corporations in my area are:

3. The nearest local office of the Small Business Association (SBA) is:

4. The address of the local chamber of commerce is:

5. The address of a trade group or professional association in my field is:

6. A women's network that might be helpful to me is:

7. One other local organization (SCORE, university extension, adult school) that could supply information is:

STEP 3: Determine local regulations and fill in the table boxes:

Item	*Address and Phone*	*Date "To Do"*	*Date Done*
1. Call the city or county clerk to find out what regulations pertain to the use of a fictitious name.			
2. Find out if my city requires a business license.			
3. Contact the appropriate state offices to find out how to collect and forward state sales tax.			
4. Contact the Internal Revenue Service for information about filing my federal income tax.			

Item	*Address and Phone*	*Date "To Do"*	*Date Done*
5. Contact the appropriate state offices for information about paying state income tax.			
6. File for my employer identification number.			
7. Contact the appropriate regulatory agencies:			
a. fire			
b. health			
c. zoning			
d. planning			
e. environmental science			
f. commerce			
g. other			

STEP 4: Use the following table to compute your start-up costs.

Item	*Cost*
1. Licensing fees	
2. Stationery, cards, brochures	

Item	Cost
3. Phone, utilities	
4. Rent, leasehold improvements	
5. Business account fees	
6. Accountant, attorney, other professional fees	
7. Office supplies and equipment	
8. Supplies necessary to manufacture my product	
9. Labor	
10. Inventory	
11. Insurance (liability, fire, theft, auto, bonding, employee)	
12. Test marketing of my product	
13. Advertising, marketing, promotion	
14. Dues for trade and professional associations, networks	
15. Travel	
16. Books, courses, specialized training	
17. Other	
	Total:

STEP 5: Prepare your financial statements. They should include the following:

1. Personal financial statement (assets and liabilities)
2. Cost-of-living budget
3. Money needs for first three months
4. Projected profit-and-loss statement
5. Cash flow projections
6. Balance sheet
7. Resources: trade and professional associations, suppliers, Robert Morris Associates' *Annual Statement Studies*, National Cash Register's *Expenses in Retail Business*, and Dun & Bradstreet's *Key Business Ratios*

STEP 6: Develop your marketing ideas.

Item	*Date "To Do"*	*Date Done*
1. Establish advertising goals and budget.		
2. Explore local possibilities: newspapers, shoppers' specials, flyers, radio spots, window displays, billboards, community organizations, and bulletin boards.		
3. Explore trade-related resources such as industrial directories, trade shows and expositions, trade publications.		
4. Consider advertising in special-interest magazines that reach your target audience (See *The Standard Periodical Dictionary* and *The Encyclopedia of Associations*).		
5. Evaluate a direct-mail campaign.		
6. Sponsor civic or charitable events.		
7. Evaluate special seasonal promotions.		
8. Teach or lecture at a local college or adult school.		
9. Develop a free seminar to introduce your product or service.		
10. Write articles in local papers, trade magazines, journals.		
11. Speak before local chambers of commerce, women's groups, trade associations.		

PREPARING A BUSINESS PLAN

Completing the exercises provided will supply you with sufficient information to start a business plan. Formalizing your ideas by putting them down on paper will give you a clear picture of what you are doing, how you will do it, who will help you, to whom your product or service is directed, how much it will cost, and what your returns will be. Although preparing a plan is often time-consuming, you have already done half the work. Now you need to organize your information in a coherent, well-written form.

You may already own a business and have avoided writing a business plan. Perhaps now is the time for you to start. For your venture to grow and prosper, you must establish some systemized view of its purpose, structure, goals, and budgetary needs. In addition, a good business plan is the most persuasive evidence to bankers and investors that you know what you are doing.

Don't include your résumé in the business plan; rather, describe your qualifications and those of your management team in terms of the applicable experience that each has had. Banks and investors look for expertise in your particular field. If you are starting a business in which you have had little prior experience, include in the section on the management team those skills you have developed that are transferable to this new enterprise.

You probably will need the advice of a lawyer and an accountant to complete your plan. The women I interviewed stressed the importance of obtaining the best professional assistance at the outset; the financial forms that you need must be done carefully and accurately. However, before seeing your legal and financial advisors, obtain sample forms and go over them so that you understand what information you must provide. Your professional advisor will then assist you in filling out the forms and interpreting what the different numbers mean.

The Bank of America's *Small Business Reporter* booklets, particularly *Steps to Starting A Business* and *Financing Your Business*, contain sample forms. You can order these forms from Bank of America, Department 3401, P.O. Box 37000, San Francisco, California 94137. Your local bank also should have loan application packages which include these financial forms.

Although your business plan is a selling tool, it is not advertising for your business. The goal is to communicate your understanding of your venture and your industry, and to present a well thought out plan of action. Keep your plan factual and avoid unnecessary adjectives.

The outline that follows illustrates one format you might follow—write one or two paragraphs for each section. Be as concise as you can, using simple English and checking your grammar and spelling. Type the final plan on good bond paper.

A. Your product or service
   1. What will you do, for *whom*?
   2. How will you do it?
   3. What will your position in the industry be?
   4. Why are you *unique*?

B. Your market
  1. *Who will you sell to? Who* are the *end-users?*
  2. *Where* are they?
  3. *How clearly* can you *describe* them?
  4. *What* is the *size* of this market?
  5. *What* is your *share* of this market?
  6. *Why* would they *choose* you?
  7. *What* is the *growth* potential?

C. Your competition
  1. *Who* are they?
  2. *Where* are they?
  3. *What share* of the market do they have?
  4. *How* are you *different?*
  5. *How* can you *convince* investors that you will be able to *compete effectively?*

D. Your management team
  1. *Who* is your management team?
  2. *What* are their qualifications?
  3. *What* are their duties?
  4. *How many* employees will you have?
  5. *What* will they *do?*

E. Your distribution methods
  1. *How* will you sell your product or service?
  2. *How* will you a*dvertise* your product or service?
  3. *What* unique *marketing ideas* do you have?

F. Your sales forecast
  1. *What* are your monthly and/or annual sales *projections?*
  2. *What economic trends* could affect your projections?

G. Location
  1. *Where* is your business located?
  2. *What* are the *benefits* and *drawbacks* of this location?
  3. *Which competitors* are nearby?

H. Operations and research and development

  1. How will your product be *made*?

  2. How will your service be *delivered*?

  3. What are the possibilities for the *future*?

I. Your organization's structure

  1. How will your company be *organized*?

  2. What type of *legal structure* will you have?

  3. Who is on your Board of Directors?

J. Financials

  1. Profit and loss statement

  2. Projected cash flow

  3. Balance sheet

K. Final questions

  1. Does your business plan *inform* and *excite* prospective investors?

  2. Do you *show* your *understanding* of the business in your plan?

  3. Does your plan *reflect* your excitement, determination, integrity?

  4. Is your plan written in *simple* English?

ENTREPRENEURSHIP AS "RISKY BUSINESS"

The following exercise offers a series of questions that will help you evaluate the risks involved in your proposed business venture. If you are not totally unafraid to take risks, don't be discouraged—Chapter 2 noted that the most successful entrepreneurs are not simply wild gamblers. In managing their businesses, these entrepreneurs focus carefully on those things which they can control and gamble only on the rest. Thus they minimize the risks involved and make their situation as manageable as possible. Now look at your business plans and answer the following questions:

1. What factors in this situation are you sure about?

2. What factors can you control?

3. How do you plan to control these factors?

4. Carefully identify the unknown factors.

5. Which of these factors are beyond your control?

6. How might these factors affect your success?

7. What concrete steps can you take to reduce or eliminate the risks associated with these factors?

8. What resources can you use (people, money, knowledge, equipment, physical space) to put your ideas into effect?

9. What do you stand to gain from this situation?

10. What do you stand to lose?

11. In the final analysis, how much of your present plan is really a gamble?

PART 4

Women Entrepreneurs at Work

CHAPTER 8

Women and Financial Success

Many of the new entrepreneurs turned to business ownership because they wanted to earn more money. Stuck in low-paying, dead-end jobs, they were eager for more opportunity, greater challenge, and higher pay. They believed that, once on their own, their earning potential would be unlimited. Yet after starting their enterprises, a large number encountered a problem they had not anticipated: They did not understand how to make money. Although lack of business training often contributed to this problem, another equally important factor undermined their financial success.

Running a business as a profit-making venture requires behavior that many women find inappropriate and "unfeminine." Because of the distorted mirror images around her, the woman entrepreneur may have difficulty charging what she is worth and demanding the payment that she is due. As she sets her prices and develops her fee scale, negotiates contracts and collects past-due accounts, she may experience ambivalence and self-doubt. For many of the new entrepreneurs, inner conflict between the need to be conventionally feminine and the need to make money directly affected the management of their business enterprise.

Sally Solomon, owner of a financial planning service, described this situation best: "I think we women really want to please. I remember myself as that type of person. I wanted to please others, to take care of their problems and do favors for them. As a result, it was very hard for me to say I was going to charge for my services. Although I was an expert in my field, I did not relate my expertise directly to money."

The women in my study were aware of the damage caused by such attitudes, but changing their self-images was often a difficult process. Even while they worked to modify their behavior, clients and business associates often unwittingly undermined their efforts. Many people still rely on the old mirror images and expect stereotypically feminine behavior from every woman they meet. When dealing with a female entrepreneur, such people may unconsciously reinforce the patterns that she is trying to break. Learning to make money therefore involves confronting both individual conflicts involved in internal changes and larger social forces that work against such changes.

The American people have always enjoyed a love-hate relationship with the self-made entrepreneur. A financially ambitious man is regarded with both admiration and distaste—admiration for his initiative and will but distaste for his greed and ambition. This ambivalence dissolves into outright disapproval or worse where women are concerned. Solomon noted with some discouragement, "There's only one word we have for a woman who works for money, who expects to be paid, who thinks highly of herself, and who succeeds, and that's *mercenary*. There are many positive things about a woman like that, but there is no positive term to describe her."

According to psychologist Phyllis Chesler, our society believes that money, like sex, "is something that is supposed to happen to women. . . . Ladies are not supposed to work. Ladies do not have to labor in public for vulgar cash."[1] The desire to make money is thus at direct odds with our cultural view of the feminine ideal. This ideal, which suggests that women are childlike, delicate, incompetent, and in need of protection, masks the reality of poverty and economic need in women's lives.

Every woman brings her personal views and problems about money to this greater cultural framework. Whatever attitudes she has developed from her particular family background and upbringing will come into play here. Learning to make money thus involves sorting through a multilayered complex of associations and injunctions, a process women find more difficult than do men. Although men also face personal problems and social ambiguity regarding money, women must in addition reshape their very definition of femininity to succeed. And they must do so in the face of cultural pressure to maintain old patterns. In Chapter 8 we join several interviewees on their journey into the world of money and profit. Their stories show us how at least one group of women successfully confronted the barriers found in that world.

LEARNING TO MAKE A PROFIT

Alice Bennington was born and raised in St. Louis during the years of the Depression. Her father was an entrepreneur who had developed a successful chain of grocery stores in the greater St. Louis area. The family was not hit as hard as some by the economic difficulties of the times. Bennington attended

Washington University, where she majored in art history. Soon after World War II, she married a Navy man and settled into raising a family of her own. Like many women at that time, Bennington did not think of a career. The mother of four children, she relocated her home as her husband's work demanded, eventually settling near Chicago.

While her children were young, Bennington spent considerable time doing volunteer work in her affluent Chicago suburb and eventually was appointed to the local planning commission. As the years passed, she became more and more absorbed with the problems of urban development and began taking courses at the University of Chicago, eventually earning her master's degree there.

In ten years of community service, Alice Bennington had developed extensive contacts and experience. Together with another volunteer, a woman trained in landscape architecture, she decided at age forty-two to open her own consulting business in urban planning and environmental design. Now fifty-six, Bennington appears knowledgeable, authoritative, and self-confident, but her story reveals that this confidence was slowly and painfully won.

"My partner and I," she began, "unfortunately had the same attitude toward making money: We didn't believe in it! To succeed in business, you must have a commitment to making money, or there will be absolutely no opportunity for growth. We had trouble understanding this. Running a business is like a thermodynamic principle—just to stand still you have to make a profit. Otherwise you're going to go under."

Over the years, Bennington learned to charge fairly for her services. However, mastering this lesson required that she confront the inner conflicts that stood in her way. "It has always been difficult," she continued with a shake of her head, "for me to be tough and assertive about money. This was one of the major hurdles I had to overcome. When I have to demand payment, I feel like I'm somehow losing some important female attributes. You must be willing to accept the fact that it's OK to be assertive, and it's fair. Being able to put your hand out and say 'Give me the money' is perhaps the most important thing. Yet I feel like I'm losing my own sense of being attractive as a woman."

Because Bennington had little formal business training, she lacked the confidence to manage the financial side of her firm. Her reluctance even to try handling this important job led to a serious mistake. "It took us a long time to figure out how to handle the financial end of the business," she noted. "We hired a man to be our business manager, and he proved to be an absolute ass. He was incompetent, a bean counter, and he had no sense of what it cost us to run the business. I don't know how we ever found him, but before we knew it, we were going down, down, down."

Both Bennington and her partner were married when they started their firm, and the security of having a husband to pay the bills proved to be yet another disadvantage. "We were second wage earners," she declared, "and this also was a problem. It was an advantage in that we didn't have to make full salaries to survive, and we were able to weather some pretty hard times. But we didn't have that critical kind of motivation to make money. We had to get over our working assumption that tomorrow we could always close the door, that our husbands were there to care for us. To be successful, one simply has to have the will to make money.''

As her business began to fail, Bennington's determination not to give up prompted her to examine that failure. She discovered that her desire to be self-sufficient and manage an independent enterprise was in direct conflict with her view of femininity and appropriate female behavior.

Bennington resolved her conflicts by committing herself to the business and its survival. She separated the desire to make money for herself from the necessity of making it for the business, and this new commitment helped counter her belief that making money was immoral, especially for a woman. Once she clarified her purpose, it was easier to be assertive about charging and collecting appropriate fees. Although Bennington is now making an excellent profit, she still does not feel completely at ease with the money-making side of business enterprise. For her, making money and being feminine may always be opposing forces.

When asked what problems they faced in running a business, many other interviewees responded with stories about handling and making money. Like Alice Bennington, they experienced conflict between their need to be assertive about money matters and their contrary need to be feminine. This conflict arose most frequently when they were negotiating contracts, pricing services, and collecting past-due accounts.

REAL WOMEN DON'T MAKE CONTRACTS

Barbara Jennings is a young woman whose success has been closely tied to the computer revolution. Now thirty-two, Jennings runs a rapidly expanding systems analysis firm. She was raised outside of Boston near the famous Route 128 electronics industry and always hoped to go into a technology-related field. Her background includes a degree in computer science and six years of writing software and developing in-house systems for a large insurance firm. After her first child was born, Jennings decided to do a little consulting before returning to her regular job. Her initial experiment soon became a full-time occupation, and she now handles several major contracts a year with insurance companies throughout the New England area.

As head of a growing consulting firm, Jennings is required to negotiate contracts on a regular basis. Although well-prepared to handle the technological side of her business, initially she was far from ready for the intricacies of the negotiation process: "I'll never forget those first few contracts," she stated emphatically. "The things people told me were absurd. They made comments like, 'Don't you trust us?' and 'We wouldn't do anything to harm you.' One man told me that his company made no written agreements with anyone while another said that the maximum profit we should make was 5 percent because that's what we'd make if our money were in a savings account! And they did it with a fatherly kind of attitude, like, just listen to me, and I'll help you."

Jennings soon learned to stand up for her own interests, and, during our conversation, she was adamant about several important points. "Before you go in there," she cautioned, "you must figure out what you want from the contract. Decide what is important to you, what you can give up, and what you really need. You have to be flexible and willing to give and take, but you can't compromise if you don't know your own bottom line. Otherwise it's too easy to be swayed by their fatherly attitude."

Jennings strongly advises other women to evaluate every job carefully and watch out for hidden costs. "Before we sign a contract," she continued, "the scope of the work is mutually defined and agreed upon by our people and the client. The job may involve two meetings to analyze what needs to be done, but as the project develops, we meet here, we meet there, and you begin to give a little, saying you want to keep the client happy. That is bleeding money from your business. It may not be a major hemorrhage, but it's bleeding a slow death, and at first it seriously depleted my business.

"Now I say, 'We'll be glad to do this for you, but it's not in the scope of our present contract. Would you like to authorize us to do it? If so, I can give you an hourly rate or a new contract.' You absolutely must monitor the true cost of being in business. It is essential that you get paid for your time, and most clients understand that. After all, they're in business, too, and will respect you more if you don't give yourself away."

Although Jennings can easily give such advice today, she developed her strategy after several painful experiences. "I quickly learned," she concluded, "to let people know I was going to protect my interests, but that wasn't always easy for me to do. Now I'm much more assertive and straightforward about charging for my time, and if people don't like it, they can find someone else."

The stereotypes that Barbara Jennings encountered are obvious. Men at the negotiating table will certainly try to gain the same concessions from other men as they do from women. However, they may use different tactics. Accustomed to interacting with women in other contexts—as fathers, husbands, or sons— they may assume a protective stance toward any woman regardless of the situation. In the business world, such a stance gives men license to take advantage of women under the guise of helping or protecting them. Since women are still taught to rely on men for support, the female business owner may well cooperate with her client's behavior even though it puts her at a disadvantage.

Another factor contributes to this situation. Women today comprise more than 95 percent of the "helping" professions—the secretaries and receptionists; the practical nurses, private child care workers, and dental assistants; nurses, bank tellers, and private household workers.[2] Women in such jobs are charged with meeting other people's needs while receiving low wages. Women are also the primary care givers at home, where they work long hours for free.

A women who moves from a female-dominated service job to business ownership must be prepared to change her outlook toward money. When she starts her own firm, the woman entrepreneur moves into a world where charging for time and services is both necessary and expected. However, she may retain the psychological framework necessary to function in her former world, a world where serving others for little or no money is the norm. If she is to succeed in her new role, she must change that framework—a difficult task for many women.

Jennings notes that her first inclination was to "keep the client happy," and this was best accomplished by accommodating his or her needs rather than looking out for her own. Men may expect accommodating behavior from women business owners and unconsciously work to elicit such behavior, but, as Jennings notes, they also respect the entrepreneur who behaves in a "businesslike" fashion. To do this, the businesswoman must discard counterproductive behavior, like the desire to please even at her own expense, and replace such behavior with a clear picture of what she wants. For Alice Bennington and Barbara Jennings, this meant understanding that running a business involves making a profit and that making a profit requires charging for time.

Why does profit making continue to be a problem for some women entrepreneurs? The work of psychologist Sandra Bem provides some answers to this difficult question. Back in the mid-1970s, Bem conducted a series of experiments with 1500 students enrolled at Stanford University. Her goal was to find out how persistently young people of both sexes adhered to stereotypic sex roles.

In the first experiment, Bem set up a job-related situation. She offered each student several activities to choose from: Some activities were clearly male-associated, and some were female-associated. Bem explained that while they were engaged in their chosen task, they would be photographed and then paid for their time. She predicted that "masculine men and feminine women would consistently avoid the activity that was inappropriate for their sex, even though it always paid more." Bem's prediction proved correct, and she notes that "such individuals were actually ready to lose money to avoid acting in trivial ways that are characteristic of the opposite sex."[3]

In another experiment, Bem arranged a situation in which the students were faced with a clearly bothersome request. During a brief phone conversation, each participant was asked to spend two hours completing a questionnaire without pay. The caller made the request in such a way that he assumed the answerer would say yes. The results were clear: Two-thirds of the "feminine" women could not refuse, whereas fewer than one-third of the "masculine" men had the same problem.[4]

When transferred to the negotiating table, the implications of Bem's work are clear. If it is difficult for young students to act even in trivial ways inappropriate to their sex, how must mature men and women feel when they must discard sex-linked personality traits and lifelong roles in situations that directly affect their economic survival? For a woman to succeed in business ownership, sex-role expectations must be at least somewhat modified, and this modification must occur on a cultural as well as on a personal level. Until this change takes place, both men and women will find negotiating with one another awkward and difficult.

It is hardly surprising that Alice Bennington, Barbara Jennings, and their clients initially related in stereotypically defined ways. It is also no surprise that both Bennington and Jennings experienced conflict when they tried to replace a conventional approach with one more appropriate to their business role but less appropriate to their sex role. The difficulties involved in this process are further compounded by the absence of any guides, cues, or models to assist in defining these roles anew.

When discussing these issues, Bennington shared the following story, laughing in retrospect but still aware of how serious the underlying problem really is: "We were presenting our proposal to the head of an important city committee, when my young assistant rose to put up a map. The committee chairman rose, too, and offered to help her. She replied, 'No, I have some pins right here,' and he said, 'You're really prepared. You must have been a good Girl Scout.' Her answer was, 'No, I never made it past Brownies,' and he reacted with, 'Oh, my wife has been very active with Scouting for years.' And this was during our proposal to redevelop an entire section of the city! He was desperate to relate to us in some way and didn't know how to respond to us as colleagues."

As the number of women business owners increases, changing sex-role expectations will become easier, and the figures are encouraging: More than 30 percent of all self-employed people are women, and the percentage increases every year. As the number of women entrepreneurs grows, they will be more visible to one another, to other women, and to the general business world. As they succeed, these women will form new mirror images that allow women greater strength, independence, and freedom.

A WOMAN LABORS . . . FOR NOTHING

For both experienced and new entrepreneurs, one question arises again and again: How much money should they charge? No matter what the business, pricing is a difficult issue. Almost every interviewee had a story to share or a lesson to teach, and nearly all had reached the same conclusion: Whatever the fee, it is probably not enough.

Underpricing their goods and services was a persistent problem even for this successful group of women. Emily Franklin's story shows how one interviewee quickly reversed a negative situation. Raised in northern Alabama, where her great-great-grandmother was well-known as a rebel slave who worked with the underground railroad, Franklin attended Spelman College in Atlanta, then moved north to St. Louis, where she got her first job as a legal secretary. Restless and eager for change, Franklin was clearly a job-hopper. She soon moved on to Denver, where she continued working in the legal field. After five years in Denver, she moved south again to Houston. Two years later, she decided to open a business that specialized in office support for the legal profession.

As she looked back on her experiences, Franklin laughed ruefully. "I gave away my services in the beginning," she declared with disgust, "and when I finally realized what I had done, I resented myself for being so stupid. My husband kept telling me that I should double my fees, but I almost went under before I listened to him."

Nine months after opening her doors, Franklin was struggling to make ends meet, and her husband's words made her evaluate everything about the business. "I had worked in the field for eight years," she noted, "and was pretty well paid. I thought I knew what a fair price for my service would be, but I was mistaken. I started calling around to find out what other people charged and even wrote to several women in Denver who had started similar businesses. One woman replied in detail and offered lots of helpful suggestions. She also gave me the name of another woman right in Houston who suggested that I join the Professional Association of Secretarial Services. Contacting other people and joining my professional association were two things I should have done *before* opening my business."

Franklin advised other women to check out the competition prior to starting their own firm. She also stressed the importance of letting unprofitable work go. "At first," she recalled, "it was almost impossible for me to turn a client down. But then I got tired of working long hours and making so little money. Now I have reset my fee scale, and if someone doesn't want to pay, they can go elsewhere. I learned that if I let a bad job go, something better always turns up. I also set clear financial goals. Last year, I envisioned doubling my salary. The next thing I knew, I was working like crazy, and I doubled my salary. But without a number to reach for, I don't think I would have done it."

Emily Franklin had trouble in another area as well: receiving payment on time. Confronting customers and clients about past-due accounts is a problem for any entrepreneur, but for women the problem may be compounded by negative stereotypes. Collecting money often requires a firm and persistent effort, an effort that may reap evasion and hostility before the actual bill is paid. Whereas the persistent man is seen as "only doing his job," the persistent woman becomes "a nagging witch," "an old hag," or "an aggressive bitch."

Facing this issue offered Franklin an opportunity to examine her own beliefs about appropriate feminine behavior: "It was really hard for me at first," she explained. "I tried to please everybody and rarely got any money in advance for a job. Then I would bill and bill and bill, but people had all kinds of excuses why they couldn't pay. It often got embarrassing to be so demanding. So what I did was flip entirely to the opposite way. It was absolutely necessary.

"Now clients pay me a flat $150 as soon as the contract is signed. That gets them used to writing checks to me right away. Then we have a strict payment schedule, and I control when the money will be paid. I provide a really good service, the best in town. That's what I'm hired for. If they don't want to pay me, then I don't want their work, and I make that clear. I don't feel guilty about that any more. I deserve the money."

Remembering her great-great-grandmother also helped Franklin overcome her reticence. "I come from the South," she continued, "and was taught to be quiet and hold my tongue. People don't like aggressive women, especially aggressive black women. But now I don't care. My great-great-grandmother had the courage to go for what she wanted, and if she could, I can too. I'm not in business to be liked by everybody. If I were, I'd have a lot of work, but I'd never be paid."

What other advice does Emily Franklin offer? "You have to be assertive," she noted, "there's no question about that, but that doesn't have to mean obnoxious. Be honest with people and tell them you expect honesty in return. Ask them why they can't pay, when they expect to pay, how you can better arrange payment. Most of all, don't give up. Phone, write, and keep after them until you get what they owe."

Once the new entrepreneurs overcame their initial reticence, they developed many acceptable ways to collect overdue money. To their surprise, they often found that a little pressure applied firmly, politely, and consistently brought good results. Although demanding money is difficult, a major portion of the problem was brought about by their own idea of what was proper and appropriate for the situation. After they accepted that being paid well for their efforts and being feminine were not mutually exclusive, their problems around money issues diminished. As their self-images changed, their ability to develop effective money-making strategies increased, and their businesses became more successful.

The new entrepreneurs' success indicates hope for the future. By modifying their own behavior, these women are simultaneously helping to modify the destructive mirror images that keep women poor. As these images change, women will experience less conflict around pursuing the money that they need and want. Although this cycle may take many years to complete, the interviewees have made an inspiring, ground-breaking start.

CHAPTER 9

Breaking the Credit Barrier

When asked what their major problem was in getting started, the new entrepreneurs gave a brief reply: money. Like most women today, they had few financial assets to help them capitalize a new business venture. Most relied on personal savings, accumulated retirement benefits, and family loans.

It is no secret that women still earn about 60 cents for every dollar earned by men, that when men and women occupy the same professional status men earn more, that the interviewees themselves were underpaid and undervalued. Women continue to be employed in chiefly low-paying jobs with little hope for advancement, and one major study concludes that "jobs held mainly by women and minorities pay less at least in part *because* they are held by women and minorities."[1]

Trapped in the lowest-paid echelons of our society, women lack power, visibility, and the means to support themselves adequately, much less the opportunity to amass sufficient capital to start a business. Moreover, with so few assets, they do not have the collateral to obtain even the smallest loans without considerable harassment. Carol Harvey, head of a video production company, has worked with many large corporations on both promotional and training projects. Her observation regarding this situation was made with some rancor: "From what I have learned," she noted, "women make the mistake of asking for only $700. If we asked for $70,000 or $70 million, that would be a different proposition. One major airline was just forgiven $25 million, including interest, for the next four months by all of their bankers because they have a negative cash flow. So they pick up $25 million free of charge."

Carol's voice rose with emotion as she recalled her own difficult experiences as well as those of her friends. "I can't pick up $2500 with a negative cash flow!" she exclaimed. "The banks have got to be so sunk into your business that they perceive a risk of losing everything if they say no to you. None of us women has got enough money to play that kind of game. You have to be able to say, 'Guys, you're going to lose the million you gave me unless you give it to me for another year at the same interest.' And we women just can't do that."

In contemporary U.S. culture, individual power and worth are frequently measured in monetary terms. How much money particular people earn or control is directly related to how much power and respect they command. Because women control so little money, they remain all but invisible on the U. S. business scene. Even when women surface to present their case, banks and other financial institutions hardly notice them. As psychologist Phyllis Chesler has noted, "Not to earn money directly in a money culture is equivalent to nonexistence."[2] Any ambivalence a woman has about becoming independent is reinforced by an economic situation that fosters financial dependency. Her sense of helplessness and vulnerability are increased by lack of monetary power, and a vicious cycle is thus maintained. Just to start a business, not to mention making a go of it, the prospective entrepreneur must face these facts and the attitudes which support them.

BECOMING VISIBLE:
THE SAGA OF LUCY WARNER

For Lucy Warner such a confrontation came early in her business venture. Born and raised in western Maryland, Warner came to business ownership after fifteen years of travel and various job experiences. Her work was concentrated primarily in the apparel industry. More a job-hopper than a job-keeper, she rarely stayed with one organization for more than two or three years. By her middle thirties, Lucy had worked for two large department stores, a national clothing store chain, a major garment wholesale house, and a well-known designer and manufacturer of women's sportswear. Her broad experience included every aspect of manufacturing, distributing, and selling women's clothes.

After three years in her last position, Lucy was once again ready for a change and decided to start her own retail store. Her long-range goal was to provide a unique clothing service for executive and professional women. At the outset, she used personal savings to finance her enterprise, but she soon needed money to expand.

Warner's story began when she went to her local Economic Development Corporation for assistance: "I was optimistic when I first went to the EDC," she noted, smiling at the memory of her initial enthusiasm. "They help new businesses with advice and loan information, and I was sure they would help me. Ann was my advisor, and she was wonderful, but the first bank she sent me to said they would give me $5000 if I would put up an additional $10,000.

That was absurd! If I had had $10,000, I wouldn't have been in there talking to them! So I decided to try another bank, and that one was more receptive.''

At the outset, Warner realized that she would have to make some compromises. Getting everything that she wanted was simply not possible. ''I had some collateral,'' she continued, ''but not enough, so they wanted to put the loan through the SBA (Small Business Administration). I didn't like that because of the paperwork and the extra 2 percent they charge to process such a loan. But when I saw they wouldn't waver, I agreed and then spent two full weeks filling out all the forms. I hand-delivered them to the bank and was assured that the SBA would process it all within ten working days.''

Throughout the loan process, Warner was determined to get what she needed. She carefully monitored the progress of her application and kept close watch on the calendar. ''After ten days,'' she declared, ''I asked Frank, my loan officer, if he had heard anything, and he said, 'Nope, but it's not time to worry yet. I'll call you when it's time to worry.' After seventeen working days, I called Ann, and she found that Frank had gone on vacation. Well, I marched over to the bank and said, 'What's the problem?' John, another loan officer, told me that Frank had been very busy, had probably had a couple of hundred-thousand-dollar loans to process, and had made a decision which to do first—mine or theirs. And it obviously wasn't mine. John said he would tend to it immediately, and I returned to the store.''

At this point, Warner made an important decision. She refused to accept second-class treatment and immediately contacted the bank to protest. ''I thought about what had happened,'' she continued, her eyes flashing and her hands making quick gestures, ''and was very angry. So I called the head of the commercial loan department, told him I didn't like the way my loan was being handled, said I wanted to come talk with him, that my store was across the street, and that I'd be there right away. I didn't take a breath, and he didn't have a chance to say anything.

''When I got there, he and John were in his office trying to figure out what they had done wrong. I pointed out to them that Frank had told me my loan had been processed when in fact it hadn't been, and that we had lost seventeen working days. They were very embarrassed because of the delay and said, 'How much do you want and on what terms?' I said I wanted $10,000 for five years, and not through the SBA. My loan closed the next day.''

Instead of remaining quietly passive, Lucy Warner stood up for her rights, and by doing so, she got what she wanted. ''I was very pleased,'' she concluded with a smile. ''It really worked to tell them that I expect better service. Who do they think they are? I am 5-feet tall and a woman business owner. That usually surprises people. First they're thrown by a female business person. Then they don't expect her to be 5-feet tall. I made it work to my advantage by being prepared, by speaking forcefully, and by demanding the same service that they give everyone else.''

Small, female, and comparatively moneyless, Warner was indeed invisible to the banking community. They far preferred to serve larger, more lucrative clients first. In addition, Frank, the first loan officer, assumed a typical protective stance where Warner's interests were concerned: "Don't worry," he told her, "I'll take care of you." Although many women would have relied totally on the loan officer's judgment, Warner did not. Instead, she depended on herself and her own judgment of what was reasonable rather than on Frank and his promises.

What else about Warner's behavior is outstanding? She knew what she wanted and didn't hesitate to go after it. Contrary to our cultural belief that money is supposed to "happen" to women, Lucy did not wait for the money to come to her.[3] When offered unreasonable terms at the first bank, she was quick to turn them down and continue her search. Treated unfairly by a loan officer, she didn't assume a martyr or victim stance but rather acted assertively to protect her interests. In both voice and approach, she retained control of the situation, and, at the end of the incident, she not only got what she wanted but also felt good about not permitting powerful people to treat her unfairly.

The prospective entrepreneur must be prepared to handle incidents like the one described by Lucy Warner. Four steps will help her avoid the economic discrimination still confronting many women today: (1) understanding your credit rights, (2) searching for the best bank, (3) courting the banker, (4) providing the necessary collateral.

UNDERSTANDING YOUR CREDIT RIGHTS

In the past, women have found it almost impossible to obtain either personal or business credit without the cosignature of a male relative. Thanks to the Equal Credit Opportunity Act, passed in 1974, that situation is no longer entirely the rule. The law clearly states: "It shall be unlawful for any creditor to discriminate against any applicant on the basis of sex or marital status with respect to any aspect of a credit transaction." It applies to mortgage financing as well as consumer and commercial credit, and it governs the practices of all credit-granting institutions, including banks, retail businesses, oil companies, and credit card companies.[4] If credit is denied, an applicant is entitled to a written explanation from the lending institution.

Although a step in the right direction, the law itself did not establish any far-reaching regulations to carry out its mandate. Instead, it gave the Federal Reserve Board the power to formulate such regulations. The Board, in turn, interpreted the law and established requirements and exemptions under Regulation B, the section which applies to women and credit. Although the wording of the law is clear—creditors may no longer deny applicants credit because of sex or marital status—the law itself primarily protects those women seeking to establish personal credit. Women in need of business credit are virtually excluded from Regulation B's protection.[5] In her analysis of the Equal Credit Opportunity Act, Lily Pilgrim notes:

The thrust of the federal law is restricted to consumer credit. The justification of the Federal Reserve is that a woman seeking business credit is more sophisticated than her consumer sisters; and, in the final revision of Regulation B, the Federal Reserve refused to prohibit creditors from inquiring about an applicant's marital status in a business credit transaction.[6]

The experience of the interviewees indicates that banks discriminate against women especially in demanding the cosignature of a husband if the applicant is married. Even though such a requirement is now illegal, many banks still "suggest" that if a woman really wants a loan, she had better bring her spouse along.

Liz Gausted, owner of the fast-growing Liz G. Maternity Fashions, vividly remembered such incidents even when she had adequate collateral. "The banks are somewhat chauvinistic," she noted with understatement, "in terms of what they expect from women in business. Every time I've gone to them, they've asked me to have my loan cosigned by someone else. In my case, since I'm married, they've wanted my husband to do it, but it's no different for a friend of mine who is single. We both have consistently refused, but they ask us every time, no matter what size the loan or how reliable we've been in our repayment."

Liz's story was echoed by two other successful entrepreneurs. Angela Warshawski, head of AW Electrical Contractors, was vehement about keeping all loans in her own name even though the bank pressured her to do otherwise. "My husband is well-respected in the business community," she declared, "and has good credit, so naturally the bank thought he would be the one getting the loan. When I filled out my application, they wanted him to cosign, but I raised such a stink that eventually they backed down. I had lots of experience, a solid business plan, and some assets of my own. Why should he have to sign for me?"

Sandra Miles, president of a large marketing concern, has long been involved with the women's movement in her state. In her capacity as a feminist leader, she has heard many tales of outright discrimination: "I helped write the equal credit bill for our state," she declared, "but I know that discrimination is still in full-blown practice, especially for women business owners. It's not so bad for retail customers or home loans, but when it comes to entrepreneurs, I hear bad news from everybody."

These stories illustrate the problems that women still encounter in spite of recent legal changes. Any entrepreneur, male or female, will face enough obstacles in obtaining needed capital without the added burden of discrimination. It is understandable that a lending institution wants assurance of a borrower's willingness and ability to repay borrowed funds. However, where women are concerned, the lenders assume that they are less willing and less able than men to meet their obligations.

The old view of women as incompetent and in need of male protection still lingers in the financial arena despite evidence that women are more creditworthy and reliable about repaying their debts. Such harassment not only prevents women

women from gaining more economic power but also requires the expenditure of valuable time and energy.

NO EQUITY LOANS GIVEN TODAY

Ruth Abrahams's story is even more shocking than those of Lucy Warner, Liz Gausted, Angela Warshawski, and Sandra Miles. Raised in Southern California, where her father made his fortune in real estate, Abrahams moved to the neighboring sunbelt state of Arizona after she graduated from UCLA and started her own career in real estate.

First an agent and then a broker, Abrahams eventually became interested in commercial development and slowly began acquiring small pieces of land. She earned a good salary and invested as much as she could in property with long-term commercial potential. Obtaining mortgages had never been a problem for her, but one day she encountered a clear case of discrimination. She described the incident with remarkable calm: "I needed some cash to complete an important transaction," she noted, "and decided to take a second mortgage on my home. I went to the bank that had the first mortgage and asked, 'Can you give me a second?' The loan officer took my application, and in two weeks he called me back and said his bank wasn't giving any equity loans. I said, 'None at all?' and he replied, 'None.' So I said, 'OK, I want you to put it in writing that your bank is giving no equity loans to anyone. I'll be right down to get that piece of paper because I intend to see whether your bank is discriminating against women. I made a written application for the loan, and I want a written answer.' "

Like Lucy Warner, Ruth Abrahams did not hesitate to stand up for her rights, and she went to the bank prepared for a confrontation. "The loan officer came out with the manager," she declared in a quiet voice, "and they asked me to sit down. The manager told me that they were giving equity loans so they couldn't tell me in writing that they were not. When I heard that, I turned to the loan officer and said, 'Did you hear what the manager said to me?' In effect I had his boss calling him a liar right there in front of me.

"I simply cannot accept being treated as second-class," she continued with conviction. "The choice is what you're going to do. A lot of women are too naive to understand what is being done to them and then too compliant to speak up. In this case, it was such a blatant lie that I spotted it right away. Sometimes the lies are too subtle, but when I recognize them, I fight back. I don't deserve to be treated like that, and they have no right to do it. I burned up a week's worth of creative energy dealing with them, but I won't let such things beat me down."

Ruth Abrahams clearly understood her rights: If she made a written application, she was entitled to a written refusal. She also recognized a faulty story when she heard one. That the bank was giving no equity loans whatsoever seemed not only unreasonable but also absurd. In addition, Abrahams did not automatically believe that the man in charge would take care of her needs, nor did she allow a male voice the deference that many women give it. Her underlying assumption was that she could best protect her rights by first understanding them and then by demanding them in a firm, knowledgeable manner. Although Ruth Abrahams lost valuable time and energy over this incident, she did not lose either her loan or her self-respect.

For women who have not yet reshaped their attitudes regarding appropriate male and female behavior, reacting as Ruth did might be impossible. How many of these women have failed unnecessarily? Suffered unneeded conflict, embarrassment, and confusion? Blamed themselves for unreasonable refusals? Avoided business ownership altogether because of such incidents? We may never know the exact figures, but until such discrimination stops, the answer is, "Too many."

OF BANKS AND BANKERS

Women interested in business ownership frequently ask me about my resesarch. They are interested in the problems other women experience, especially in the area of money and finance. One reaction I typically hear is, "It would never occur to me that I could choose a bank. I just assumed that you were lucky if a bank chose you." Like young girls at a dance, these women are waiting to be selected. They do not realize that alternatives exist if a bank treats them unfavorably.

For Christine Stewart, owner of Stewart Travel Agency, pursuing alternatives meant going from bank to bank until she found one who would gamble on her success. "When I needed my first loan," she remembered with a laugh, "I interviewed ten loan officers. Nine of them were pretty negative, but the tenth decided to work with me. He was very helpful, and I worked hard on preparing my loan package. After everything went through, he looked at me and said, 'I don't know what ever made me decide to give you a chance, but I'm glad that I did.' I have all my accounts at his bank now, and we still joke about the way our relationship began."

After she has chosen her bank, the entrepreneur must then establish a good working relationship with the bank personnel. This involves a sustained and active effort to publicize her business, its progress, and its goals. Once again, don't wait for the bank to initiate contact, and do maintain a clear information exchange. Most banks require at least a yearly financial statement to bring them up to date on the economic position of the business. Many women chose to file one quarterly instead and to share other important developments as well.

In addition to keeping the bank updated on her finances, the woman business owner must actively publicize her firm's growth and development. This means introducing herself to the bank manager, stopping by to see her or him or the loan officer on occasion, and sending any good publicity that her business has recently had. The new entrepreneurs occasionally invited their bankers to lunch. When they held holiday parties, company picnics, or receptions for special clients, they included the bank manager on their guest list. And if they achieved new milestones or special community recognition, they were sure to let their banker know.

For Rona Smythe, owner of an elegant Scandinavian furniture store, such a sustained campaign worked in her favor when she wanted a loan to expand the business: "We have worked very hard to develop a good relationship with our bank," she declared. "I send them financial statements every quarter to show them that we are operating at a profit. When we set our new marketing plans, I send them those. I also include any promotional literature I can—articles that have appeared about us in the press, our new brochure, the company newsletter, anything that will keep them up to date about our growth and development. If I'm in the neighborhood, I'll drop in and say hello.

"When we applied for a loan to renovate our store," she continued, "we put together a special book on the business. It included every piece of free publicity we've had, articles that called us 'trendsetters' and the 'best in the area.' That helped the loan officer sell our proposal to the loan committee. Then when we had our opening, we invited him to come. Whenever anything significant happens, we keep our loan officer informed. That builds trust and also shows him that we are serious about the business."

A few women found such an active campaign difficult. They were either unaware of its importance or reluctant to "butter up" a banker to get what they needed. Such reluctance reflects inexperience in managing the public relations aspect of business ownership as well as a confusion of motive. For Smythe, educating others about her business and its development was an accepted part of her role. Moreover, she did not view it as manipulating others to get what she wanted but rather as building trust through communication and exchange of information. A loan officer who was thoroughly familiar with the progress of her business would be more likely to push her cause than one who was unaware of what she and the business had been doing.

THE PROBLEM OF COLLATERAL

Prior to opening a business, a woman should assess her credit rating to determine how much money is in fact available to her. If she has never borrowed any funds or obtained credit in her own name, she must at least apply for and use one or two bank credit cards. A number of the women interviewed followed this procedure when they realized that they had no credit history whatsoever. Borrowing small amounts of money and then repaying them promptly are good tactics for building personal credit.

When a prospective entrepreneur applies for a loan, the bank will almost certainly request some form of collateral. Since women control so few financial resources, they generally do not have sufficient equity for substantial loans. The woman entrepreneur must therefore be especially imaginative in her search for ways to secure the money that she needs. When confronted with the problem of collateral, the new entrepreneurs were very inventive in their solutions:

- "They asked me for a second mortgage on my house, and I didn't mind doing that. It got me the money I needed."
- "I put up $2000 in bonds that I got as gifts when I was younger."
- "I had inherited some stocks from my mother so I used those."
- "We got our suppliers to guarantee that they would buy back all our inventory should we fail. The bank was satisfied with using the inventory as collateral."
- "About a year after we opened, I got a loan on my accounts receivable. The bank gave me 75 percent of what my monthly receivables were."
- "After Don offered to sell me the business, I asked him to put in a good word for me down at the bank. He told them, 'This girl has her act together.' "
- "I sublease part of my office space to another business, and the bank took over the lease as collateral."

Whether it was personal contacts, private assets, accounts receivable, equipment, real estate or inventory, these entrepreneurs explored every resource at their disposal. However, the interviewees fell into two groups. The first group was willing to risk personal assets to secure the needed loan. Aware that money meant growth and growth led to more money, these women were willing to gamble extensively on themselves as well as on their business venture.

Not every woman shared this point of view. For some, putting up private assets was impossible. Although willing to risk business failure, these women could not gamble their home, savings, stocks, or other personal resources. Having some reserve as security was of overriding importance to them even though it meant little or no business growth.

The most controversial aspect of the loan process was the decision whether to accept the cosignature of a husband or other male relative on the loan application. For some women, success on their own was of primary importance, whereas for others the presence of a male cosigner did not detract from the independent nature of their effort. The decision to allow a cosignature is clearly a personal one. Particular women who felt very strongly about this issue generally found another way to obtain the financing they needed. Their reasons varied from "I won't let them get away with these demands" to "This business is all mine, and my husband is in no way responsible."

Yet the price that women continue to pay here is the inability to obtain meaningful sums of money. Their businesses therefore often remain small, and they are unable to increase either their personal or their collective economic power.

A STUDY IN TRUE INDEPENDENCE

Norma Jenkins is the oldest child of a prosperous Atlanta family. Her father, a successful accountant with a large practice, had many contacts in the community where he worked. She attended law school after college and continued to expand a side interest in gourmet cooking and cookware. This interest eventually developed into a large and lucrative import business.

Married, divorced, and a mother by age twenty-six, Norma was very clear about her motives: "I was fortunate to expand my interest in gourmet cooking," she began, "just before the craze for the 'new' American cuisine. In the mid 1960s, I travelled extensively in France and was always picking up special utensils there that I couldn't find anywhere else. After I finished my law degree, I got a fellowship to study at the London School of Economics, and I decided to keep on looking for unique cookware to bring home. So I borrowed $500 from my father, took my grant and my son, and went off to London. During my vacations, I returned to France and purchased some things that I sold to friends after I returned home."

Jenkins's import business soon took over her life, and she obtained increasingly larger loans to help her expand. "Since that worked so well," she continued, "I borrowed $3000, and my father cosigned the loan. With this money, I went back to France and started investigating importing cookware on a bigger scale. I also perfected my language skills and learned all about shipping and customs regulations. When I finally went home, I continued importing things on a small basis and started working for a local law firm. After two years, I decided to leave the law and build up my import business. Once again I asked my father to cosign a loan, this time for $50,000."

For Jenkins, having a well-to-do father with solid banking contacts was an advantage not to be overlooked. Since the age of sixteen, she had wanted to be financially independent and never wavered from this goal. After college, Jenkins put herself through law school even while she cared for her young son. The era was the early 1960s, and Jenkins was as atypical of her generation as she was of the other interviewees. Although a few aspired to a career other than marriage, only one other woman mentioned financial independence in particular as a youthful goal. For Jenkins, financial independence was a part of her life plan: "When I was in high school," she noted, "I wanted to be a professional. I wanted to do this because it was demanding and selective, and I thought it would be good to be trained. You never know what is going to happen to you, and I wanted to be trained in order to have some financial security. That was twenty-five years ago, and feminism wasn't even popular then.'' Jenkins believed that it was necessary to learn how to take care of herself. Throughout high school, college, travel abroad, and the early stages of her business, she never lost sight of this goal.

Because she was clear about her priorities, Jenkins was able to separate two critical issues: dependence on her father to take care of her as opposed to using her father's position to take better care of herself. In her own mind, she was not relying on him for support but was enabling herself to move into a whole new financial sphere where she would be able to gain economic power and respect in her own right. Jenkins's alternative was to use valuable time and energy struggling against a system that doesn't allow women to acquire any degree of wealth and then punishes them for this disadvantage by witholding credit from them. She did express anger that women were still forced into a dependent role, but she did not let that anger prevent her from acting on her own behalf. For Jenkins, true independence was doing what was best for herself as opposed to emotionally reacting to a situation she could not change.

An alternative would have been to insist on establishing her business totally alone. Had she chosen this option, she might have ended up feeling victimized. Since she had little inventory and no other assets, a $50,000 loan would have been out of the question. Without such an infusion of capital, her business would have remained much smaller. Although she would have been independent of her father, she would not have been independent of the near-invisible status that she enjoyed as a woman with little financial power.

THE BIG PICTURE: MOVING TOWARD ECONOMIC POWER

Norma Jenkins was able to see the "big picture," including the overall potential for growth and real financial independence. In her case, depending on her father was not the issue. At stake was whether she would gain the economic power to do what she really wanted with her life. "I took the loan in this manner," she declared, "because my name was on it too, and it gave me access to credit in a local bank. My name on that note established a credit record for me on a very high level. After two years, the bank turned the loan and my line of credit over to me. Now I have that, and it is a major asset.

"When you're going to start a small business, you must look at your assets. I had the advantage that my father was in business and knew a lot of people. Having him stand up for me is no different from using other contacts in the business world. If you know people, they introduce you to other people and help you get jobs. I have learned to pull on all my talents and contacts in order to succeed."

With her large capital investment, Jenkins was able to expand her business tenfold. She soon had sufficient money not only to buy her own home but also to expand her business interests into commercial real estate. At this time, she controls over $1 million worth of assets and enjoys unusual status as a businesswoman in her community. In a culture where money means power, Jenkins believed that she had to gain control of greater financial resources to exert any meaningful influence on behalf of other women. Her belief has certainly been validated. Local politicans now court her favor, and she actively works for legislation to counter the very laws that she found so objectionable.

Unlike Norma Jenkins, many women are not yet psychologically independent of male protection, and their frame of reference still includes the image of a protective male figure. This is true even if they work and are economically self-sufficient. Like the violet by the stone, they are half-hiding from complete self-reliance, which includes an inner belief that they can stand alone. This problem is compounded by the continued pressure to conform to an outmoded feminine ideal, an ideal that identifies femininity with dependency.

Business ownership is one of the most independent endeavors a woman can undertake. It requires that she change her view of so-called feminine behavior and cultivate her active, independent side to the fullest. As she works to make her business profitable, the woman entrepreneur will encounter issues of dependency, both psychological and financial. Her undertaking therefore becomes a personal as well as economic journey, and different women are on different places along the path.

To complete this journey, each woman must confront the conflict between her need to be psychologically protected and her need to be financially independent. She must determine when a male cosignature signifies dependence and is therefore unacceptable and when it is a positive step toward her goal. She must decide if accepting assistance in the form of contacts, money, or recommendations is truly helpful or if it is only detrimental to her progress. I believe that once a woman has developed a certain level of psychological independence, her ability to use every resource at her disposal will increase. But until that point, she will do well to consider the circumstances carefully before joining with parent or spouse to further her cause.

Psychological dependence can also keep a woman from using what money she does make to expand and grow. She may amass a certain degree of wealth, but unless she becomes psychologically as well as financially independent, the woman entrepreneur will not amass the power, control, and influence necessary to stand apart from male dominance. Money and power are definitely linked together, but the woman who makes money yet psychologically still needs protection will hardly be capable of using that power effectively, either for herself or on behalf of other women. For the woman business owner, these issues are critical: To survive she must confront them one by one and decide where she stands.

PRACTICAL TIPS TO ASSIST YOU

The following three-part checklist will help you choose a bank, prepare your loan application, and maintain a good relationship with your banker.

A. How to choose a bank.
1. Remember, you are the bank's business. . . . The bank needs *you*.
2. Find out if the bank's policy includes financing a business the size of yours.
3. Ask if the bank is familiar with your type of business.
4. Assess the bank's financial annual report to determine if its investment strategy is liberal or conservative—or ask people in your community or at a women's group for this information.
5. Make an appointment with a bank officer to discuss your business needs and plans—don't drop in unannounced.
6. Remember that bankers tend to be conservative. Dress appropriately.
7. Bring your business plan, marketing plans, financial statements, and brochures. Be prepared to discuss honestly both the strengths and weaknesses of your company.
8. Don't wait until you are desperate to plan your approach.
9. After your initial meeting, assess the responses you received (helpful, indifferent, patronizing, discouraging, honest).
10. Listen to your own intuition about a particular person and turn down banks that respond to you negatively.
11. Use any contacts you have for recommendations or introductions.
12. Understand your credit rights. If you are unsure why your loan was denied or if you suspect discrimination, request a written explanation.
13. Don't get discouraged. Remember that some women try several banks before finding the best one to work with.

B. What to provide the loan committee. (Good bankers will help you collect these items, because it is to their advantage to work with you to facilitate the loan and ensure approval. Banks often have their own forms or format that they want you to use—Ask at the outset.)
1. A good credit record and evidence of increasing profitability are basics.
2. Provide a carefully prepared business plan. To their disadvantage, many women do not complete this step. A business plan takes time and effort to prepare, but it shows the bank that you are serious about and understand your business.

3. Income tax returns and financial statements also must be carefully prepared with the help of a CPA or other financial advisor.

4. Your loan request must indicate how much money you want, what it is to be used for, and how the loan will generate more income so that you can repay the bank promptly. You must convince the bank that you will be able to meet your loan obligation.

5. Use positive publicity and other information that makes your business come alive and stand out to personalize your company in any way that you can. Show why you are unique, who wants your product or service, why you are in demand.

6. You must show adequate collateral to the bank, such as personal assets (stock, savings, home), inventory, valuable business equipment, accounts receivable, debts owed you, leases that you hold, real estate.

7. Recommendations from colleagues and other business associates should accompany your proposal.

C. Follow-up activities.

1. Drop in to see your banker from time to time.

2. Invite her or him to lunch.

3. Send your banker your company newsletter, a new brochure, and other pertinent information about your company's growth and development.

4. Provide the banker with quarterly financial statements.

5. Forward any new marketing plans.

6. Let your banker know when you reach a special or new sales goal.

7. Keep a record of any free publicity you get. Organize it into a book and include it with your financial statement.

8. Invite your banker to company parties, events, outings.

9. Remember, personalize your company in any way that you can. Keep your banker up to date on all business developments.

CHAPTER 10

Learning to Mind the Store

Once she opens the door to her business, every entrepreneur wants to succeed. Armed with energy, drive, and determination, she hopes her enterprise will grow and prosper. As she embarks on this new course, she must be prepared to handle a wide variety of tasks and, inevitably, she will make her share of mistakes. How can a woman capitalize on her strengths and decrease her weaknesses to avoid the most common pitfalls? Understanding the four entrepreneurial functions will help her approach business management in a productive, new way.

Starting and managing a business involves four different but related functions: innovation, organization, leadership, and expansion. Entrepreneurs are versatile, and one of their outstanding strengths is the ability to generate new ideas. Innovation is therefore one function that the dynamic and creative business owner rarely finds difficult. However, because she has so many good ideas, the typical entrepreneur may lead her business in many different directions at once, losing her focus and allowing a haphazard pattern of growth.

A certain amount of chaos is typical of any new venture, but many entrepreneurs resist organization far too long—they may have a strong intuitive sense of where their business is heading, but they do not formulate specific goals. *Planning, goal setting,* and *structure* often are not in their vocabularies. Even while leading their company into new expansion cycles, they neglect to develop the literal organization necessary to facilitate continued growth.

INNOVATION IS NOT ENOUGH

Formulating specific goals was a problem for Ingrid Schofield, the charismatic leader of Advanced Micro Products. Schofield grew up in the industrial Northeast, the only child of a professional couple who divorced when she was two. Trained as an electrical engineer, she migrated to the sunny Southwest and found work with an electronics company in the Dallas area. Schofield was captivated by the newly emerging computer industry, and in her spare time she worked on developing a unique modem. Like many other aspiring young engineers, she was eager to start her own business. At twenty-nine, she quit her job and set out to establish Advanced Micro Products. Today, her firm is a leading manufacturer of modems and other telecommunication devices.

When I met Ingrid Schofield, her highly profitable company was four years old and growing fast. Her comments showed her to be a creative person who easily managed the innovation function but could not impose structure on her rapidly expanding concern. Getting organized was one of her most persistent and troublesome problems: "I am a very forward-looking person," she began. "To me, it's the future that's interesting, and I have a great deal of trouble paying attention to the past at all. Sometimes I can't even remember what I did two days ago! In fact, once I've done something, I don't want to talk about it any more. I'm on to the next idea."

Schofield's ability to look ahead was definitely an asset. She spotted upcoming trends, anticipated the needs of her customers, and encouraged new product development. In short, she was a gifted and innovative entrepreneur. However, she was unable to use the company's history to avoid future mistakes. She also resisted analyzing either the firm's operating structure or her specific role in the overall organizational scheme.

"Somebody's going to have to get in here," she continued, "and provide the scientific management, but I'm just not ready for it. I hate putting people in little boxes and telling them what to do. It traps them and stifles their creativity. I deliberately haven't made an organizational chart because I don't want to box anybody in. When someone asks me about this, I say 'Just wait. We're going to find out as we go along what each one of you can do.'

"People want to know what I expect. I tell them, 'Don't ask me that. Go out and do something that's really interesting. It may not be what I expect of you, but that's OK.' My staff loves the freedom and creativity that this policy allows. All kinds of good ideas come out of it. On the other hand, they pay a great price in terms of ambiguity. Nothing is certain around here, and people don't like that either. They prefer to have some limits and parameters in order to know where they stand."

At this point, Schofield knows that she cannot avoid organization much longer. Her company is expanding too rapidly, and the business is becoming too chaotic. "There's no end to what I can do with this business," she noted with pride, "and that's why I can't see the end result. Developing a structure would mean rigidifying everything. I'm not dying to write it all in stone because I want to be free to go in any direction that seems suitable. I don't want anyone telling me I can't do this or that because it's not on target. But I know this situation can't last forever. I really need someone to come along behind me and pick up all the pieces and put them into place. I just haven't found the right person to do it yet.''

ASSESS YOUR INNOVATION SKILLS

Innovation is one of the fundamentals of the entrepreneurial process. The ability to generate new ideas is essential to small-business growth and development. Creative entrepreneurs like Helena Rubenstein and Mary Kay Ash have changed the face of U.S. business. Rubenstein was among the first of the great cosmetic manufacturers, whereas Ash's unusual marketing strategies are now widely imitated by other organizations. The following exercise will help you assess your innovation skills.

1. What percentage of my time do I spend on innovation?

2. What innovations am I considering at present?

3. How do these innovations fit in with my present business goals and structure?

4. Who, if anyone, helps me fill the innovation function?

5. Could I use more help in this area? If so, who should help me and how?

6. To what extent do I encourage and listen to innovative ideas from my staff?

7. Do I sacrifice organization for innovation? If so, how does this affect my business? What can I do about this problem?

8. How skilled am I at getting other people excited about my new ideas?

9. Overall, how effective an innovator am I?

GETTING ORGANIZED

Although Ingrid Schofield could generate new ideas, she lacked important organization skills. Eventually, she hired a consultant to help her develop some acceptable structure. He analyzed the company's different operations and helped her understand that these operations fell into broad general groups. To start, he recommended that she organize her company along loose functional lines: finance, production, personnel, marketing and sales, training, and operations. This recommendation enabled her to understand the overall scope of her business and to determine where she needed new people before hiring them.

A true entrepreneur, Schofield was not particularly comfortable with the management of routine, daily tasks. Coordinating work was not one of her strengths. Getting good people to assist her with this aspect of her business was the next logical step. As she engaged in this process, Schofield slowly realized that structure and creativity were not mutually exclusive. In fact with a more orderly structure to support her, she had more freedom to do what she did best: create, innovate, and inspire her staff to bring ideas to life.

A forceful and charismatic person, Schofield continued to set the tone for the business. This allowed continued freedom for her employees but within broadly defined limits. Included in each person's job description and yearly objectives were "stretch goals" that allowed them to reach out and grow. Schofield encouraged them to use their imagination and rewarded them for doing so, and, consequently, she continued to get the new ideas that were so important to her company's growth.

STOP AND GO MARKETING:
THE ROAD TO DISASTER

For May Wong, owner of Wong's Direct Mail Service, getting organized involved a new understanding of the marketing process. Wong was pulled into business ownership by a lucrative contract offer that she couldn't turn down: "I worked as the assistant to the director of a major San Francisco direct-mail firm," she recalled, "and was well-trained in the field. After my second child was born, I decided to take a leave of absence. A couple of months later, a friend who worked for a big hotel chain called and asked if I would do some independent work for him. It turned out to be a much bigger job than he anticipated, and I had to hire two other women to help me. Eventually, I focused more on coordinating and running the project, and I took on several more employees. By this time, I had moved out of my home into an office. Some savings helped me computerize my operation, and the next thing I knew, I was managing seven people and rushing to get all the work done."

May Wong well remembers the initial excitement she felt as her business grew and expanded. However, fifteen months after that pivotal phone call, Wong's Direct Mail Service faced imminent disaster. Her initial contract was drawing to a close, and Wong had no new business. "I'll never forget how I felt," she continued, shaking her head, "when I realized that in three months there would be no more money coming in. I started letting people go, and then analyzed what had gone wrong. That first job was so big that I became totally involved in expanding my operation in order to manage the work. I never thought about developing any future marketing plans. The whole experience made me realize that a consistent and systematic marketing effort is essential to business success.''

Stop-and-go marketing is one of the most common mistakes a new business owner can make. Concerned with delivering her product or service, she may overlook the necessity of developing an ongoing marketing plan and of hiring people to implement that plan if she cannot. ''When you are overwhelmed with work,'' Wong noted, ''it is easy to forget about getting new customers. That is one mistake I won't ever make again.''

Once she started marketing her business, Wong encountered another problem. People often did not want or need her service, and she experienced feelings of self-doubt that she hadn't anticipated. Such feelings can easily interfere with the marketing process if they are not recognized and resolved. ''I quickly learned not to take rejection personally,'' she stated emphatically. ''If you knock on 100 doors, you're going to get ten people to talk to you and maybe give you an appointment. And you're going to get two or three to sit down and actually give you some time and consideration. You may end up with two jobs from those 100 calls. Now you can either internalize that and say, 'They don't like me, my work is no good,' or you can say, 'Not everybody needs what I have,' and go out and work harder.''

Once Wong faced these problems, her business entered a positive growth cycle. Although awarded other major contracts, she continued cultivating old clients as well as developing new ones. She also diversified her market mix, seeking several smaller jobs so she would not become too dependent on one firm for all her business. As she successfully completed each project, her confidence increased. She realized that her work was excellent, and this realization helped her depersonalize rejection more easily. If one prospective client didn't need her service, then another one would. Today, May Wong runs one of the most respected direct-mail services in the San Francisco Bay Area. By catching her mistakes early and organizing her marketing effort, she avoided closing the door of her business as quickly as she had opened it.

ASSESS YOUR ORGANIZATION SKILLS

The following exercise will assist you in developing your skills as an organizer. Answer each question carefully.

1. What is the legal structure of my business?

2. What is the working structure (a rough organizational chart) of my business?

3. For the coming year, what are my company's goals in these areas?

    a. Sales

    b. Marketing

    c. Production

    d. Staffing

    e. Training (self and staff)

    f. Other

4. What plan have I developed to help me meet each goal?

5. Who will help me implement this plan? What will their duties be?

6. How will I know if I have reached my goals?

7. What percentage of my time do I spend on these activities?

    a. Planning

    b. Organizing

8. Overall, how effectively do I handle the organization function?

BECOMING AN EFFECTIVE LEADER

Women and the Web of Connection

Stepping into the role of leader is both difficult and easy for the woman entrepreneur. Recent research on the psychology of women sheds some light on why. Psychologists such as Carol Gilligan, Jean Baker Miller, and Lillian Rubin have made significant discoveries regarding the importance of relationships in women's lives. According to these researchers, women identify themselves in terms of their relationships to others and make ethical decisions based on how their actions affect the people around them. Women seek to create a continually expanding web of connections and feel most comfortable when they are at the center of this web, surrounded by family, friends, and coworkers.[1]

    Forming a web of connections is a positive and absolutely essential process for a successful venture. Such a web contributes to the development of a unified staff and broad-based clientele. Women are especially adept at reaching out to other people and weaving them into a familylike network. This helps them to to build a sense of joint endeavor with their employees and to develop a feeling of loyalty and affiliation throughout their business.

This ability to make connections also enables some women to pull seemingly disparate pieces of information together into a new whole. Cathy Denton, owner of Young Totes, Inc., summed it up this way: "My greatest strength is my absolute sense of the connectedness of everything. Everything I do has bearing on everything else that I do, on everything that you and other people do. This sense also enables me to recognize patterns, cycles, and relationships that other people don't see."

However, a tendency to build and maintain connections also has its dangers. A woman can easily become caught in the web, unable to separate herself from the relationships she has made. Her own boundaries and sense of self may become meshed with those of individual employees, or even of the business itself, thereby obscuring her vision. Should this occur, she will lack sufficient distance to evaluate people in an objective fashion, and her ability to lead will be seriously diminished. In addition, her sense of self-esteem may become tied to the overall success of the firm or to the opinion of individual staff members.

Cathy Denton: Learning to Be the Boss

Now thirty-nine, Cathy Denton started her manufacturing firm seven years ago. At that time, she made her six-year-old daughter, Jenny, a special tote bag to use when visiting her grandparents. The colorful bag was shaped like a round doll whose arms came up to form a handle. Jenny Denton loved the doll and found it comforting during moments of homesickness, and her mother appreciated the roomy compartments for her child's clothes and other belongings. Creating an individualized bag for her daughter eventually led Denton into a new business venture. Today her highly successful Young Totes, Incorporated, boasts a varied line of carryalls for children under the age of thirteen.

However, Denton remembers a time when running her business was not so easy: "Leadership did not come easily to me at first," she remembered. "It was difficult to learn how to be the boss. One thing that got in my way was that I like to be liked. When you're the boss, that's not always possible. I have to constantly be aware that it's OK if I don't win the popularity contest this month. It's far more important for me to make the best decisions for the business, or everyone here might be out of a job."

From time to time, Denton had to set a policy or insist on a procedure that wasn't popular with her staff. Although she considered their objections and suggestions, she sometimes had to make a decision that they didn't like. Occasionally, she personalized their disapproval and allowed it to undermine her self-confidence. This in turn weakened her ability to manage the business: As long as employee opinion contributed to her sense of self-esteem, she could not be an effective leader.

Cathy eventually learned that the top person isn't always liked and that this was no reflection on her personally. She also realized that leading others meant substituting guidance for friendship. "Once you reach a certain level," she continued, "employees are no longer friends, and you have to stop treating them that way. It was difficult for me to stop talking about personal matters with everyone over coffee or not to be chummy with people after work, but I finally realized that this wasn't appropriate. It's hard enough for me to say, 'You're not going to get your raise because you didn't produce such and such.' It would be almost impossible for me to say that to a friend. My talents are best used in guiding others to do the best possible job, and then pulling back and letting them do it."

Firing was another area that was difficult for Cathy: "I was much too soft-hearted at the beginning," she declared, "and couldn't fire people. I remember one sales rep who never met his quota. He just couldn't close a sale. Eventually, he was such a drain on my financial resources that I had no choice. It was fire him or go down the tubes. Now I tell myself that firing is sometimes necessary even if it hurts me to do it."

Yet Denton still believes that the human touch is important to running a good business. "I try to balance the business and personal sides," she stated, "without letting my emotions get in the way. I watch things and listen carefully. Sometimes when I walk into a staff meeting, I know something is wrong. Men want to get right down to business, but women are willing to take the time to pick up feelings between people. I think I have an advantage because I am a little bit more sensitive to these things. Women are also more compassionate, and I hope we always stay that way. I want my business to succeed, but not at the expense of every person here."

Good leadership requires distinguishing between sensitivity to employee needs and sensitivity to employee rejection and dislike. As soon as Denton realized this, her leadership skills improved. She understood the importance of considering special staff problems without letting staff opinion influence her judgment. For example, flex-time was one policy that she endorsed to meet the family and commuting needs of her employees. Giving people some flexibility of work schedule decreased tardiness and absenteeism and increased both productivity and morale.

Denton also accepted the necessity of maintaining some distance between herself and the people who work for her. Although certain staff members think she is too distant, she no longer lets their attitude affect her behavior. A naturally warm person, she has now achieved a comfortable balance between friendliness and the professional disinterest necessary to make sound business decisions. Secure in her position as company leader, she does not need anyone's approval to do what she believes is best.

The challenge for today's woman entrepreneur is to use her strengths, her empathy, understanding, and concern for others and not to allow her need for approval or her feelings of connection to obscure her judgment. To meet this challenge, she must first understand that personal feelings can distort perception and prevent clear assessment of a given situation. When this occurs, individuals interpret the reality before them through a filter of emotional needs. Without some understanding of this process, a woman may unwittingly allow those needs to influence her decisions. Her wish for approval, desire to take care of her staff, or tendency to merge her boundaries with those of others will then control her behavior, thereby decreasing her effectiveness as a leader. To succeed, she must understand these issues and work to separate business from personal concerns.

DEVELOP YOUR LEADERSHIP SKILLS

Certain practical strategies will help develop your skills as a leader and will enable you to maintain objectivity in situations where you could become emotionally involved.

At the time of hiring, you should clarify company policy regarding vacation time, sick leave, overtime, and evaluation procedures. Consider drawing up a brief written policy statement and giving it to all new employees. Such a statement will avoid misunderstandings and reduce the possibility of an emotional response to difficult personnel problems. While personal concern is an important consideration, it should be balanced by clear, objective standards that are understood by staff and management alike.

Job descriptions, goal setting, and specific, measurable objectives are other tools to help you manage your employees more effectively. Ingrid Schofield did not like confining staff members within narrow job descriptions. She felt that this would inhibit creativity and individual initiative. However, she understood the price that she paid: Her employees went off in many different directions at once, bringing chaos and instability to her business.

Sharing company goals and setting objectives for each employee will make you a better leader and will diminish emotional involvement in personnel matters. Defining expectations in measurable terms makes it easier to assess if those terms have been fulfilled. By contrast, evaluating performance is almost impossible when the conditions are vague and imprecise. May Wong remembered this as yet another mistake that she made as she developed her new marketing strategy: "I hired a young woman named Fran," she explained, "to take care of my main marketing effort. She came on just when we were winding down our first big job, and all I wanted her to do was get out there and get some new clients as quickly as possible. Initially, we didn't take the time to develop guidelines regarding how many jobs she was supposed to bring in and in what time frame."

Wong's marketing manager set out with instructions to go "get some new clients quickly." Such a fuzzy goal produced problems for both Wong and her new employee. Without more specific objectives, neither of them could evaluate whether Fran was in fact doing a satisfactory job. In precisely such situations a woman's empathy, need for approval, or need to please may come into play and negatively influence an assessment of her employee's performance. In addition, without specific sales goals, Wong could not monitor the growth of her business.

Specific objectives would have helped Cathy Denton fire the salesman who could not close a sale. Had she set out her expectations clearly, she would have soon realized that he was not meeting them. Without such factual evidence, she was unable to appraise the situation accurately. As a result, her emotions gained control of her behavior, and she lost sight of what was best for her firm. The new entrepreneurs agreed that definite goals helped them to avoid emotional involvement in employee performance reviews. They also believed that regular evaluations were essential. Checking on staff progress even informally helped them identify problem areas and generate solutions before such drastic measures as firing were necessary.

In addition, the interviewees found that keeping employees informed and being honest about business goals and problems helped avoid conflict. As Cathy noted, "When something bothers me, I talk it out and try to be clear. I also have few secrets. If we have a bad month, everybody knows, and we all work harder. I also want to understand my people's goals so I can help them move ahead. But if someone wants to be president of the company some day, I'd better know about that, too!"

ASSESS YOUR LEADERSHIP SKILLS

The following exercise will help you evaluate your skills as a leader. Answer each question carefully.

1. How would I describe my supervisory style—friendly, distant, autocratic, "hands off," controlling, demanding, etc.?

2. How does my style affect my interaction with employees?

3. How does my style affect my ability to manage my business?

4. What do I expect from my employees?

5. To what extent am I getting what I want from my employees?

6. Have I clearly defined staff jobs?
   a. If not, how can I do so?

   b. If so, how much latitude do staff members have within individual job functions? How much autonomy and responsibility?

7. How would I characterize the working environment of my business—chaotic, orderly, rigid, warm, open, etc.?

8. How does this environment affect employee productivity?

9. What provisions do I make for employee growth and development?

10. How do I evaluate staff work? How is this evaluation communicated to individual staff members?

11. Is it difficult for me to separate friendship and business?

   a. If so, how does this problem interfere with my capability to lead this business effectively?

   b. What can I do about this problem?

12. Overall, how effective a leader am I?

EXPANDING YOUR BUSINESS: WHICH WAY TO GO?

Every successful business owner inevitably faces the question of expansion. Perhaps she has achieved a new level of recognition in her community or field, and this generates more business. She could also find herself in the forefront of a fast-growing industry or service, such as computers, video entertainment, child care, or health care, with people clamoring for more of her product or service. Another avenue of expansion could involve an innovative idea or some natural outgrowth of her original business.

No matter which avenue she chooses, three potential problems might occur. The first hazard is too-rapid growth that lacks the structure or planning necessary to support a larger business. The second problem involves the lack of clear business direction. Moving in too many unrelated directions at once is often tempting to the creative, innovative entrepreneur. Although a given idea may be good, you must understand how it relates to your particular business or you will lose focus and scatter your energy. The third problem concerns making money. Will more business mean more profit? If not, you will be wasting precious time and resources, and your expansion plans should be dropped.

Pat Pulaski: Bigger Isn't Always Better

Pat Pulaski, a vivacious black woman, owns two commercial art stores and a poster shop. She also manages a framing operation and supplies artworks on a wholesale basis to interior designers and retailers. Her business is located in the Baltimore area, where she moved just before starting junior high school. "From the time I was young," she recalled, her eyes sparkling and her voice enthusiastic, "I wanted to be involved with art. My family didn't have much money, and I was grateful for the public museums and universities where I could get an education for almost nothing. Those museums were good for my soul, and I wanted to bring art to the people in any way I could."

When she was thirty-three, Pulaski left her job with the city of Baltimore and withdrew her retirement benefits. Her goal was to start an art shop where people could purchase inexpensive reproductions or modestly priced original works, but she decided to work first for an art gallery to get some experience in business management. After two years with a Washington store, she moved back to Baltimore, ready to start her own shop.

"I found a location in a popular suburban shopping center," she recalled, "hired a helper, and set up the store. My art work came all framed from a supplier in Washington, and I was the shipper and receiver. Every few weeks, I drove to Washington to pick up new work. Soon I discovered that people sometimes liked a picture but not the mat or frame. Making a change involved taking the piece back to Washington and then picking it up again. This got to be too time consuming, so I asked my sister if she wanted to help me. We bought some mats and a mat cutter and set ourselves up in the basement of my parents' house. If someone wanted a blue mat instead of a grey one, we changed it for them."

At first, Pulaski's business expanded in a natural fashion: She added a custom-matting service that directly supported the product she sold. Soon, she started expanding her product line as well, buying unframed artwork directly from artists or other suppliers. "I took the unframed art down to the man in Washington," she noted, "and he continued doing most of the framing. But then I said to myself, 'He's not doing that because he likes us. He's making money. If we did that, we'd be making the money ourselves.' So we gradually expanded our custom-matting service into a full-scale framing operation. Eventually we found some space in a big warehouse and set up a manufacturing site just to frame our product."

Before renting the warehouse, Pulaski sat down and planned her operation carefully. She balanced her anticipated expenses against the money that making her own frames would bring in and realized that this new business would indeed be profitable. With careful sales and cash flow projections in hand, Pulaski obtained a small loan to help her set up a new site. However, her calculations also showed that the manufacturing operation would use only half the available space. Since she had the room for storage, she decided that expanding into wholesale art merchandising was her logical next step. Pulaski started selling framed pictures to other stores, and soon she was working with interior designers as well. At this point, her business had expanded from a popular art shop to include a successful framing operation and a substantial wholesale venture.

During her fourth year in business, Pulaski saw yet another opportunity to grow. At that time, Baltimore's harbor area was being renovated into an attractive shopping complex, and she was offered a desirable location for another store. "Once again," she declared, "I looked carefully at whether such a move would be profitable, and I decided to give it a try. It was a small but very well-placed spot, and the Harbor Place people were giving the whole operation lots of good publicity. I could see that it was going to be a major tourist attraction, and I wanted to be part of it, but I decided to get more specialized. At this location, we sell only posters, and it has been quite successful."

Throughout her expansion efforts, Pulaski avoided the three major problems that we described above. However, when she opened a third store, her business faltered. "I decided to expand into the Washington area," she noted, "and opened a shop in College Park. However, this proved to be a mistake. College Park is a university community with a different type of market, and it also was too far away. As I look back on it, my first store was the most successful, and the framing/wholesale side of the business has also gone very well. The poster shop has done OK, but my third store doesn't break even."

In analyzing her situation, Pulaski compares her operation to those of the major retail chains. "When you're a big outfit like Penney's or Sears, you have hundreds of stores. If one of them doesn't make money, they can absorb it. But when you've got only three stores, and one of them doesn't do well, that causes real problems. Now I realize that we have been dissipating our energy, spending too much time on the location that does the least business. We would be better off concentrating our efforts on making our two best stores even more profitable."

Pat Pulaski now understands that more outlets don't necessarily mean more money. They mean more work and greater expenses as well. "We have a much greater volume of business," she noted thoughtfully, "and a lot of money and inventory goes through our hands. But as you grow bigger, your expenses grow bigger too. When I look at the bottom line, I'm not making a whole lot more money. Now I support twenty-five people instead of three. Personnel issues—hiring, firing, promotions—take up more time, and we have more employee benefits to pay. My inventory is also huge, and I need help coordinating the overall operations of the firm. Growth has brought greater challenge and more work but not as much money as I would have liked."

Pulaski handled this situation by hiring a marketing specialist to analyze her potential College Park clientele. She hopes that by understanding her new customers better she will be better able to meet their needs. The type of art that she stocks in her Baltimore stores is not suitable for this new location, and Pulaski now realizes this. She knows that expanding into a different geographical area may require a different kind of inventory and a fresh sales campaign. She plans on keeping this third store for another year to see if she can't turn the situation around. If it doesn't become more profitable, then she will close down and keep her business centered in Baltimore.

ASSESS YOUR EXPANSION SKILLS

The following exercise will help you understand the expansion process. Analyzing your business will allow you to assess whether your present expansion plans are appropriate and feasible.

1. What are the natural avenues of expansion that I foresee?

2. To which of the following do these avenues relate (be specific in your answers):
   a. Markets

   b. Products

   c. Services

   d. Spin-off businesses involving a new market, product or service

3. How much will expansion increase my volume of business?

4. How do I plan to handle the projected increases?

5. Will expanded volume bring greater profits? If so, how much? If not, why?

6. What kind of plan have I developed to help me through this expansion phase?

7. Do I have enough of the following resources to enable me to undertake the projected expansion?
   a. People

   b. Money

   c. Equipment

   d. Space

   e. Other

8. What resources do I still need, and how can I get them?

9. What percentage of my time do I spend planning for growth and expansion? Is this enough? Too much?

10. Overall, how effectively do I handle this function?

ENTREPRENEURSHIP: A CONTINUOUS CYCLE

Innovators provide the creative spark that gives birth to new business enterprise. They have a special ability to move beyond the existing order of things and generate something unique and different. This may be a new product or a new means of making that product, the discovery of an untapped market or a special strategy to reach that market, a different concept of organizational design, an unusual service, a new management technique, or any one of a thousand other ideas. Dynamic and creative, the typical entrepreneur is always moving on to the next idea.

However, a new venture cannot succeed on innovation alone. Creativity provides the leavening that makes the business rise, but organization brings the structure that holds it together. The second part of the entrepreneurial cycle is thus imposing some order on the often chaotic young firm. As a business grows and matures, it also needs a strong leader to guide its development. Most entrepreneurs are charismatic people with an almost evangelical belief in their ideas. This enables them to inspire others to bring those ideas to life. However, good leadership involves mastery of the organizational process and sound management techniques, and this is where many entrepreneurs encounter problems.

Once she has put her ideas into effect, the typical business owner may become restless and bored. As her business stabilizes, she will turn to new avenues of expansion to find continued outlets for her imagination. Expansion completes the entrepreneurial cycle, which then starts again with a new innovative concept. The four functions thus interrelate, each one depending on the next for its successful development and completion. A sound understanding of this process will move the aspiring entrepreneur further along the road to entrepreneurial success.

C H A P T E R 11

Sexual Harassment in the Entrepreneurial World

The date was September 21, 1979. Billye Ericksen was looking forward to attending a golf tournament at the Los Altos Golf and Country Club.* As vice president and general manager of a well-respected Silicon Valley firm, she had been invited by the Electronics Representation Association to attend this industry-sponsored event. At the time, Ericksen was employed by Capacitor Sales Company, an electronics distributorship that she subsequently took over and renamed CAPSCO.

It was a typical California day—hot and sunny, and Ericksen was getting ready to join three male colleagues whom she had invited to accompany her. She enjoyed a good game of golf, but she also knew that serious business would be conducted on the fairway that day. Like any professional, Ericksen understood that attending such events would enhance sales as well as better her golf score. Leaving her office that morning, she never dreamt the day's outing would catapult her into California legal history.

"There wasn't anything unusual about this event," she recalled as we talked in her modern, functional office. "The Electronics Representation Association had rented the club's facilities for lunch and golf, and I arrived with my three guests, one of whom was a male factory representative and the other two CAPSCO employees. We sat down together with another rep to have lunch, and the

---

*Because of the historic nature of this case, Billye Ericksen has allowed me to use her real name.

waiter immediately came up to our table. I thought he wanted to take our order, but instead he asked me to leave the Grill because I was a woman. I was so stunned that I didn't do anything. I thought I had misheard him. But then the manager came and made the same demand.''

Ericksen was indeed the only woman present at the event, but this was not unusual. The electronics industry is still male-dominated, and she was accustomed to working almost exclusively with men. Although aware that sex discrimination was still a major problem, Ericksen had never experienced such an incident before. "I was mortified, hurt, and humiliated," she continued, "and the men I was with felt embarrassed to be with me. I went out on the terrace to eat my lunch and then stayed to finish the day to spare them further embarrassment. One of the sales reps was part of my golf foursome, and he kept saying, 'Forget it, stop talking about it.' He was really uncomfortable. After all, who wants to work with someone so unacceptable that she can't share a common table?''

The events that followed this incident moved beyond harassment to outright intimidation. When Ericksen filed suit against the Los Altos Golf and Country Club, her boss at Capacitor Sales began receiving threatening phone calls: "One sales rep for a factory whose products were distributed by Capacitor Sales called my boss, who was then owner of the company. This sales rep made several threats, telling him, 'If you don't shut that broad up it will cost you business.' The Electronics Representation Association didn't stand behind me either. Many of their members also belong to the club, and they just wanted the whole thing covered up. It was clearly a collective effort to 'show that bitch not to take on the good old boys.' My boss was really wonderful and backed me up 100 percent. Incidentally, he is Jewish and had exerienced a lifetime of discrimination. He was sickened by what was happening.''

Billye Ericksen's case went to trail on March 31, 1982, and on April 12 the jury found against her. The trial was a horrible nightmare, and she had to endure further insult and humiliation. "There were many terrible things done at that trial," she stated with surprising calm, "but three stand out. In the two years between the incident and the court date, I had bought out the company. I had also become engaged. The defense attorneys came after me in the most vicious manner possible. They brought one stockholder onto the witness stand and asked him if I had slept with him in order to get control of his stock. Their implication was that I had slept my way into taking over. I had to sit there day after day with my three children and fiancé and listen to this type of character asassination.

"Then during the first week of the hearings two of my major factories cancelled their contracts with us," she noted. "A company such as mine distributes products made by others. For CAPSCO, this means the capacitors and resistors that we market to the major electronics companies on behalf of the manufacturers. The two factories involved were associated with people directly related to the discrimination incident. Our business depends on a good personal relationship between our company and factory sales reps. The reps control which distributor gets the factory's line, and in my case the adverse publicity affected how these men felt about me and my company.

"Finally, we lost the case because of this opening statement made by the defense: 'What would you do if you had a mountain cabin and the government told you who you must rent it to?' The objection to this statement was sustained, but its impact on the jury could not be reversed. The Los Altos Golf and Country Club does not allow its women members into the Men's Grill. However, when it rented its facilities to the Electronics Representation Association, which is a public group, it was no longer a private club. The real issue is that once you have put your facilities up for rent, you are not allowed by law to discriminate against individual members of any group that might rent them."

Despite the harassment both to herself and her company, Billye Ericksen-Desaigoudar has achieved remarkable success. Her personal courage can only inspire other women faced with similar discrimination, and her business acumen is equally impressive. When I first entered CAPSCO's spacious Sunnyvale headquarters, the many plaques and awards commending the company for outstanding performance caught my eye. Today, Ericksen not only owns one of the top distributorships in Silicon Valley but also works tirelessly on behalf of women's rights.

After losing her case, Ericksen filed an appeal, which was finally settled in May 1985. Once again, she lost. "One of the judges of the appellate court," she explained, her eyes flashing and her voice strong, "told my attorney, 'Offer her money. She's a business woman, she'll take money.' They just wanted me to settle out of court. My response was, 'The money is not what's at stake here.' The judge then made the following statement: 'The mood of the court is conservative, she will loose her case in appeals.'

"My mood is not conservative," she declared with passion. "The time to end sex discrimination has come. I am only symbolic in this case. The discrimination happened to every woman and man who believes in equal rights. The person singled out that day in essence was you as well as me. I appealed again, this time to the California Supreme Court, and they just agreed to hear my case. Since they accept less than 8 percent of all appeal requests, that in itself is a major victory. I will keep on fighting as long as I have to. It may take some time, but we are going to win."

SEXUAL HARASSMENT: MYTH OR REALITY?

Whenever the topic of sexual harassment arises, I hear the same question: "Don't you think that's a thing of the past now?" I find that people no longer believe women are harassed simply because of their sex. In fact, when asked what problems they had encountered as women business owners, even the new entrepreneurs generally replied, "I have never been held back because I am a woman." Their initial sense was that discrimination was not a problem.

However, even a casual reading of their stories reveals that sexual harassment is a fact of life for any woman working in the entrepreneurial world. What happened to Billye Ericksen-Desaigoudar is extreme but not unique. It illustrates the deeply embedded negative attitudes still prevalent in our society toward women in business. Such attitudes lie behind the many unpleasant and unnerving incidents that arise too regularly throughout an entrepreneurial woman's life.

Although the discrimination that Ericksen-Desaigoudar experienced did not cause her to fail, it brought untold personal suffering. It demanded time, money, and energy that would have been far better spent on managing her company, and it caused a serious loss of business income. In short, the negative impact on her life was, and still is, almost incalculable.

Every woman interviewed had encountered some form of harassment. In fact, harassment is so much a part of a woman business owner's daily life that she is hardly aware of the time and energy she spends dealing with it. Entrepreneurs of both sexes must confront and solve business problems, but the woman entrepreneur must handle sex-related issues as well. Such issues demand her attention in countless small ways and detract from her concentration on other, more pressing problems. For a large number of interviewees, the problems were directly sexual in nature.

BUSINESS AND SEX DON'T MIX

Men and women will experience sexual attraction to one another no matter what the setting. As one woman noted, "People react to each other sexually, be it male to male, male to female, or female to female. You just have to be aware of this fact." A certain amount of attraction between the sexes is natural and may be acknowledged as such. Nevertheless, the new entrepreneurs are quick to caution: Business and sex don't mix.

Because of early conditioning, men and women alike may behave in a way that is inappropriate. Women have been taught to attract men through the use of their sexuality, men to treat women as sex objects. Consequently, there is considerable potential for sex-related problems in a work environment. Some women try to achieve a certain end by unconsciously using, in the words of one interviewee, "little feminine wiles." They may dress too seductively or flirt too much, as if they were trying to win a date rather than close a business deal. Many men respond to a woman's looks rather than her expertise or make unwelcome advances because they view the woman involved as a sex object to be conquered. Despite social changes in recent years, the stories of the new entrepreneurs show that this is still true.

Jenny Van Buren, owner of a large, international business, was emphatic when she discussed this issue: "There is no question that there is a sexual problem," she told me without hesitation. "You will have a pass made at you under most any circumstances, and the problem is to forestall the pass before it comes. It is difficult for me to attend conferences without my husband because the old standard still holds: If you're there by yourself, you're free and available. I entertain in foreign hotels quite frequently, but, God knows, I can't have a bed in sight. So I end up with a suite with a separate room that has no connotation of a bedroom. I need to talk to clients, but I can't afford any misunderstandings."

Although Van Buren does not believe that her ability to succeed is seriously hampered by this situation, she frequently has both the problem and possible strategies in the back of her mind. These thoughts subtly detract from her concentration on business affairs. Every time she is invited to visit a client's suite, she must weigh the possibilities of a sexual advance. She must consider the best place to meet dinner guests to avoid embarrassment or misunderstanding. And she must be prepared to defend her presence without escort and to project the feeling that she is loyal to and trusted by her husband. Frequently asked why her husband "allows" her to travel alone, she replies with good humor: "He has a full time job, too, and is busy taking care of his own work."

Should any "slip up" occur, the new entrepreneurs believe their credibility would be seriously and permanently damaged. Since many men still do not take women business owners seriously, the old view prevails: A woman alone among men only wants sex. It is up to the woman involved to counter this belief and show that business is her foremost goal. The following three stories show how the typical entrepreneur handles these issues.

Edith Kilsteen is the owner of a large automotive supply shop. It is a business that she entered by chance. Disgusted by the small salary she was earning as a secretary, she gladly accepted an offer to manage the office of Readi Auto Supply. Several years later, her boss, Phil, suffered a heart attack and decided to retire early. He urged Kilsteen to take over the firm.

Kilsteen remembers many incidents and sarcastic comments when she first entered this highly male-oriented industry. She was also aware that she was being watched carefully for possible mistakes: "When I came into this business," she declared, "I was the first women to attend the automotive training school given by one of our manufacturers. I knew a lot hinged on what happened to me, because if I didn't behave well, I could ruin it for other women for the next ten years. I wore collars up to my chin and shirt sleeves down to my fingers, rarely smiled, and was very quiet, like ice-water-in-my-veins. I didn't want anyone to misunderstand why I was there."

Kirsteen well remembers the attitude of the other students at the school, all men. "They were shocked to see a woman," she continued. "I could just feel their disdain. Their attitude was, 'If this is Phil's playmate, he ought to leave her home.' I was living with the stigma of being a secretary accompanying the boss. If I was with him, I had to be his girlfriend. It never occurred to them that I was there to learn the business."

Louise MacFadden, owner of an import-export firm, voiced a similar opinion.

She, too, felt that men often assumed she was looking for sex; it was up to her to change this perception and to avoid possible misunderstandings. Louise frequently travels alone, making the run from her Manhattan office up to Providence or Boston several times a month. "Sometimes I take the 6 a.m. train," she declared, "and I always display my briefcase in a conspicuous fashion. I want people to know that I'm traveling on business. Otherwise, they see a woman alone and think I'm a target for their advances. Things aren't quite as bad as they used to be, but many men still think a woman who isn't home by the fire is out looking for trouble."

Maria Santori, a well-known designer and manufacturer of jewelry, felt the weight of such attitudes even at mid-day. Some men view a simple business lunch as a potential sexual encounter. "Oh, I still run into men who want to be cutesy-pie over lunch," she noted scornfully. "If I meet over lunch, I always bring my briefcase. Then I get out my notebook immediately and start talking business. They get the message. A woman still has to be real careful how she comes across. If you're halfway attractive, men will come on to you and try making a pass. Or maybe they tease you to see if you're open. Some guys go to the opposite extreme and are real cold because they don't know how they're supposed to deal with you. I am naturally a warm person, but I've learned to control exactly how much of that warmth I'll let through. I don't want any misunderstandings to interfere with my business."

Such situations are so woven into each woman's experience that she deals with them almost automatically. Yet they are constantly in the back of her mind, a little-noticed but ever-present source of irritation. No man can understand the drain on a woman's resources that such treatment as a sex object causes. It is impossible to imagine a man making the following statement: "Usually someone will react to how I look first, and then discover I'm competent. When I was first introduced to the president of my bank, I could see him thinking, 'Wow, you're gorgeous. Let me get to know you.' " The burden rests with the woman in this vignette to prove that she is capable as well as beautiful because the man involved cannot see beyond her physical and sexual exterior. The typical entrepreneur still must communicate to the men around her that lunch doesn't mean a date, a conference is not a sexual playground, and business is her first and foremost goal.

DRINKS, DINNER, . . . AND BED

Some women encountered problems in the course of doing business that were much more serious. The following stories are a sample of the extent to which men still harass women sexually. In such instances, the men involved were not employers who were using their position to force favors but were themselves executives or business owners doing business with a peer.

Today, Melissa Aviles owns an independent insurance company located in a major Midwest city. When she first started out in the industry twelve years ago, insurance was a predominently male field: "I'll never forget my first convention," she noted with chagrin. "There were very few women, and during several discussion groups, I had to speak before an all male audience. One guy in particular really came after me. He called me at my hotel at midnight and asked if he could come over and have a drink. I said, 'It's midnight and I'm trying to sleep. You cannot come over.' He said, 'Oh, that's OK if you're in bed,' I told him *no* several times, and he kept arguing back. Finally, I told him I had to get some sleep.

"A few years later, a group of us was sitting together at another convention, and that same man looked at me and said, 'Remember that meeting? You were so pretty when you were up there and did such a fantastic job of handling yourself. Everybody there wanted to get into your pants, and we had a bet going to see which one of us would make it.' I was glad he told me even while I was angry. Inside, I thought, 'You rotten creeps.' He meant it as a compliment, and telling me was a gesture of acceptance. But his words were really double-edged, because personally what he said was insulting."

Over the years, Aviles has learned to be frank about where she stands on this issue. "When someone at a meeting asks me to meet him for a drink," she continued, "I let him know where I stand. The last time anything happened, this man called me way beforehand to see if I was even going to go. When I said yes, he asked me to meet him for a drink the first night of the convention. I suggested that we meet in the bar with a group of other agents and all have dinner together, but he didn't want that. Then I could see where he was coming from. I told him, 'As long as you don't expect me to hop in bed with you later, I'll meet you at 5:00 to say hello. Then I'm having dinner with everyone else.' That just eliminates any problems before they start."

Yvonne Fletcher, head of Conference Planning Associates, was considerably more angry when she shared her story. "You know," she confided, her voice betraying the emotion she still felt, "men have only one thing on their minds when they look at a woman. I've been in an executive's office discussing the progress of a major conference that his company is cosponsoring, and he'll be saying, 'You've got great tits,' or 'I just love seeing you in that thing.' I hardly bother to reply and usually say, 'Why, thank you' and go on. I just let him get his little kicks and do his macho thing and think I'm soooo attractive and soooo flattered. I'm not going to let that get in the way of my doing business. I don't have to go to bed with him. I just have to say thank you when he likes my tits. I'm sure he thinks of it as a compliment and doesn't begin to see how inappropriate such remarks are."

All the women to whom I spoke were grateful to have an opportunity to unburden what had often been traumatic experiences. For Deborah Janacek, it was a chance to vent angry feelings that she had held for several years. Janacek now owns a dealership from a major manufacturer of heavy equipment. Her customers include anyone in need of Caterpillar-type tractors, dump trucks, backhoes, and other such vehicles. Although she deals almost exclusively with men, the people who purchase her product are not her worst problem: "I have had the most trouble with my factory rep," she noted with disgust. "He doesn't believe that women should be in business, especially his type of business, and he lets me know it. Every year, he has a sales contest, and every year he changes the rules so I can't win. One year I set my goals to win, and I did. I knew he didn't like me, but I wanted to try anyhow. At the awards meeting, he called me up there to get the award, and he leaned over and kissed me right on the mouth. I was furious. Then he made a joke about how there weren't many dealers around who he could kiss. I wanted to slug him. He was careful to steer me away from the microphone because he knew I would grab it and have a few words."

Gail Monteux, head of TechnoCrat Computers, told the last story that we will share here. Like so many other women, Monteux learned a painful lesson early in her career. "I discovered real quickly that it wasn't wise to meet anyone for a drink on business," she exclaimed. "Men might be able to do it, but I can't, at least not after 4:30, because they're never going to talk business. I've had men look me straight in the eye and say, 'I don't want to talk about this. I'd just as soon fuck you.' And I've had to say, 'Well, that's real nice and I appreciate the compliment, but I'm here to talk business.' I just let the remark go by, like he'd told me he liked the color of my dress. It had no more attachment for me than that."

ACT, DON'T REACT: KEEP YOUR GOAL IN MIND

The psychic toll on these women is obvious. Their first reaction was anger, and justifiably so, but they learned to hold the anger and not respond to the situation in this manner. All of the new entrepreneurs agree that the best way to handle such incidents is to ignore them, to have no "attachment" whatsoever to the spoken words, not to snap at the bait, and to remain businesslike and disinterested. Teresa Yee, owner of a prosperous Boston typesetting firm, noted, "Men still make remarks just to see if you pick them up. If you don't, the guys drop them. If you're offended or react in any way, they will definitely follow through. I just leave their little remarks hanging in the air rather than accept or respond to them."

Some women are understandably angry that men still treat them in such a fashion. They resent being viewed as sex objects and dislike wasting energy on sexist situations. For many, not reacting still requires considerable self-control. Even when they were aware that anger was not the best response, these women were occasionally unable to contain their vexation. All of them understood that, once provoked, they could react in an indignant, confrontational fashion.

One woman vividly remembered losing her temper, though she quickly realized that such behavior accomplished nothing other than venting her feelings: "I don't make appointments with men late in the afternoon anymore," she declared emphatically. "Most men don't give a damn if you're single or not, because most of them are married anyhow. They want you to have cocktails, then dinner, and then maybe bed. Well, I'm not interested in that.

"I remember one week where I had four late appointments," she continued, her voice rising, "and every guy made a pass. After the fourth one did it, I really railed into him, called him every name in the book, asked him about his cute wife and how many kids he had and what he expected to prove by all this. If I'd had a gun, I probably would've shot him. I was just livid. He really got more than he deserved because he was the fourth one to do it that week. I finally said to myself: 'Don't blame them, just don't set yourself up.' "

This woman recognized that losing her temper offered some release of frustration, yet she simultaneously understood the cost. In personal terms, she was livid and shaking, and she experienced an emotional assault on her system. The drain on her energy is clear. Where her business was concerned, she undoubtedly lost a client as well as the opportunity to teach that client the same lesson in a different way. However, as long as such harassment continues, both men and women will suffer the personal and financial costs.

Over the years, the new entrepreneurs have learned that reacting with rage and resentment is not to their benefit; they also recognize that adopting male-associated characteristics of dominance and aggression is not productive either. Instead, they realize that remaining calm and flexible, and acting on their own behalf is the best possible course. By keeping their goals clearly in mind, they are better able to reach those goals.

However, the interviewees do not excuse the unpleasant incidents that they encountered. On the contrary, all wish that men were less sexist in their perception of women. Nevertheless, they believe that unbridled anger will only continue the vicious cycle. Since men are unlikely to drop their mode of behavior first, many women feel that the only way to change the situation is to modify their reaction.

The new entrepreneurs feel that professional behavior, not verbal retaliation, is most effective. In general they would agree with Teresa Yee, who willingly shared her philosophy: "If a man needs to make remarks to me," she declared with conviction, "that's his problem. It's his ego that's involved, not mine. If I give that man a lecture, his consciousness isn't going to be raised. But if I do a good job, he will continue to respect my work and what I can do for his business. He still knows that what I am doing is right, and that I'm not compromising my professional knowledge."

By responding in this manner, Yee no longer allows any male to control her behavior. She believes that reacting to a man's words, rather than acting in her own interests, means she has allowed him to steer her off course and away from what is best for her business and herself. "The minute you argue with someone else in your mind," she continued, "they've got power over you. The minute what others think is important, they have some sort of control over your life. I'm not talking about being truthful and honest but about reacting to others and arguing with them in our minds."

Teresa Yee's viewpoint does not in any way take a "blame the victim" stance. Instead, it allows that each woman has a certain amount of individual control in a given situation. In other words, although injustices occur and discrimination exists, we are not powerless to counter these negative forces in our lives. The new entrepreneurs recognize that even though some factors are beyond their control, many others can and should be governed directly.

This attitude is well illustrated by an incident which Yee experienced when she first started her business. "For a long time," she recalled, "I was the only woman in my professional association, and I was always asked to take notes at meetings. At first, I was so tickled to be accepted in any way that I was glad to do it. Then I began to see the real advantages. The person who keeps the records gets to know who the key people are. She isn't out on the fringe with no insight or knowledge about the important things. I learned who gets things done and who has authority. Then I began to think, 'I don't care why they're doing this. I know why I'm doing it.' "

Instead of reacting to the situation and chafing at her role as secretary, Yee was able to find the advantages and use them on her own behalf. She made valuable contacts and was always current regarding important events. People had to contact her for names and dates, and she became a clearinghouse for important organizational information. Over the years, she gained both respect and visibility, and she eventually became president of the group. In this instance, Yee acted for herself instead of reacting to the motives of the group, and in the end she changed the group's view of sex roles in the most effective way possible: She became its leader.

Acting instead of reacting also affects a woman's personal behavior. The new entrepreneurs are aware that friendliness may be misinterpreted, that a smile may be viewed as an invitation, and that warmth may be misleading. However, they realize that too distant a demeanor is also inappropriate. In her discussion of these problems, Teresa Yee noted, "I'm generally cautious about making sure that my intentions are clear and that I'm being friendly because I'm friendly and not because I'm coming on. It's important not to lose sight of who I am as a person. I like to smile, and I like being warm. When I'm sincere about this, people react in a positive way."

The new entrepreneurs believe that it is important for them to be who they are, to remain amicable, if businesslike, and not to become cold simply as a reaction against potential sexual advances. They believe that if they are clear about their goals, then the men around them will also be clear. This may not avoid all unpleasant situations, but it certainly helps establish a new male-female rapport based on mutual business endeavors rather than sex.

OTHER WOMEN, OTHER MEN'S WIVES

The new entrepreneurs not only encountered problems with male colleagues and clients but also found that other women misinterpreted their intentions. Sophie Zedecke was unprepared for this problem when she entered her field. A medical physicist, Zedecke started a genetic engineering firm together with a friend who is a biophysicist. Attending scientific conventions is a normal and expected part of her job. Like most of the interviewees, Zedecke knew that sex-related issues can arise during the course of a meeting or seminar. However, she was surprised to find that it was not the men but their wives who presented the problem.

"When you go to conventions," she explained, "you learn a lot from talking to other people, and that is really important. Well, if the spouses are there and I'm the only woman attending for business reasons, I have a choice. I either go and stand with the guys, who are my colleagues, or go over with the wives and talk about diapers and recipes. That doesn't help me with my business. If I go with their husbands, I imagine all the wives wonder what I want with their men. I'm probably imagining that because I don't know what they really think, but it still bothers me."

Zedecke soon developed a successful strategy to handle this situation. "Now when I travel," she continued, "I try to get invitations to the man's home and become friends with his wife. That takes a lot of the charge out of the fact that I'm a woman. They understand that I don't want their husbands. All I want is to do business and preferably with my clothes on. I also make my goals clear. What you are looking for is evident to other people, and I make sure they all know what I'm there for. Over the years, that has worked very well for me."

When Zedecke first encountered the wives' hostility, she had two options: act or react. The latter meant yielding to the wives' disapproval and consequently joining their group. With this choice, she would have forgone the work contacts that she needed. Her other option was to stay with her colleagues and feel uncomfortable. Either way, she allowed someone else's opinion to govern her behavior; therefore, she was not free to act in her own best interests.

Zedecke fortunately recognized her participation in this incident. Her conflict was caused as much by her own doubt regarding her position as by any real disapproval from her colleagues' wives. As she gained experience, Sophie was able to establish and then accept her role with greater ease. She also learned to focus on her business goals. This in turn enabled her to do what was best for herself and her business without any feelings of discomfort. As a result, she soon established rapport with the women and accomplished necessary business transactions with the men, and her problem eventually disappeared.

MAY WE SPEAK TO YOUR HUSBAND?

Another major problem faced by the new entrepreneurs is the issue of credibility. Establishing themselves as serious business people was often a time-consuming task. In addition to facing all the problems of starting and maintaining a business, they had to face continual challenges to their credibility simply because of their sex. The interviewees had to ignore not only sexual advances but also condescension, male superiority, unpleasant jokes, and even disdain. Through hard work and perseverence, they slowly replaced such negative behavior with acceptance and respect.

Since the new entrepreneurs are trailblazers, they have few markers to guide them. For some, the feminists of previous generations had already somewhat eased their paths. Several women noted with gratitude that certain fields were already more open to them because of others' efforts. One woman, who established her own public relations firm five years ago at the age of twenty-six, noted, "I feel very lucky that I'm in a younger generation of women who are starting their own businesses in this field. The other women, the pioneers, they had it tough."

However, in spite of earlier successes, women today still must overcome the view that they are not serious about their work. This perception is based on old beliefs that women are childlike, weak, and in need of protection, that they are emotional and lack business skills, and that the real wage earner in the family is male not female. The following comments show that for women of every age, "proving" themselves is a difficult process.

"I'm the only woman landscape contractor in our area. When a male client first calls on me, it takes me 20 minutes to convince him that I'm not some rich man's wife playing with flowers and landscaping as a hobby. My age may have something to do with it. They see a woman in her forties as a garden club lady who does these things for fun or for a crusade, like an environmentalist."—Tommie Roth, age forty-four, landscape architect

"I'm almost forty now, but when I go out and meet new people they say, 'We were expecting someone older.' Sometimes when people come in the store they say, 'May we speak to your husband?' They just don't believe that I know what I'm doing."—Rona Smythe, age thirty-eight, owner of Scandinavian Furniture Designs

"I think there is a problem being a young woman, especially since I look about ten years younger than I am. It's one thing for people to hear me on the phone, but when I get to a construction site, people think, 'Who's this kid coming here and telling me what to do?' I try to sound confident as best as I can. Once I speak, their attitude usually changes because they see that I know what I'm doing."—Angela Warshawski, age twenty-nine, electrical contractor

For the older woman, overcoming the image of hobbyist or dilettante is the primary problem. Whether married, divorced, or single, she is perceived as playing store while her husband earns the real income for her family. Since most of the interviewees either support themselves from their business profits or make substantial contributions to the support of their families, this view is obviously erroneous. Yet for the majority of women, a minimum of one to two years of effort was necessary to change this perception.

The younger woman faces a slightly different problem. A man is more likely to assume a mentor role with a youthful male colleague than he is with a female. Remembering his own youth, he may identify with a younger man and feel a sense of kinship and rapport. A young woman does not enjoy such an advantage. Instead, she may meet with doubt regarding her ability and experience. She may even encounter a fatherly attitude, which is especially detrimental if she must maintain a position of authority.

Stereotypes about age were not the only barriers that the interviewees had to overcome. They frequently experienced a direct challenge to their professional knowledge and expertise as well. This was especially true for women working in male-dominated fields such as engineering, manufacturing, computer science, construction, architecture, and industrial supply. Amanda Johnston is a software consultant who helps manufacturers computerize their operations. It is her job to go into a factory, identify the key problems, and then develop a system to handle them. She finds that both managers and laborers alike are suspicious of her ability to do the job.

Johnston recounted the following incident as typical of the attitudes that she encounters: "Recently I was talking to a manufacturer," she declared, "and I was trying to get out of him what he really needed. Every time he used a word that was not part of the normal English language, he'd look at me to see if I understood. He'd even quiz me, saying, 'Now did *you* understand *that*? Can *you* do *that*?' To me that kind of thing says, 'I don't believe you know what I'm talking about.' "

Alicia Markham also works in a technical field. As the owner of a medical supply company, she must deal with the sales reps of the factories that manufacture the equipment which she in turn sells to doctors and hospitals. "Some of the men I deal with are inclined to belittle my role in this business," she stated in a matter-of-fact tone. "They are often reluctant to talk about the technical aspects of the equipment with me because they don't believe that I understand what they are saying. Sometimes they ask to see the president. When they find out that's me, they are really surprised. Most of them won't be outwardly disrespectful, but they sometimes won't help me in any way either. That not only makes my job more difficult but also decreases their own sales. If I can't get the service I need from them, I go elsewhere."

The new entrepreneurs of every age believed that hard work, humor, flexibility, and a willingness to learn were the best antidotes to these problems. On occasion, a particular woman brought a trusted male staff member to meetings with hard-line customers. This did not happen too often, but in such cases, the women involved did not want to spend any more effort on convincing people of their expertise. Although many women believed that they had to work harder than a man to prove themselves, they did not feel that this had been an insurmountable barrier. Some felt understandably resentful at having to spend so much valuable time and energy on overcoming sexist attitudes, but the majority felt that the effort had been worthwhile.

Tamara Arnold, partner in Management Training Systems, spoke for the majority when she made the following observations: "The 'Hey, toots, where's the boss?' 'I am the boss.' is slowly passing. People are now a lot more professional in dealing with us. They have done their homework and know a little about our business and what we've done. I also think women are being taken a lot more seriously than they used to be. There are a lot of us out there working very hard and being very dedicated and professional. Men are getting accustomed to this and aren't so threatened by the things we represent.

"My general approach has been to handle everything with grace rather than any kind of adamance. It doesn't work to be tough. Being yourself and being gracious in dealing with some of the slights to your sex in a humorous way is much better and easier. It's paid off to let it all roll off our backs. A number of people who were terrible to us in the beginning have come around and become good clients. We don't get any more of the, 'What are you girls doing down there?' We've even been able to chide some of our worst tormentors about the way they used to treat us. They know we work hard and have a service they like. And that is very, very nice."

Choosing to follow such a course rather than reacting with anger or helplessness not only opened new doors for each woman but also contributed to her sense of personal empowerment. The more a woman learns to act on her own behalf and do what is best for herself the greater her power will be. And with increased power she will succeed in advancing both her own economic cause and the cause of women everywhere. Although sexism may still affect such a woman negatively, it will not hold her back. Through working in the entrepreneurial world with clarity of purpose and concern, she will help change that world forever. Whether or not they intended to, the new entrepreneurs have already initiated that change.

THE DEVELOPMENT OF PERSONAL POWER

Although the women interviewed offer a broad range of models, nearly all of them have placed their anger in a new perspective: They don't waste valuable energy responding to obvious slights. Although they may feel angry within, this feeling no longer controls their behavior, thereby interfering with their business success. Instead of reacting emotionally to sexist incidents, they keep their business goals in mind and act as calmly as possible to further their own best interests. This may mean filing a law suit like Billye Ericksen-Desaigoudar, stating an opinion frankly like Melissa Aviles, or simply letting comments roll off your back like Teresa Yee and Tamara Arnold. Whatever path they chose, the new entrepreneurs were unanimous in their belief: Women become empowered when they act on their own behalf with a clear goal in mind rather than reacting against another person's behavior.

However, none of the interviewees discounted the emotional drain that sexual harassment caused. They simply believed that it was better to find more constructive outlets for their feelings than angry confrontations. These women shared their experiences with family and friends, were active in sports or fitness programs, participated in networks and professional groups, wrote articles, organized protests, and looked to other entrepreneurs for support. They also exercised one important prerogative of owning a business: They "retired" clients, customers, suppliers, reps and other people who were too unpleasant, simply refusing to do business with them.

You, like all the women interviewed, have undoubtedly experienced sexual harassment. Perhaps avoiding an emotional reaction is still difficult for you— you don't want to let anyone "get away" with bothering you, yet you don't want to lose control either. The following exercise will help you evaluate your behavior in such situations.

Think of an incident that caused you an unpleasant emotional reaction and answer these questions about it:

1. Who was the person involved? Is this someone who harasses you often? How does he bother you?

2. What was your reaction to the incident? Were you taken by surprise? How did this affect your behavior?

3. Is this a person you have to deal with frequently? If so, why? What is your goal in doing business with him?

4. Look at your answer to the first part of question 2. To what extent were you reacting *against* the person involved? How angry were you? How did you express your anger? To what extent was the other person controlling your behavior? Did you feel helpless? Frustrated? Outraged? Victimized? If so, what could you have done to change these feelings?

5. Look at the situation again. What did you want to get out of it? Did you get it? Were your best interests served by your behavior? If not, how could you have behaved differently to get what *you* wanted?

6. Was the situation serious enough to warrant a formal complaint, law suit, or other legal action? Should you consider "retiring" this person and not dealing with him at all in the future?

7. What constructive outlets do you have for expressing anger generated by sexism in your life?

Remember, the goal here is to gain control of sexist situations by acting to achieve your goals. Keeping these goals in mind will help you develop the best behavior in a given situation. Like the new entrepreneurs, you can learn to act on your own behalf and get what you want rather than feel powerless and at the mercy of your tormentor.

PART 5

Building Relationships That Work

CHAPTER 12

The Entrepreneurial Marriage: Choosing Interdependence

Jeanne Blackman is just twenty-nine and has been married for six years. Her business, The Willow Cafe, is a fast-growing restaurant and catering service known for its fine fresh ingredients and original gourmet dinners. When she started out three years ago, Blackman worked at home; cooking for special events was her primary focus. However, she soon outgrew the family kitchen, and now she manages a successful restaurant in addition to serving her catering clientele.

Blackman has found success as an entrepreneur; she also has a happy marriage. Because of their strong commitment to the relationship, she and her husband, Dick, have confronted and worked out the problems that inevitably arose. According to Jeanne Blackman, the independence necessary to succeed as an entrepreneur is not always compatible with traditional marital roles: "When I first moved to the restaurant," she remembered, "our marriage underwent a tremendous strain. I wasn't sure we were going to make it. When the business was in our home, Dick could drop in and say hello, and we saw each other more often. Even though I was working, I could stop and fix us something to eat, and I did about 70 percent of the housework. I was more available to him, and he was used to that.

"After I moved the business," she continued, "I was much more absorbed in my work, and things began to deteriorate. Dick was really unhappy with the changes that were happening. One day, we said to ourselves, 'We'd better take hold of this situation and make sure our marriage survives.' So we started making a real effort to set aside time for ourselves, and to talk things out. Dick also has had to change his perception of me and and of women's roles in general. I don't fill the traditional wife role any more, and that hasn't been easy for him to accept. It's in the home where a woman's career rubs against tradition daily and hourly, and that's bound to cause some conflict. A man who doesn't feel real comfortable with himself is going to have a lot of trouble adjusting to these changes and the kind of independence that his wife may want.

"I feel independent," she concluded, "in that I know I can take care of myself. A lot of money goes through my hands each month, and I make financial decisions that most women don't ever have the chance to make. But I'm very much dependent on Dick for support and for caring about me as a person. I value the love and affection that our marriage brings. To me, the trick is to fulfill my need for support without losing my sense of independence. Marriage can help a woman do this as long as she is aware of the pitfalls."

Jeanne Blackman's story raises issues that were important to all the new entrepreneurs. Ninety percent of the study participants married; about half eventually divorced. Of these, roughly one-third married again. During the course of the interview, almost every woman was eager to discuss her experiences. The issue of marriage and independence stood out as an important concern. The typical woman wanted to have a loving partnership; however, she wondered how she could achieve such a relationship and still have the autonomy that she desired.

The new entrepreneurs' stories suggest that if a woman wants to maintain both her independence and her marriage, she must be prepared to overcome certain barriers that may stand in her way, including: (1) possible pressure from her husband to conform to the traditional wife role; (2) unwillingness of a partner to accept her as an independent equal; (3) inability of her spouse to accept change—either within himself or within her; (4) her own fear, hesitancy, and ambivalence about standing alone; (5) broader social forces that still reinforce old mirror images.

These problems arose in the lives of the new entrepreneurs in a variety of combinations. However, their marital patterns fell into roughly three categories. One group of women were *child wives*. These women grew more and more dependent on their husbands and gradually lost their sense of self. Since most of the child wives held paying jobs, the dependency that they experienced was more psychological than financial. Over the years, their confidence gradually diminished, and they grew to believe that they could no longer survive on their own. This belief was clearly encouraged by their husbands. For the child wives, marriage thus enhanced negative mirror images and undermined their ability to stand alone. Only by seeking divorce could these women reassert their independence and reclaim control over their lives.

The women in the second group were *self-developers*. For these women, the demands of marriage often conflicted with their growing sense of independence—the situation for Jeanne Blackman. As Blackman's business grew so did her need for autonomy and self-control. Threatened by these changes, Dick Blackman reacted by pressuring his wife to conform to old roles. However, instead of finding divorce the only solution, the Blackmans worked to resolve their differences. Like all the self-developers, Jeanne Blackman was able to continue growing within the boundaries of the marriage, and her husband grew along with her.

For the self-developers, three factors made growth within marriage possible. First, both partners valued the relationship and did not want to lose it; second, neither believed that the problems were insoluble, and both worked hard to find satisfactory solutions; third, the husbands were open to the changes that their wives required. In fact many of these men wanted to change themselves as well. Both partners were thus able to grow and develop together, and the marriages remained intact.

The third group is composed of women who became *independent partners*. Almost from the start of their marriages, these women established a true partnership with husbands who would accept nothing less than full equality with their wives. The women in this group chose men who truly valued and encouraged their independence.

On the following pages, we will meet a variety of women and observe how they handled issues of independence within marriage. The stories presented here suggest that although roles are changing, such changes are occurring very slowly. Marriage still exerts pressure on women to become dependent and thus helps perpetuate outmoded mirror images. In general, however, the new entrepreneurs overcame this barrier.

THE CHILD WIVES

Karen Swenson is thirty-four, divorced, and the owner of Kinergetics Fitness Center. She was born in Michigan, where her father was a successful dairy farmer. The only daughter among four children, she was destined to be a nurse: Her mother and maternal grandmother were both nurses, and they expected her to follow the same path. In high school, Swenson was very precocious, graduating at sixteen, participating in anti-Vietnam War demonstrations, and making friends with people five and six years older than she was. Although unsure of her future, she knew one thing: She didn't want to be a nurse.

Already very independent, Swenson left home at seventeen and moved to Ann Arbor to attend college and be near the center of student activism. After the turmoil of her adolescence, she planned to settle down and put herself through school. During her second year at the University of Michigan, she met and married a young law student who was also active politically. He worked part-time at a legal aid center and frequently brought clients, coworkers, and fellow activists home.

Swenson describes her marriage this way: "I met my husband," she began, "when I was nineteen and working my way through college. At first, he was all for my staying in school. He even offered to help me pay for it, but that didn't last for very long. What he really wanted was someone he could control, someone who would cook and clean and do everything for him. He began bringing friends home and expected me to take care of everyone. I'd get back from work at 1:00 in the morning and want to go to bed because I had to get up and go to class in the morning. They would all be there drinking beer, playing cards and waiting for something to eat.

"After a while," she continued, "he began laying this trip on me that I'd ruined his career because he had to support me. Well, that wasn't true at all. If anything, I was supporting him. I handed over every check I earned just like I was a little girl. All of a sudden I started thinking, 'Hey, I don't need you to take care of me. I can make it on my own.' I woke up one day and realized I wasn't a little girl anymore, that I could take care of myself. Then things started getting physically violent, and one morning I just picked up everything I had and walked out."

When she left her husband, Swenson did not appeal to her parents for help. It was important to her that she make it on her own. "I couldn't afford much," she remembered, "only a really cheap apartment with cockroaches and all that. I learned alot about life during this period and about taking care of myself. You know, my family was very middle class, and I grew up out in the country where I was pretty sheltered. My job didn't pay very much, but I earned enough to get by. I dropped out of school for a year and slowly worked my way up to a better position. A couple of years later, I finally graduated from college."

Vera Bloom is fifteen years older than Karen Swenson, but her story is not very different. Like Swenson, she, too, became a child wife. Bloom married in her middle twenties after finishing college and working for several years as an architect with a large firm. Today, she is the divorced mother of two sons, and she works out of her own office.

In Bloom's case, marriage meant a personality transformation that she never could have dreamed would happen: "As I look back on it now," she recalled, "I realize that I had a very bad marriage. My independence was gradually destroyed, and I'm still not sure how that happened. My husband encouraged me to have a job, but I was supposed to do everything else as well—the house, the kids, the shopping, everything. At the same time I was working so hard, he belittled my efforts. No matter how hard I tried, I couldn't do anything right.

"Eventually, things got so bad that I thought of leaving. But whenever I mentioned this to Kurt, he undermined my efforts. He kept saying, 'You need me, you can't save money, you'll never make it without my support and my help. You don't know how to stand alone.' Somewhere inside I must have believed him, or I would have left sooner. Over the years, I became more and more depressed. Eventually, I couldn't get out of bed, and I spent all day sleeping.

My job went down the tubes, the house looked terrible, and I couldn't even take care of the kids. At that point, I realized it was time to do something.''

Bloom decided to see a therapist and subsequently entered into intensive counseling. "Soon after I made this step," she declared, "it was like a grey cloud lifted off of my life. With the help of my therapist, I gradually understood what had happened. Over the years, I had lost all my confidence, and my independence was destroyed. I realized that I had been this pretty neat person once, but not after I was married. Then I was just a total incompetent blumpf who couldn't do anything right.''

In less than a year's time, Bloom's situation improved remarkably. She slowly got in touch with the bright, strong person she had once been, and her sense of confidence and independence returned. This enabled her to confront her husband with her dissatisfaction and leave the marriage. "That took a lot of courage," she noted with pride, "but it was necessary for my survival. It also took courage for me to start my own business, and I'm really proud of what I have done.''

An "Adjustment" Theory of Marriage

For Karen Swenson and Vera Bloom, marriage had a negative impact on their journey to independent enterprise. Both entered into relationships where the men undermined their autonomy and fostered traditional roles and dependent behavior. Instead of helping them develop strong new mirror images, their husbands did just the reverse. Although each woman continued working, neither was able to maintain the psychological independence necessary to control her own life. As a result, Swenson and Bloom experienced a loss of confidence and started believing things about themselves that were obviously untrue. Their distorted self-perceptions intensified their feelings of dependency and further decreased their abilities to manage their own lives.

Even while she supported her husband, Swenson thought of herself as his "little girl." Bloom believed her husband when he told her, "You need me, you'll never make it without my support, you can't stand alone." The stories of Swenson, Bloom, and the other child wives suggest that economic independence is not the same as psychological independence. Until a woman develops an inner belief that she can stand alone, she will not experience true autonomy. Developing such a belief is very difficult because of the distorted mirror images that surround her. To change these images, she must restructure her definition of femininity and create a new picture of what it means to be a woman. Instead of helping her with this process, marriage may do just the reverse.

In her article "The Paradox of the Happy Marriage," sociologist Jessie Bernard analyzes why this is so.[1] Bernard notes that marriage requires women to "adjust" to a certain standard of behavior, a standard that reflects the negative mirror images of the feminine ideal. Instead of allowing for any real independence or self-determination, marriage often encourages docility, helplessness, and dependency, thereby reinforcing stereotypic "feminine" characteristics and per-petuating stereotypic roles. Because the influence of sex-role stereotypes is so strong, even an independent woman who wants to take care of herself may eventually adjust to the expected model. This was certainly true for Bloom and Swenson.

Marriage demanded that these women abandon their drive for independence and conform to an outmoded feminine ideal. In adjusting to these demands, both Swenson and Bloom lost touch with their active, self-directed side, and their ability to take charge of their lives was seriously eroded. Their self-confidence diminished, and they grew to doubt their ability to stand alone. As a result, each woman temporarily perceived herself to be more dependent that she actualy was, and this self-perception undermined her ability to control her own life.

Yet neither woman experienced a permanent subordination of her drive for independence. This was true for all the child wives. The first step in reclaiming control over their lives was recognizing the destructive changes that had taken place. This step was usually prompted by a pivotal incident that served as a catalyst for a new awakening. For Karen Swensen, it was physical violence that pushed her to leave her marriage. Vera Bloom realized that she had become totally immobile, and, subsequently, she sought counseling. No matter what the incident, it enabled these women to see their situation for what it was: They had become trapped in a net of dependency and were no longer able to stand alone. At that point, each woman took responsibility for her situation and decided to make a change. The fact that they were economically independent contributed to their ability to take this important step.

The importance of economic independence is supported by other research findings. In their book *American Couples*, psychologists Philip Blumstein and Pepper Schwartz make the following observation:

> It may seem unconscionably cynical to say that wives stay in marriages because they cannot support themselves outside them, but our data show there is some validity to this. We think many unhappy wives stay married because they could not maintain a decent standard of living alone. Women who can support themselves can afford to have higher expectations for their marriages beyond financial security, and because they are more self-sufficient, they can leave if these are not met.[2]

Karen Swenson was young and still in college, yet she knew that she could pay her way. Once she overcame the internal barriers that kept her dependent, financial independence enabled her to make a complete break from a destructive situation. Although her earnings were not high, she was determined to take care of herself. The same was true for Vera Bloom.

With the help of her therapist, she realized that she had contributed to the family income for years even while her husband insisted that she needed him to survive. After reconnecting with her strong, independent side, Bloom returned to work and subsequently left her marriage. Financial independence helped both Swenson and Bloom move on once they had achieved the psychological independence needed to stand on their own.

THE SELF-DEVELOPERS

The women in the next group were "self-developers." These women were able to resolve issues of independence and self-determination within the boundaries of their marriage. Success in this endeavor depended on the readiness of both husband and wife to change to accommodate the wife's growing need to be on her own.

The story of Marjory Higgins stands in promising contrast to the experiences shared by Karen Swenson and Vera Bloom. Higgins grew up in Trenton, New Jersey, and met her husband, Bill, when they both were still in high school. After her graduation, she started working in an insurance company. She and Bill continued dating and then married four years later. At that point, the couple decided that Bill Higgins would attend graduate school in Maryland to complete a Ph.D. in economics and that Marjory would support them through this period. After Bill finished his doctorate, Marjory stopped working and had two children within a three-year period. Her husband obtained a job as an analyst with the Department of Labor in Washington, D.C., where they have made their home for the past twenty years.

Here is how Marjory described her marriage: "When my first child was born," she recalled, "there was no doubt that I would stay at home. After working so long, I felt ready to have Bill take care of me. But the next thing I knew, I was climbing the walls with dissatisfaction. I didn't understand what was wrong with me. Bill was bringing home good money by then, but I just wasn't comfortable, and that caused a certain amount of strain in our relationship."

Around this time, Marjory Higgins rediscovered an old love—painting. She had been considered a talented artist in high school but had never thought of pursuing an art-related career. However, when she found herself with a little spare time, she started developing this interest: "When my children were small, I spent hours sketching and designing. Eventually, I volunteered to teach painting to some kids over at our church. When I took an art class at the YWCA, I met an instructor who encouraged me to continue my studies."

Thanks to the urging of her teacher, Higgins decided that she wanted to go back to school. At this point, she and Bill sat down to discuss what this would mean for both of them. "At first my husband felt threatened," she explained, "but then he realized that it was his turn to reciprocate. He said, 'OK, it's your turn to go to school.' I enrolled at a local art college and got totally involved in design work. As I progressed, I got a student internship with a large firm and started earning a little money again. That meant contact with all sorts of new people, staying out late once in a while, and becoming more independent."

During this period, Higgins really grew and changed. She enjoyed having some life of her own apart from the family, and the professional success that she experienced increased her sense of confidence. After graduation, she was hired by the firm with which she had completed her internship and was offered a respectable salary.

However, Higgins' relationship with her husband, Bill, began to deteriorate: "The whole situation got pretty tense," she remembered with dismay. "At first Bill was very jealous of my success and of my being out there meeting other people. We had a lot of disagreements over where I was heading. But he has grown in his profession, too, and now there are a lot more women working in his field than there used to be. He has learned from them and sees that I still have places to develop. We always laughed about how we argued from the day we met, but that ability to disagree and talk things out has helped us survive. For a woman to go through something like this and stay married, she has to be very clear about what she wants. She also must have a husband who will grow and change along with her. In order to get what I needed, I had to restructure my life, and, fortunately, Bill was willing to go along with that."

The marriages of Marjory Higgins, Jeanne Blackman, and the other self-developers reflect issues of growing importance to U.S. couples. Today, nearly half the labor force is female; due to changing economic and social trends, more and more women are combining paid employment with marriage.[3] Nevertheless, although many men welcome their wives' economic assistance, they have more trouble accepting changes in the old mirror images that the wives' employment may require.

In their nationwide study of couples in the United States, Philip Blumstein and Pepper Schwartz found that married women make compromises and adjust to the demands that their husbands' careers pose. Such compromises occur even when a wife is unhappy with her situation. Men, however,

> . . . do not seem to make the same kinds of adjustments. Even after many years of marriage, a husband who is angry about disruptions caused by his wife's work does not accept it as an inevitable part of their marriage. . . . While the man may be more than pleased to see her out in the work force helping to support their household, he may not be so ready to bear the costs of her efforts. By expecting her to work but giving no quarter for the demands of her work, he is asking her to be "superwoman," and few women can comply.[4]

Disruption within the household and the demands of changing roles are not the only issues that today's dual-career couples must face. A husband may oppose his wife's employment for deeper psychological reasons. In her book, *Intimate Strangers: Men and Women Together*, psychologist Lillian Rubin suggests that men are threatened by independence in women because they fear abandonment. "This is what haunts so many men," Dr. Rubin notes, ". . . the fear that a woman will become 'more independent inside herself,' that she'll come not to need him so much that she'll be free to leave.''[5] When such a fear arises, some men may react by using manipulation to keep their wives dependent—clearly the case for Karen Swenson, Vera Bloom, and the other child wives. By contrast, the self-developers did not encounter such deep resistance to their growing need for independence.

When Marjory Higgins was ready to reassert control over her life, Bill Higgins responded with mixed feelings. On one hand, he supported her efforts to develop her talents and increase her skills. On the other, he was threatened by the changes that he perceived. After returning to school, Marjory Higgins not only grew personally but also achieved success in her chosen profession. The demands of her work began to conflict with her responsibilities at home, and she started contributing to the family income once again. As an accomplished professional, she no longer depended on Bill Higgins to take care of her, and he found this threatening.

The Higginses valued their relationship and worked hard to resolve their problems. As Marjory Higgins noted, their ability to disagree and then compromise helped them stay together. Although doubtful at first, Bill Higgins was ultimately open to accepting the changes that his wife needed. Eventually, he saw that the situation offered him the opportunity to grow and develop as well. Marjory Higgins was also clear about what she wanted and communicated this to her husband. The Higgins' marriage thus grew into a relationship based on interdependence and mutual support rather than on dependency, fear, and control.

Although all the interviewees valued the love and caring that marriage could offer, they also valued their independence. They hoped to achieve some personal autonomy without sacrificing the companionship and mutuality that a close relationship offers. For the child wives, this proved to be an impossible task, at least within the marriages they had already experienced. By contrast, the self-developers resolved these issues successfully. The women in this group were able to achieve personal growth and increased autonomy without leaving the relationship. Paid work, a willing husband, and an inner belief that they could stand alone helped them in this endeavor.

THE INDEPENDENT PARTNERS

A third group of women, the "independent partners," offers further hope that old mirror images can be changed. Even after marriage, these women continued to strengthen their independent side. From the very beginning, they established an equal partnership with a husband who would himself accept nothing less. Instead of reacting negatively to their wives' need for independence, these husbands supported it. Although the independent partners compose only about 20 percent of the sample, they provide inspiring examples for others to follow.

Carolyn Terman is representative of the women in this group. From the time she was in the third grade, Terman wanted to be a teacher, a goal that she fulfilled upon graduating from college. Her love of children and concern for their development eventually led her to establish a nursery school, and today she runs a chain of day-care centers that is rapidly expanding throughout the South. Terman was raised in Oklahoma but has since settled in neighboring Texas. Dallas serves as the corporate headquarters for her fast-growing business.

Although she dated many men, Terman decided against an early marriage. She was preoccupied with her career and never met a man she felt would understand her need to manage her own life. That remained true until, at the age of thirty-seven, she met Frank Jacobson, a recent widower and successful partner in a major Dallas law firm.

"Soon after we started dating," she noted with a smile, "I realized that Frank was getting serious about our relationship. I told him, 'You know, my heart beats for Sunnyside Child Care. I think you should line up ten other women you are interested in marrying and pick the one whose heart beats for you.' I didn't realize it at the time, but my putting a roadblock in his way was nothing but encouragement. He was very persistent, but all along, I made it clear that I had to keep on running my business, and he said that this didn't bother him a bit. Some men don't like independent women, but Frank believes a woman should be able to take care of herself."

Terman and Jacobson married after a ten-month courtship, and equality characterized their relationship from the start. "Things have worked out reasonably well," she continued, "in part because I was clear about what I needed before I got married. Frank also never wanted to be a father figure to me. I don't think he wanted the responsibility of having me get my life's satisfaction from him. He has encouraged my work, and accepted it, even though there are times I know it is hard for him. I live and breathe this business, and there are a lot of men who wouldn't like that. He is very supportive of the fact that I have my own career and can take care of myself. I wouldn't settle for anything less in a man, and I think that's what he wants in a woman."

Throughout Terman's story there runs a real sense of reciprocity and respect. She clearly views her husband as a partner not a father figure, and he regards her as an independent individual in return. In their relationship, Frank Jacobson never assumed the role of provider or protector. Instead, he respected Terman's need to take care of herself and understood the work that a demanding career requires. From the outset, Carolyn Terman was clear about her needs. Both psychological and financial independence were important to her. Her goal was to establish a relationship which would allow her that independence while providing the love and support that she also desired.

A woman must have a certain level of independence to become an entrepreneur. She must have confidence, persistence, and self-reliance to succeed on her own. By contrast, marriage has traditionally demanded that women assume the role of protected dependent, thereby undermining the very qualities necessary for business success. This certainly was true for the child wives. For these women, marriage placed barriers on the road to entrepreneurship instead of offering the necessary support. However, both the self-developers and the independent partners were able to work out issues of independence within their marriages. Paid employment, inner confidence, and the support of a willing partner all contributed to their ability to accomplish this task.

Today, women like the new entrepreneurs are refusing to accept the "adjustment standard" of mental health once necessary for success in marriage and are working instead toward equal partnerships. It is encouraging that both the self-developers and independent partners, who together represent about half of the sample, achieved such relationships. Thanks to the efforts of these, and other, independent women old mirror images are slowly changing. For such changes to continue, we must offer the upcoming generation of women strong role models and early training in independence, responsibility, and excellence.

All women, no matter what their age and upbringing, should realize that they, too, can change distorted mirror images and forge a new standard of independent behavior. As the new entrepreneurs have shown, no woman has to adjust to old standards to have the relationship she desires. The stories shared here indicate that marriage and independence can be compatible, and such compatibility is essential for the woman who hopes to have her own business. A relationship that undermines confidence and self-control will only deter her progress toward independent enterprise. Discarding old mirror images and developing new ones to take their place requires strength, courage, and determination. For today's aspiring entrepreneurs—and their husbands—this is not an impossible task.

CHAPTER 13

The Entrepreneurial Supermom: Exploding a Myth

Lucinda Jarvis is both an entrepreneur and a mother. Her highly profitable wholesale operation provides goggles, helmets, shields, and other safety equipment to construction and manufacturing companies; she numbers many *Fortune* 500 businesses among her clients. Jarvis has two children, a son and a daughter, and she finds running a business and a family a continually challenging task.

Like many of the new entrepreneurs, Jarvis knows that both business and family demand more attention than she can give: "There's definitely a conflict between a happy family and a very successful business," she noted. "A few years after we started, we passed the 5 million mark in sales. But we could have grown much faster. My family often has to come first, and so my company has grown more slowly than it could have. The demands on both sides are very heavy, and I frequently feel split in two. It seems like I'm always trying to find a happy medium."

The problem that Jarvis describes is a primary concern to all women business owners who have, or hope to have, a family. What, in fact, does a woman with the responsibilities that business ownership demands do with her family? What sacrifices are involved to find the "happy medium" that Lucinda Jarvis describes? And is it possible to care for both children and enterprise, much less have time for your husband or partner as well?

The woman who is both entrepreneur and mother has to make some important decisions about how she will divide her time. None of the interviewees felt the choice was easy, and few were able to choose business over family without some conflict and guilt. Their stories indicate that even if a woman runs a large and profitable enterprise, she still also takes the primary responsibility for running the family. This dual role leaves her feeling fragmented and exhausted, never able to devote her energy fully to one endeavor or another.

Yet all the entrepreneurial mothers feel that business ownership offers them a number of advantages that are not so readily available in a more traditional job. When the need arises, they can arrange for flexible hours, schedule visits from their children, or provide part-time jobs for older sons and daughters. Their stories reveal that entrepreneurship brings at least seven positive advantages that most working mothers do not enjoy:

1. Children of entrepreneurs can visit the workplace at any time. Such visits offer a unique opportunity to learn about the business world.
2. Children are encouraged to help at the family business. Such work allows them to develop unusual skills and positive work habits at an early age.
3. Assisting with a family business helps children develop a greater sense of responsibility and independence.
4. Children who visit their mother's business have a greater possibility of understanding her work and the demands made on her life.
5. The woman business owner can, when necessary, create a somewhat flexible schedule.
6. An entrepreneurial mother offers children an interesting and unusual role model.
7. Children who help their mother at work develop a sense of sharing in a family endeavor.

On a practical level, balancing family and business is difficult at best. It requires a skillful juggling of time, energy, and attention. On a personal level, a woman may experience conflict as well. Our culture regards motherhood and business success as mutually exclusive. Each is considered to require different skills and abilities, and thus a woman viewing herself in the mirror marked "mother" will see an image that is incompatible with the one viewed in the mirror marked "entrepreneur." This attitude further heightens her conflict, exacerbating any divided feelings she already has.

In addition, motherhood is so tightly woven into the feminine ideal that women who choose business over family are regarded as unfeminine. If the conflict between independence and femininity is strong, then that between having or not having a family is stronger still. Then, even if a woman decides that she really wants children, her struggle continues around how much of her time and energy she will devote to their care. These issues surfaced again and again in the stories of the new entrepreneurs.

BABY OR BUSINESS: AN AGONIZING CHOICE

The problems faced by many of the mothers interviewed are clearly anticipated by Lisa Tedesco, a young woman who is presently considering whether to have children. Born and raised in Boston, Tedesco grew up in a close Italian family whose clannish tendencies extended even to the businesses they owned. Her parents ran a prosperous restaurant where Tedesco worked after school from the eighth grade on. Tedesco well remembers a sense of family effort to make the business work. Her grandmother babysat so Tedesco's mother could participate in managing the restaurant; her uncle, an accountant, assisted with the books; another uncle, a building contractor, appeared whenever plumbing or electrical work needed to be done.

It was no surprise to anyone when Lisa Tedesco joined her sister, Pam, in starting a distributorship for the products of a major telecommunications company. While Lisa Tedesco was building her career as a high school physics teacher, her sister worked as a service representative for a high-tech company on Boston's Route 128. When she saw an opportunity to establish a wholesale service in a new area, Pam Tedesco decided to act. Both women were ready for a career change and correctly believed that the telecommunications industry was a growing field with good financial prospects. Within two years of starting the business, they had grossed over $2 million and were well on their way to a large and prosperous firm.

An obviously dynamic, organized, and systematic person, Lisa Tedesco met every challenge the business offered with a new achievement. When the bills mounted, she found a way to pay them off; when a new line of equipment was returned with problems, she learned to fix it herself; as the business grew in size and assets, she found good people to hire and trained them to take over routine tasks. No problem seemed too large for her to tackle, and she actually enjoyed facing new obstacles as they arose. Each difficulty presented her with the opportunity to achieve something bigger and better.

The problem of children, however, was one that Tedesco hesitated to take on. When I first met her, she had been agonizing over her decision for several months: "My husband is currently in graduate school," she explained, "finishing his Ph.D. in mathematics. Recently he came home and said, 'I want to have kids.' I couldn't believe what he was saying, and it scared me to death. I like the idea of having children, but I don't know how I'd find time to do it. Sometimes things get pretty wild around here, and I hardly have time to do what I need to do. All my problems would be magnified a thousand fold with a child. I don't know how we could continue to expand. Building this business takes almost all of my time."

Tedesco tried to imagine herself with a baby; realistically, she wondered how she could integrate yet another responsibility into her already busy life. "We have to move to a larger place," she continued, "and I thought that I might find a big office with a little one behind it for the baby. Then I could have my child right here with me. But I don't know what I would do if I were sitting here having a meeting and the baby started crying. That requires a whole different kind of thinking.''

Child care was another problem that she could not solve. Like most of the other interviewees, she was divided as to what solution would be best for her child. ''The lady across the street from me has a nursery,'' she noted, ''but I don't know how I feel about taking kids to nursery school all day. Morally, I have a problem with hiring someone to take care of my children. I'm amazed I have that attitude, but I do. I come from a very family-oriented background and have these real strong tapes in my head about what you do with your kids. Perhaps it is because my mother stayed home with us when we were small. Then when she went to work in the restaurant, my grandmother helped out.''

Tedesco's husband, Jack, has promised to help, but she has some doubts about how realistic his offers are. ''Jack says he's all geared up for it,'' she declared, ''that he's prepared to make a time commitment especially while he's still in school. He studies at home and figures it would be the perfect situation. Right now, he does 90 percent of the housework and about half of the cooking. He says, 'Oh, I'll take care of the baby,' yet when I add up what he already does, I think he's promising more than he could deliver. He has two more years of school, but then he'll have a regular job and be home less. I can't imagine never having children, yet right now I can't imagine doing it either.''

Lisa Tedesco is typical of the young career woman who has postponed child-bearing in favor of developing her work skills. As she approaches her middle thirties, she knows that she must decide soon and thus finds herself facing a difficult dilemma.

Although the situation is not as hopeless as she presently feels, Tedesco is wise not to gloss over the difficulties. The new entrepreneurs did find adequate child-care arrangements and were often very grateful to the dedicated men and women who assisted them. However, they still experienced many of the same conflicts that Tedesco anticipated. As entrepreneurs, they wanted to develop the best business possible; as mothers, they wanted to be involved with the care of their children. For most, finding a happy medium often felt like an impossible task. This is the dilemma of today's entrepreneur, and it has no easy solution.

ROLE CONFLICT AND CULTURAL PRESSURE

Because the boundaries of traditional roles are so limiting, women like Lisa Tedesco often see childrearing as a burden and source of conflict. If the role of motherhood were more open and flexible, these same women might see the joys and opportunities that it offers. Nowhere does Tedesco mention the benefits that she would derive from having children. She only notes the added problems they would bring. However, she is quite clear about the pleasures of running a business: "When I say that I have my own company, everyone thinks it's very exciting. I took an idea, started with nothing, and made it into something. That has been exciting and given me lots of confidence."

In her discussion of motherhood, Tedesco does not exhibit the same excitement nor does she see the same potential for growth and respect. Her hesitation is well-founded. Although our culture defines womanhood in terms of motherhood, it then denigrates the mother role. Women who choose not to have children are viewed as unfulfilled, unwomanly, or unfeminine, and women who choose motherhood are relegated to an unfavorable, even invisible, status. Unpaid, powerless, and dependent, the housewife-mother enjoys the least respect of any worker in our society.

This fact became painfully clear to me during the years I remained at home with my children. In the intellectual university community where I lived, raising a family was granted little or no interest whatsoever. The question, "Well, what else do you do?" inevitably arose, and the woman who responded, "Nothing," was regarded as little more than just that. This was during the late 1960s and early 1970s when the value of family in general and children in particular was seriously questioned.

Even the feminist movement of that time did little to help. Its encouragement to get a job, or better yet, to get a divorce, only reinforced the negative image. If women were "free" of the shackles that family and children represented, they would somehow be transformed into new, independent people. This point of view contributed to the denigration of those women who genuinely enjoyed mothering and wanted to be at home with their children for some period.

I thought that I was perhaps imagining these negative attitudes toward motherhood until I spent a year in Brazil. During that time, people constantly admired my children and then praised me for having them. At the beach, on the bus, in the street, both men and women fondled the children's hair, smiled at me, and said, "How happy you must be to have these wonderful boys."

At that time, I was teaching English at a university in Rio de Janeiro. To my surprise, my colleagues and supervisors alike praised my family as well as my work. I felt reinforced both as a mother and as a professional, and a new pride, that of motherhood, developed within me. Upon returning to the United States, I immediately noticed a difference in attitude. Children were a burden, a responsibility, something to be cared for without compensation, financial or otherwise. At work no one ever inquired about my family, much less admired my children. Such talk was considered unprofessional and unsuitable for the woman eager to get ahead.

It is thus easy to understand why a woman in Tedesco's position would hesitate to choose mothering children over managing a business. The former activity would bring little positive reinforcement from the culture around her compared to the admiration and self-respect she felt in the latter. Because she was unable to resolve the issue of child care, Lisa believed it was impossible to be both a mother and an entrepreneur. She therefore chose to stay temporarily with the role she knew gave her the most satisfaction.

Lisa Tedesco is hardly unique among the new entrepreneurs. Almost half do not have children, and most of these indicated that they do not plan to have any in the future. The fact that so many energetic, talented, and successful women choose business over family indicates that the problems Tedesco described are very real. Role conflict, physical and emotional strain, a fragmented, harried life, and cultural devaluation of mothers all contributed to their decision to remain childless.

THE ENTREPRENEURIAL MOTHERS

While Lisa Tedesco was agonizing over the issue of motherhood, many new entreprenuers faced the very problems that she anticipated. How did these entrepreneurial mothers fare? Although all were glad that they had had children, few were able to work out a truly satisfying arrangement for themselves and their families. Only one woman described herself as a "Supermom," who gladly arose at 5:00 in the morning to do her housework before starting her business day. The single mother of two teenagers, she apparently had avoided the strain described by the other interviewees, who often felt tired, fragmented, and guilty as they tried to manage the many responsibilities typical of the entrepreneurial mother's life.

Juggling Baby and Business

Betty Lewis owns a construction company that specializes in building new homes and remodeling old ones. She is also the mother of an eight-year-old daughter named Judy. Lewis's husband Jim is an engineer with the state Department of Roads who works a regular eight-hour day. Lewis doesn't feel that Jim understands the demands of her life: "I would have liked more than one child," she declared, "but I knew I couldn't handle it. My husband is very proud of my work, and he certainly is willing to listen to my business problems. But as far as child care is concerned, he's old-fashioned in his views and thinks that it is my responsibility."

Because she is balancing two jobs, Lewis often feels divided and harassed: "Jim just doesn't understand how complex my life is," she continued. "If there's a doctor's appointment, I go. If there's a school conference, I go. Whenever there's a problem, I'm the one that stops work and tends to it. He has no idea how that interrupts my concentration. One minute I'm absorbed in planning a major construction job, and the next I'm on my way somewhere with my daughter."

Despite the difficulties involved, Lewis's desire to participate in her daughter's care is genuine. From the very beginning, she looked forward to enjoying some of the satisfactions and joys that motherhood offered. "I never wanted to give Judy up every day from eight to six," she declared. "I have tried to make myself available during the day, but that sometimes has been very difficult. One year, I helped with a playgroup. Every other Wednesday after school I got Judy and her best friend, and we did something together. The friend's mother took them the alternate weeks. Then last year, I participated in a car pool. On the days that I drove, I put a stickpin with a little note on the side of my dress saying '*car pool*,' so I didn't forget to go. I picked the kids up, delivered them to whatever class they had, and rushed back here. I've used the perks of being a business owner whenever I could, but I just can't take time away any more."

Soon after Judy was born, Lewis realized that she would have to make some important decisions. "At first," she explained, "Judy was with me a lot of the time. She was in a day bed in one corner of the office. Then I'd rush her to the baby-sitter, rush back again, and try to do a little work. That was intolerable. She wasn't getting good care, and I wasn't giving good service. I knew we were in trouble one day when she was about two. We had a client come for a special visit, and Judy didn't want to be there. I had to drag her along with me. She took one look at the client, and kept saying, 'Go way lady, go way lady.' At that point, I reluctantly made other arrangements for her care."

Although her daughter is now in the third grade, Lewis still has not solved her dilemma. "Sometimes I feel like I am abandoning her to one service or another," she noted with dismay. "After school, she goes to swimming lessons or gymnastics or dancing lessons until I can pick her up at five o'clock. Then we go to the grocery store to get something for dinner. It's really hard to juggle all these responsibilities. There are days when I sit here and say, 'Now which day is it? Where is Judy? Where should I be right now?' But I guess it's all working. Judy has a desk here and knows that she is part of this operation. My employees jokingly call her 'Madame President,' because she wants to take over the company when she grows up."

Mobilizing Family Talent

A few years ago, Julie Gerstein started the first bagel shop in the large university community where she lives. She has just opened a second store and looks forward to further expansion. After becoming an entrepreneur, Gerstein started managing her family in a different way. Although she once was fully responsible for child care and household tasks, she now enlists the efforts of her husband and children.

Getting them involved hasn't been easy, but Gerstein is pleased with how her family situation has changed: "At first," she noted, "my husband resented the time that I spent at the shop. He didn't like the fact that I wasn't as available as I used to be. I also went from being a woman who scrubbed the floors every week to someone who ignored the dirt and the clutter. For a while, we had a cleaning lady who came in and took care of the worst of it, but then she got sick and had to stop working. At that point, I sat my sons down and told them, 'The house has to be cleaned, and I'm going to pay someone to do it. Do you want the job? If you take it, you can't fool around. The work has to be done regularly every week.' ''

Gerstein's sons accepted her offer. At eleven and thirteen, they were old enough to vacuum and dust and to clean the bathroom. ''This was a tremendous help,'' she continued, ''but there was still a lot of other work left to be done. So we tried dividing it up. I take care of the shopping and cooking, my husband does the laundry and dishes. For some reason he just can't get the permanent press clothes done right, and he has trouble sorting dark socks. Just the other morning he was out of socks and was almost desperate. 'I've got to have a pair of brown socks today,' he said, and I ran down quickly to the laundry and looked through the wash basket. But he usually sits in front of the TV and sorts laundry, and our division of labor has worked pretty well.''

According to Gerstein, succeeding as both mother and entrepreneur requires being well-organized. ''I plan my menus in advance,'' she explained, ''so I can make up a careful shopping list. Cooking can be a real problem especially if I'm held up at the shop. Even with good planning, life isn't perfect. The other night, I got a desperate call, 'There's nothing ready for supper,' and I drove home and made some stuff and then went back to the shop. (We were getting a special order ready, and I had to supervise it.) If I have to go out of town, my husband takes over. He has to get the boys up and see that they get off to school. I leave everything planned before I go, and when I return he always tells me how smoothly everything went. I just chuckle and say, 'Anyone can keep it going for a few days. Try doing it all the time, and you'll see the difference.' ''

Like many of the interviewees, Gerstein involves her children with her business whenever she can. They do occasional odd jobs and visit her to get a special snack after school. However, she still sometimes felt guilty about spending so much time on her business. ''Sometimes I tell myself,'' she noted with chagrin, '' 'Make sure you're not cheating Sam and the boys.' My sons are very independent and self-sufficient, which in the long run will be to their benefit. They also have a good opportunity to learn something about running a business if they want to. But then I think that these are just rationalizations, that I should be spending more time with them, and that what I am doing is somehow not to their advantage.''

Making It Alone

Frances Levinsky was in her middle thirties when she started her ''Women and Success'' seminars six years ago. At that time, she was the single mother of Sally and Bob, both in their early teens. Divorced for three years, Levinsky had made a good effort toward restablishing some sense of family life, but she found that the demands of work and career were too difficult for her to handle alone. So she teamed up with another woman, and today they have a "family" of their own.

"I feel I have one of the best solutions possible," Levinsky noted with a smile. "I live with another single mother whose daughter is about the same age as mine. We live in a lovely five-bedroom home that neither of us could afford alone. Every other week, one of us is 'mother of the week.' So one week, I'm on duty and Helen is totally free, and the next week we reverse. This way, the kids get good care, and we mothers have time for our work and a little social life."

Frances willingly shared her formula for making such an arrangement work. "When I'm the mother," she continued, "I'm totally responsible for the cooking, shopping, and children. If the water heater goes, I call the plumber. If someone isn't doing their chores, that's my problem. Whatever comes up, I tend to it. Then the next week, I do nothing. I'm like the husband and have no responsibility for the house or family. I once took a vacation to Mexico for a week without a qualm in the world. I knew that the children got home-cooked meals every night, and their life did not change for a minute. Their 'mother' was still with them."

Where money and chores were concerned, the two women also shared everything. "We split all the bills," she explained, "according to how many people we support. That means I pay three fifths and she pays two fifths. We have fun with this, too. If I have company one week, she serves us, and I do the same for her. Every once in a while we bring each other flowers. One time we had a beautiful candle-lit dinner for the five of us, and we served hamburgers! Once a month, we sit down and organize all the chores in advance. The kids' jobs are planned ahead of time, and every month we rotate the work. One month, my son does the yard work, one of the girls has the kitchen, someone else does the bathrooms. Then the next month we change so no one gets stuck with one chore. Each child has one night to be 'cook's helper,' and Tuesdays are 'free for all' because everyone has some meeting or activity that night."

Levinsky is an innovative and organized woman, and this helps her manage a complicated family life. "With a little organization and back up," she declared, "you can get a system like this going. We do things together in a project-oriented kind of way. It has to be a team effort, or it won't succeed. There are also certain rules, and some things are just non-negotiable. The kitchen has to be kept clean, and the same with the living room. Each person's room can be a disaster zone if he or she wants. We all have the luxury of our own rooms, and this privacy lets each of us have a place to do our own thing. Sometimes I get really tired managing all this, and sometimes I feel like a drill sergeant getting everybody to follow the rules. But by and large, it's worked for me, and I'm very grateful."

GUILT AND CONFUSION: THE STAPLES OF
A MOTHER'S LIFE

Whenever the issue of family and career arises, I hear one opinion again and again: "Owning a business is a wonderful solution for a woman. It allows her time to take care of her family and get a little money as well." This widespread belief is based on two persistent stereotypes and ignores the realities of the entrepreneurial mother's life. Owning and managing a business is as demanding as any other career. It requires time, energy, and concentration. However, where women are concerned, this fact is overlooked because they are typically viewed as second wage earners who are just "playing store."

Popular opinion is based on a stereotypic view of motherhood as well: Primary responsibility for the family's care should fall on the mother's shoulders. In her book *A Woman's Place*, sociologist Cynthia Epstein addresses this issue. She notes that "mothers have not been freed from the cultural mandate to know and see all about their children. It is not considered proper for children to be raised by anyone other than the mother."[1] Because of such beliefs, many women feel guilty when they devote more time and attention to their work than to their family. This certainly was true for the new entrepreneurs.

On one level, the interviewees genuinely wanted to participate in their children's care. On another level, they believed it is wrong if they don't. Their desire to create a family-oriented environment for their children was thus clouded and confused by guilt. This was clearly reflected in their stories. Lisa Tedesco believed that taking a baby to day care was "morally wrong," while Julie Gerstein often reminded herself that she might be "cheating" her husband and children of the care that they deserved. Frances Levinsky was able to enjoy her vacation only by knowing that her children were receiving "home-cooked meals" and a "real" mother's care.

Like all the interviewees, these women were unable to distinguish how much they want to be involved in caring for their children from how much they think they should be involved. Given popular stereotypes regarding the mother's role, it is understandable that the new entrepreneurs felt such conflict and confusion. To manage both family and business, they had to create a new, personally defined standard of mothering in face of strong social pressure to conform to the present cultural norm. Other research shows how difficult it is for women to attempt such changes.

In 1981, Sara Yogev studied 106 faculty women at Northwestern University, 61 with children and 45 without. An analysis of the child care and housework patterns of these women revealed that their husbands spent considerably less time on household duties than did the women themselves. However, only a few of the participants believed that their husbands were not doing enough. One woman even made the following observation: "My husband does much more than most husbands, but the work is still not equally shared. It is mostly mine.

I'm not sure I *want* it to be equal. I want to be with the children these unequal hours, otherwise how shall I be able to feel that I am the mother of the family?"[2]

Until such attitudes change, women will hardly be "free" to make the best choices for themselves and their children. In addition to sorting out their particular feelings about family life, their particular logistical problems, and their particular familial relationships, the new entrepreneur mothers must wade through a dense cloud of social pressure as well. Until our culture modifies its view of women, motherhood, and work, a woman's choices, and those of her husband, will be unduly influenced by restrictive role expectations, and she will continue to experience conflict about whether to have children and how to rear them.

PERFECT WIFE, PERFECT MOTHER, PERFECT WOMAN

The new entrpreneurs experienced yet another dilemma: the pressure not only to "do it all," but do it all perfectly. In her analysis of motherhood and work, Dr. Epstein explains the cultural roots of such feelings. "Women who choose careers," she notes, "react to the cultural expectations of femininity by trying to prove themselves in all spheres. They accept all the role expectations attached to their female status, feeling that to lack any is to deny that they are feminine."[3] Such women have brilliant careers, cook gourmet meals, sew quilts, nurse their babies, care for their young children, entertain lavishly, and are dynamic partners to their husbands. Our culture allows women business ownership provided that they don't neglect their other, more "feminine" duties.

This point of view is frequently reinforced in the popular press. The August 1980 issue of *Savvy, The Magazine of Executive Women*, offers a particularly good example. In an article billed as "Food and the Executive: Bringing Management Systems Home," the writer sets up a model of motherhood that few women can hope to achieve. Included in the article are an attorney, a physician, a consultant, and an upper-level manager. These women are, naturally, "tops" in their field. The main point offered is the wonderful, efficient, and gourmet nature of family meal preparation. Here is a description of the physician and her family:

> Gail Becker, head of the internal medicine department in her multispecialty group and a recent president of her county medical society, was sitting on a glassed-in porch with her husband, Doug. They were sipping Chablis while their six-month old son stretched and gurgled on a blanket on the floor amid clusters of exotic plants. The other children were busy in different parts of the spacious contemporary house—tackling homework, visiting with friends, measuring butter to add to the green peas.
>
> The dining room table was set for dinner with a cornflower blue tablecloth,

matching cloth napkins, china, and crystal goblets. A vase of long-stemmed roses served as the centerpiece and a heart-shaped cake bearing the message "I LOVE YOU" was waiting for Doug at his place. A dinner of roast beef, rice, and salad—all of which had been prepared by the housekeeper—and a loaf of Gail's homemade cracked wheat bread were ready to go on at seven. The red roses and cake were special touches because this was Valentine's Day, but the meticulous organization was Gail's norm.[4]

The attorney was described no differently. Her "meticulous organization" included planning menus eight weeks in advance and then recycling the same meals every two months. She dropped that plan, however, when her husband became bored with the repetition: "The Paynes' two children, along with Nat Payne's boredom, forced some flexibility into their meal system." Needless to say, Mrs. Payne, like the other women in this article, assumed the major responsibility for this aspect of family care. She also taught her children "how to use butter plates and how to get salad from the bowl onto a salad plate," though she "doesn't bother with finger bowls the way her mother did." Notes the author, "Most couples divide their labor in a traditional manner, with the woman (and housekeeper if there was one) doing the cooking and the man occasionally cleaning up. . . . The professional women keep some cooking duties for themselves either because of their image of what a good wife and mother is or because they like to cook."[5]

None of the new entrepreneurs came close to achieving such perfection. Even Frances Levinsky described moments of chaos and despair. A woman has only a given amount of energy and realistically can concentrate on only so many details at the same time. The picture painted here ignores the fragmentation and exhaustion that characterize so many women's lives. Furthermore, the typical family does not have the financial resources to provide for the kind of household help that the women in this article enjoyed.

Such stories still appear in women's magazines with great regularity. Obviously, their intent is well-meaning—these women are good role models for others aspiring to nontraditional careers—but the overall effect is negative. The message here is that, with the right approach and effort, every woman can fulfill a variety of roles and fulfill them perfectly. They also suggest that any woman who fails to do so is somehow not measuring up to a new standard of femininity.

This message can be devastating. Career women—and this includes entrepreneurs—who are working out acceptable new roles for themselves and their husbands are led to believe that they shouldn't even try. The new role has already been defined for them: They must not only fulfill demanding work obligations but also maintain the standards of housewifely perfection required by the feminine ideal. Such a message prohibits the development of new, more flexible approaches to family responsibilities and perpetuates the belief that a "good" wife and mother must oversee every aspect of her family's care.

CREATING A NEW IDEAL

Janine Berman publishes the most widely read newspaper in her hometown—a small midwestern city of 49,000. The history of her venture reflects her strength and determination. The *Times-Journal* had always been a locally owned publication when a Chicago-based publisher expressed interest in buying the paper. Both the employees and the city were angered at the prospects of losing the last community-oriented news publication in the area, and encouraged Berman, an editorial writer, to take over. With the support of local businessmen, she raised the money and purchased the paper.

At the age of thirty-eight, and three years after her successful takeover of the *Times-Journal*, Berman embarked on another venture: Her daughter was born in 1975 and her son was born eighteen months later. Although Berman had some of the same conflicts and doubts about motherhood as Lisa Tedesco, she solved the problem in a unique manner. Instead of trying to manage a family and a business, she married a man would manage the family for her. Her story, though unusual, indicates new possibilities for the future.

At the outset of our conversation, Berman was very clear about her goals. "I knew I wanted kids for sure, but my goal was to have a career first," she began. "I need a certain amount of congratulations for intellectual achievement, and you don't get that around the house. Once I decided to have children, I looked for a certain type of man. I subsequently met and fell in love with Tom. If you're going to have a family, choose a man who complements you. I chose someone who works part-time—Tom works four hours a day and feels great about it. I was older when I made my choice. That helps because you know yourself better and understand what you need. I couldn't manage this paper if I were married to a man as ambitious as I am. It would be very hard to have two careers and a family, and I'm glad that in our family the career is mine."

Even before she married, Janine Berman had made an important decision: She wanted to be involved with her business on a full-time basis. She and Tom talked over their needs, and both of them agreed that he would have primary responsibility for the children. "When we got married," she continued, "Tom knew I planned to work full-time. After the kids were born, it was clear that he had the extra time and it was going to be his responsibility to arrange for their care. Tom is very physically oriented, takes the kids to the park, gets them involved in gymnastics, and encourages them in that way. I'm much more intellectual and read stories to them."

Janine Berman believes that she has the "perfect" situation, though her view of perfection differs markedly from that described in the popular press: "I wanted a family with a lot of love," she laughed, "not too much order, a nice husband who doesn't resent my career, and a home where I could go to get away from the pressure. I'm too superstitious to say I have everything I wanted, but it comes close. I couldn't have done it without the right man."

At first glance, Berman seems to have reached a simple and conventional solution to the family—career problem: She found a "wife" to take care of the children. However, this solution is hardly conventional for the average career woman. The findings in this and other studies indicate that, even if a woman works full-time, overseeing the care of the children is still her responsibility. Janine Berman and her husband are unique because they have rejected stereotypic roles and redefined parenting in a personally acceptable fashion.

Unlike most of the mothers in this study, Berman has successfully avoided what sociologists call "role strain," or the pressures of fulfilling dual or triple roles simultaneously. Instead, she has chosen the role that brings her the most personal satisfaction, that of business owner, while redefining the motherhood role on her own terms. Despite cultural expectations and social pressures, the Bermans have worked out an arrangement that satisfies their personal needs. They are indeed pioneers of a new and more equal family life.

In addition, Janine Berman has not accepted Superwoman has an appropriate model for herself. Although she has household help, she recognizes that, with two small children, her home may be disorderly at times. She prefers that meals be somewhat unstructured, noting, "If we want hot dogs, we eat hot dogs. If we want to go to the park or the movies, we go. Dinner is not at 8:00 every night. Each of the kids has a separate room, and I spend time with each one alone. Sometimes I take them on separate vacations. It's totally relaxed with little structure."

The picture that Berman paints here contrasts sharply with that presented in the article we just reviewed. However, the difference is not simply that some women prefer a carefully planned home life and some do not. Most women will fall somewhere between Superwoman and Janine Berman. The difference is that one model subtly tells women that they will somehow fail as mothers and wives if they don't create the "perfect atmosphere" at home. The strain that such a demand puts on the woman business owner is obvious. The other model allows more flexibility and encourages each woman to nurture her family in the way that is best for everyone. In short, unlike the broader cultural viewpoint, Berman does not suggest that women who choose a model different from hers are failing their family.

Janine Berman also recognizes an important personal process that enabled her to structure her family and work in an acceptable fashion. She was certain about what she wanted—career first and then a family—and she was equally clear about the way in which she could fulfill her needs. Because of this clarity, she sought the type of man who would complement her needs. At no time did she ascribe her situation to luck, but rather took responsibility for bringing into her life the things she wanted.

SORTING IT OUT

When she decides to have a business and a family, every woman must ask herself, What compromises am I willing to make? The answer to this question is unfortunately complicated by many factors. At this juncture, she must assess how much she wants to be involved in her child's life and how much time she wants to devote to her business. Even if good child care is available, her own genuine desire to provide nurturing cannot be discounted. The women in this study didn't like being cut off from their children and wanted to participate in their daily lives.

In assessing her situation, the prospective entrepreneur must look carefully at the realities of her life. To what extent is her husband really willing to help? Can she rely on him to sacrifice his own work to provide the assistance that she needs? Since most men are still unwilling to make such sacrifices, she may have to provide more or less alone the care that she wants for her child. The economics of her situation may further complicate her choices, for, if her husband is the primary wage earner, he may not be able to assist her even if he were willing. In addition, preschool-age children are very demanding and cannot easily fit into a business schedule the way an older child can. Children of all ages get sick, and even the best child care may not provide the stability and family-oriented environment that she wants.

These external realities are not the only complicating factors. They are compounded by culturally induced expectations that make it even more difficult for a woman to hear her own voice. Any practical solutions she works out will be colored by guilt and anxiety engendered by sex role expectations. What she wants to do may very well conflict with what she believes she should do. In developing her individual response to this problem, each woman must work through a surrounding wall of pressures and demands to discover what is truly best for her. As long as role pressures remain as strong as they are, and the realities of each situation as complex, developing an individual response will be a difficult process.

The best possible situation will occur when women can make life decisions from an inner point of self-knowledge and strength rather than from a point of conflict and role-induced guilt. Among the interviewees, Janine Berman was the most successful in achieving this goal. Berman recognized, then rejected, the stereotypic mothering role as unsuitable for her individual life. After clarifying her own values, she was then able to create a new, more personally defined standard of motherhood that better met the entire family's needs. The more that women can succeed in this process the less that old mirror images will exert their force and the more that we will have freedom to make our decisions. In the final analysis, a woman's reasons for making a certain choice are far more important than the actual choice. If her chosen path springs from guilt and obligation, she will find it unsatisfying, and it will fail to bring the independence and freedom that she desires.

CHAPTER 14

New Pathways into the Future

Now you have met the new entrepreneurs. You have followed their journey to independent enterprise, sharing their successes, witnessing their triumphs, and learning how they overcame adversity. And you have seen how a variety of women used their individual strengths to achieve success on their own. More than anything, their stories show that independence is possible for any woman who is determined to take charge of her life.

Like the women in this study, you can choose to follow a new pathway into the future. The road to entrepreneurship is open to anyone who chooses independence as her goal. For some of you, the first step out on that road may be simply reading this book; for others, taking a class in how to start a business or interviewing a successful woman entrepreneur may be what starts you on your way. No matter what avenue you choose, you must start somewhere.

One of the outstanding characteristics of the new entrepreneurs is their ability to take action. Instead of waiting for life to come to them, these women actively work to achieve what they want. Once they have embarked on their course, they are persistent in their efforts. They do not easily give up when faced with problems to solve or obstacles to overcome. Despite the barriers that they may encounter, they keep moving along the road.

However determined they may be, the new entrepreneurs are also flexible in their approach. Their success has required that they be willing to change course when necessary to follow a different path to a goal. Essentially the message here is not to lose sight of where you are going even if you must take an unexpected turn to get there.

Success as an entrepreneur depends on many other factors as well. Creativity, common sense, knowledge of your field and of sound business practices, the ability to assess risks and to take them, and the willingness to work hard are only some of the characteristics common to the new entrepreneurs. Each participant in my study capitalized on her unique combination of traits and abilities to fulfill her entrepreneurial goals. Now let us meet one last enterprising woman. Her story represents the most outstanding experiences common to all the study participants. She will serve as one final guide to help you along the road.

Corinne Dey presently owns a successful personnel service that boasts offices in two locations. Her future dreams include opening several more branches, perhaps franchising her operation, and then ultimately selling the entire organization and moving on to yet another new venture. Dey's entrepreneurial talents were obvious even when she was a youngster. At the age of twelve, she developed a window-washing service for the shop owners near her home. A creative and innovative woman, she described herself with the following words: "I am a true entrepreneur. I have idea after idea. Sometimes I wake up in the middle of the night and write my ideas down. I love to take on new challenges and solve new problems."

From her high school graduation until she started her business at twenty-eight, Dey was a job-hopper. She worked for several large corporations, starting out as a secretary and eventually finding great success in sales. As the years passed, Dey noticed that all her employers persistently needed good secretarial personnel. During one of her midnight sessions, she came upon the "right" idea to solve this problem: "I had been thinking about starting a personnel agency," she noted with enthusiasm, "and one night it struck me how to go about doing it. Right then and there, I decided it was time to put one of my ideas into action. At that point, I said to myself, 'What do I have to lose? I don't have a husband. I don't have any children. I have a mediocre job. I can keep thinking about this forever, or I can go do something about it.' The next day, I took $300 from my savings account, got some cards, and started my business."

Dey's words to aspiring business owners are encouraging: "If you want to do something bad enough," she noted, "you will find a way to make it happen. You just have to have faith that you can get it off the ground. When I was looking for an office, this real estate agent took me to some warehouselike place on the edge of town. I knew I didn't want to be in a place like that, but the agent didn't think I could do any better. Right away, I decided not to let that experience get me down.

"There was a new building going up in an area where I was interested in locating. So I walked in there one day, gave the manager my card, and said, 'Hi, I'm Corinne Dey with Professional Personnel Service. What do you have available for office space?' I told him about my business and what I planned to do, and he said, 'How about this office in here?' He gave me a copy of the lease to take home and read, and the next day I signed it. I must have sounded pretty confident because he never even asked me for any money."

Dey remembered lack of money as another obstacle that she had to overcome. Since she had so little working capital, she approached her local bank for a loan. The response that she received was not encouraging. "The first time I went to a bank," she remembered, "I had a business plan and a projection of where I thought I'd be in a year. They didn't laugh, but the man I talked to . . . his mouth twitched a little, and he smiled. It was like being a little girl and going to your parents and telling them you wanted to do something fantastic and having them laugh because they knew you could never get the money. I could tell just from the way he looked at me that I wouldn't get the loan."

Although the bank refused her request, Corinne did not give up. Once she made the initial step, she knew she could succeed. She simply had to find another way. "After I got my office," she continued, "I decided to lease a typewriter because at first I didn't have the capital to buy equipment. I called an IBM service rep for my area, told him what I needed, and the following Friday he brought it over and we plugged it in. The only asset I had was a used car, which I sold for $2600. With that money, I hired my first employee, and then I started recruiting people. Because I had so many contacts, I didn't have any trouble getting clients."

Thanks to her persistence and self-belief, Corinne Dey has been very successful. Two years after starting her business, she was ready to expand into a second location. At that time, she returned to the bank for a loan, only this time she got a different response. "I had so much information," she laughed, "that the loan officer couldn't believe it. I had a history of my business, my present business plans, a description of my industry, where we were within the industry, what we wanted to do, my résumé, a projection from the previous two years, plus what we expected to do next year, and my tax returns. Then I invited the loan officer to come out and visit my office, meet my clients, and see the types of companies we worked for. In the end, they couldn't *not* give me the loan."

As her business grew and developed, Dey had to clarify her role. This was not an easy process: "Initially," she noted, "I wore all the hats. I did typing, answered the phone, met the clients, recruited personnel. Now my role is more of an administrator. I've gone from being an implementor and producer of the work to the director of how the work is being done. That was a struggle for me because I love working directly with clients. But the company can't go forward without a leader, and that leader has to be me."

Making the transition from follower to leader was a difficult step for Dey: "I have nine employees now," she declared, "and managing people is a real drain on me emotionally. My business associates tell me how important it is to be the manager, to set the example, to be firm. But to do that you have to set yourself apart. You no longer can be part of the group sitting around talking about what you did on the weekend. I want to be one of them, to have them like me, but that's not how it works in business. Your employees cannot be your friends, and I have learned to accept that."

For Corinne Dey, business ownership has meant personal growth as well as financial gain. "As the demands of the business have increased," she noted with pride, "my ability to take charge has grown stronger. I have convictions on what I think is right or wrong. I also have a certain way that I want people to behave with clients. After you've muddled along for a while, you develop real positions on things. Your beliefs get clearer, and you suddenly think, 'Hey, I don't like that. I'm not going to do it that way.' And pretty soon you develop your own identity both personally and professionally. For me, that's been a very exciting process."

What other advantages does business ownership offer? "Freedom," Dey replied emphatically. "I love the freedom to make my own decisions and put my ideas into effect. I like setting the pace, being the leader, taking the responsibility. I also can choose who I work with. Occasionally, people call me who are real rude and demanding. When this happens, I say that we are very busy and probably can't help them for a week or two and could we recommend someone else?"

However, entrepreneurship has its difficult moments as well. Dey found an interesting solution to one problem that initially troubled her. "Running a business can be really lonely," she noted. "At times, I desperately need someone I can call and talk to, so I established a friendship with an older woman who has had a business for years. She's helped me many times, advising me what to do and listening to my ideas. I was always reluctant to use people I knew when I had problems. I didn't want them to think I couldn't do it by myself. That's the biggest mistake I ever made. The most important thing is to realize that it's OK to ask for help. After all, other people have problems, too. As I've gained experience, I've learned to be a resource for younger women. I believe in giving back some of what I've received."

Corinne Dey is highly encouraging to the woman who wants to have her own business. "If you are a woman," she declared, "and you are knowledgeable in your field, and you can also be feminine, you have 2000 percent more going for you than a man does. I can often get in on a sales call where men can not. I can be a little more familiar with my clients than a man would feel comfortable doing and still appear professional. I can come in as a woman who is accepted in the role of being nurturing and helpful because that's how people perceive women. A man couldn't call up and say, 'I think we can really help your company,' but I can. And if someone is dissatisfied, I can sit down with him and say, 'Tell me exactly how you feel about this,' and get a good response. Women have so many strengths that they can use to succeed."

To some people, the responsibility that Dey shoulders would be overwhelming. She manages two offices, employs nine people, and services a roster of impressive clients. Her hopes for the future include opening yet another branch of her successful business. How does she feel about the risks involved? Her reply was very clear: "You know," she stated with conviction, "the only security we all have is within ourselves. It doesn't matter if you're the president of a bank or a secretary. If you're honest, if you believe in yourself and know that you do good work, then you will be OK. A business will grow and then wane; employers come and go; people get hired and fired. In the final analysis, the only security you have is your own confidence—knowing that you have something that you can survive on.

"I will always be able to take care of myself," she continued, "no matter what happens with this business. I have proved that over and over again. In fact, I think that was one reason I started my own company. I didn't do it just to get money. If that's all I'd wanted, I could have stayed in sales. I did it to show that I can get what I want and get it by my own effort. At this point, I don't even know what the word *failure* means. I will continue to make mistakes, to grow, and learn, but I won't fail because I will always have myself to fall back on."

Corinne Dey's experience offers hope and encouragement to all women setting out on a similar path. In practical terms, the steps that she took to start her business are ones that any aspiring entrepreneur can pursue. Dey saw a need, developed a plan to fill that need, and then took action to make her plan a reality. Finding the necessary funds, establishing her office, obtaining equipment, and hiring her first employee are part of the entrepreneurial process that she followed.

On a personal level, Dey recognized and used all her strengths to help her succeed. These included strengths that she identified as "feminine." To Dey, being a woman brought many advantages that enhanced her position in the business world. Her work experience was another asset that she drew on. She had important organizational and sales skills, and her many business contacts offered her a pool of potential clients. During those first months of operation, Dey learned to become an effective leader. She also recognized that she had opinions and convictions about business ownership that were valid and worthwhile. Confident at the outset, Dey increased that sense of confidence by establishing an independent enterprise and making it succeed.

IMPLICATIONS FOR THE FUTURE

Should you decide to become an entrepreneur, you will join a fast-growing group of women whose success will bring about many important changes. These changes will occur on several interrelated levels. There will be personal and psychological changes for the individual woman entrepreneur; social changes starting in her community and extending outward to adjoining towns and cities; shifts in power as women gain control of money, jobs, and resources; structural changes within businesses and corporations; and revaluation of female-associated traits and characteristics by the culture as a whole.

Psychologist Ann Ulanov writes that "we achieve our authority on the basis of actual experience."[1] For many women, that experience has included dependency, devaluation, and a diminished sense of confidence and self-esteem. Trapped in a hall of mirrors, the typical woman often cannot see and appreciate her individual strengths. As a consequence, she discounts her own voice and looks to others for validation rather than to herself. She may also have serious conflicts about independence and her ability to stand alone that generate feelings of powerlessness and low self-worth that in turn keep women from taking charge of their lives, both psychologically and financially.

For each woman interviewed, business ownership provided a different kind of experience, one that enhanced her inner authority rather than diminished or silenced its voice. Managing an independent enterprise required that she assume sole responsibility for her success or failure. It demanded that she draw on her life experience and apply what she had learned in an independent, autonomous fashion. And it tested her judgment, her efficaciousness, her abilities both to work with others and to stand alone. Any woman who moves forward to meet these challenges has an opportunity for unprecedented growth and change. The building of self-confidence, enhancement of personal power, revaluation of individual strengths, and achievement of independence are some of the positive rewards that she will garner.

Personal growth, however, is only one result of success in independent enterprise. As their businesses grow and prosper, the new entrepreneurs will play an increasingly significant role in the nation's economy. The U. S. Small Business Administration notes the following:

> Independent small businesses now employ one-half of the private sector labor force. Small firms are helping American workers adapt to the shift from a manufacturing to a more service-oriented economy. During the last recession, small firms served as a catalyst for the recent recovery by generating thousands of new jobs for the cyclically unemployed.[2]

This comment suggests that The United States's small businesses collectively make as important a contribution to the economy as do our larger, more visible corporations. Since most female-owned businesses are small firms, the potential influence of future women entrepreneurs is obvious. In the coming years, they will employ more people and generate growing revenues for local communities. Once in control of jobs and money, they will be in a far stronger position to assume the leadership roles that have been previously denied them.

Small-business ownership thus offers women a means to gain influence in their communities and to effect social changes on a broader level. This was already a clear trend among the interviewees. Owners of both small and larger businesses served on community boards and were active in community organizations. Their opinions were sought on matters affecting the development of their towns and cities, and local politicians solicited their support. As these new entrepreneurs unite, they will wield considerable economic power and influence. Soon they will be in a stronger position to affect policy and legislation on issues of concern to them as women and as business owners. One woman described this process in the following way:

> I have become known in my area as a feminist lobbyist and also as a successful business person. My name is on a few mailing lists, I get invited to a few cocktail parties, and local politicians now court my favor. That could extend way beyond myself to women entrepreneurs as a group. My women business owners network has fantastic political power that it is not using. Some day we will get organized, and then we will have tremendous clout.

Another change suggested by the life patterns of the interviewees is the decreasing importance of family and child-bearing in a woman's life. Although business ownership offers some advantages to women with children, it is not the panacea that many might suppose. Like any other challenging career, it demands as much of a woman's time and energy as she is able to give. Forty-two percent of the new entrepreneurs have no children, and most of them will probably not have any in the future. These women believe that giving adequate attention to both family and business is too difficult, and, at least for the present, they have chosen the latter.

If women continue to become entrepreneurs in great numbers, their preference to remain childless may contribute to an eventual decline in the national birth rate. An alternative to not having a family is for husbands to take more responsibility for child care so that the stresses on individual women are not so great. However, this study's findings suggest that this option is not a real possibility. Instead, I believe that future entrepreneurs will follow the path carved out by their pioneer sisters: Business over family will be the first choice of many.

WOMEN ENTREPRENEURS AND THE CORPORATE WORLD

Although the past decade has seen women gain self-confidence, visibility, and achievement, it has also signaled a period of decline for U.S. industry. The very corporations that women have been clamoring to enter have suffered decreased productivity, worker and customer satisfaction, and competitiveness with international rivals. During this difficult period, when the corporate world has needed every resource at its disposal, the business community has continued to underuse one of its greatest assets: the American woman.

Many prominent business consultants and writers argue that fundamental changes in the structure, character, and outlook of the corporate community must happen for the present economic situation to change. In general, these people suggest that our corporations:

- Develop a more flexible, process-oriented form of management
- Adopt a less linear, more intuitive type of thinking
- Be more tolerant of the chaos, apparent inefficiency, and sometime inconsistency required for innovation and creative movement
- Modify their hierarchical, pyramidlike organizations into structures that are flatter and more interconnected
- Encourage more personal, fluid forms of communication
- Develop more empathy and concern for people—both staff and clients.[3]

Even a brief reading of these suggestions reveals certain key terms: flexibility, intuitive thinking, interconnection, empathy, and personal concern—all characteristics strongly, although not exclusively, associated with women. Many business women today bring unique strengths into the corporate world, strengths that could form the foundation for a new style of leadership.[4]

Despite the positive qualities that this new style has to offer, its value remains largely unrecognized or ignored, chiefly because the male model continues to dominate the corporate hierarchy. As long as the male model remains desirable and acceptable, women will not easily fit into U.S. corporations. Many will continue to leave the corporation for independent enterprise. These new entrepreneurs will then be free to tap their personal resources, reassess their individual strengths, and fulfill their economic potential. These women will succeed on their own, but our corporations will not succeed without the balance and perspective that the new female-trait-associated model has to offer. Just as women suffer when alientated from their active, independent side, corporations also suffer when cut off from their intuitive, receptive side. The strategies recommended by today's leading analysts will encourage the two sides to balance.

This process of reconciliation will be supported by the work of the new entrepreneurs. Many woman business owners interact with the corporate community on a daily basis. They are consultants, suppliers, manufacturers, and providers of essential services who fill an important and necessary role. Such women deal successfully with the corporate hierarchy, and they do so on their own terms. Unlike their corporate sisters, women entrepreneurs are freer to embrace the model that works best for them. For many of the participants in this study, that model is one closely identified with a more feminine style of leadership.

As the number of successful woman entrepreneurs increases, their contact with the corporate community will also increase. The corporate hierarchy will thus experience strong external, as well as internal, pressure to integrate the feminine model into its structure. This cycle will help generate some of the changes that leading experts recommend as essential to the growth and survival of our industries.

The potential influence of the new entrepreneurs thus extends beyond the realm of personal growth and economic gain. These women serve as examples to other women who aspire to be independent without giving up who they are as women; they show that true autonomy is achievable for the determined woman despite psychological barriers, cultural injunctions, and practical roadblocks; they bring a new leadership style that may help revitalize our failing industrial system; and they offer our culture the opportunity to recognize and accept the value of its feminine side.

I hope that as an aspiring women entrepreneur you will join the ranks of this growing movement. Your strength and energy will contribute to exciting changes, changes that will impact your life, your community, and the broader social environment in which you live. During the past ten years, the United States has rediscovered her entrepreneurial roots. Many articles now appear in the popular press celebrating the rise of the independent business person. The primary difference between today's new entrepreneurs and those of past generations is that so many of our present-day successes are women.

If starting or building a business is part of your dreams, I wish you good fortune with your venture. The road before you lies open, well-travelled by successful women before you. With persistence and determination, you can follow that road using the new entrepreneurs as your guides. Although you may encounter unexpected barriers along the way, I hope you don't waver. Like the women whose lives you have shared on these pages, you, too, can achieve independence and fulfill your entrepreneurial goals.

APPENDIX A

Sample and Methodology

Her Own Business: Success Secrets of Entrepreneurial Women is based on the case-history method of research. At the outset of the project, I decided to collect the life stories of a representative group of women entrepreneurs through the use of questionnaires and oral interviews. Not only was a large-scale statistical study beyond my means, I was also not certain that it would fulfill my purpose—to illuminate what enables a woman to achieve the independence necessary to control her own life. Using the woman entrepreneur as a model, I hoped to discover what familial, personal, and experiential factors contribute to a woman's ability to stand on her own. A secondary goal was to provide a descriptive summary of the life patterns and trends prevalent among this fast-growing segment of the business community: the new woman entrepreneurs.

SELECTION OF SAMPLE

After choosing my research method, I then had to compile a sample. At that point, I decided on two criteria for participation: The business had to be at least 50 percent woman-owned, and the woman involved had to be the manager and leader of the enterprise. Once these criteria were met, I selected participants to ensure a widespread geographic and industrial representation. I did not want an overabundance of one type of business, and I hoped to find women from the four major areas of the country: West-Northwest, Midwest, Southwest, and Northeast-Southeast.

When I was ready to find the women I needed, I chose four sources of information: women's networks, news articles about women entrepreneurs, directories of women-owned businesses, and personal referrals. A letter describing the project and asking for volunteers appeared in network newsletters throughout the country. This initial inquiry yielded ninety-three positive replies from women eager to share their stories and participate in the study.

In addition, I wrote to many women whose stories appeared in newspapers or magazines or whose names I received from other entrepreneurs. In California, I obtained the state *Directory of Minority and Women-Owned Businesses*, and the Whittemore School of Business at the University of New Hampshire provided me with a similar directory for that state. Using these three resources—personal referrals, news media, and state directories—I personally contacted 119 women, including many in industries I felt lacked representation. I described the study and its goals, and 55 of the 119 queried indicated that they would like to participate.

As I worked to complete the sample, I read everything I could find on the subject of entrepreneurs and entrepreneurship, women and credit, sex-role stereotypes and female identity development, and the state of U.S. business today. This background research helped me gain perspective on what other issues were important besides those that concerned me personally. What information was known about males that remained a secret about females? What barriers had other people identified as holding women back? How did women entrepreneurs fit into the greater business community and what were the possibilities for the future? The answers to these questions, together with my own personal quest for information, helped me design a questionnaire which I then sent out to 148 women in twenty-eight states; 117 women completed and returned the questionnaire, and the information that they shared formed the foundation for my study.

GEOGRAPHICAL DISTRIBUTION OF SAMPLE

Participants resided in California, Washington, Colorado, Kansas, Missouri, Tennessee, Wisconsin, Illinois, Indiana, Ohio, Michigan, Florida, Virginia, Washington, D.C., Maryland, Delaware, Pennsylvania, New York, Connecticut, Massachusetts, and New Hampshire. From my pool of respondents, I decided to interview seventy women. Since I wanted as broad a representation as possible, I selected interviewees on the basis of geographical location and type of business owned. The largest number of volunteers were concentrated in the Los Angeles, San Francisco, and Central Valley areas of California; Seattle; northern Illinois; southern Wisconsin; and the Atlantic seaboard from Virginia to New Hampshire. Interviewees were thus drawn from these areas.

A recent Small Business Administration publication entitled *The State of Small Business: A Report of the President* validates this choice. Published in March

1984, this informative book makes the following statement: "Female-operated businesses are more strongly represented in some regions of the United States than in others. Proportionately, female-operated businesses are more prevalent on the East Coast from Virginia to New England, the central Midwest states of Ohio and Illinois, the West Coast state of California, and Hawaii." The sample for *Her Own Business* reflects this national distribution. Whereas respondents to the questionnaires came from all parts of the country, the interviewees are concentrated in those areas with the largest proportion of women-owned enterprises.

RACIAL AND ETHNIC COMPOSITION OF SAMPLE

In terms of racial and ethnic composition, the new entrepreneurs represent women from diverse backgrounds. Black women compose slightly more than 8 percent of the sample, and Asians and Hispanics each constitute 3 percent. The remaining women are a reflection of the U.S. melting pot culture, with families from France and Italy, Germany and Poland, Russia and Scandinavia, Great Britain and Canada, Holland and Yugoslavia, Hungary, Turkey, and Greece. Of the participants, 18.5 percent had at least one parent who was born outside the United States.

RESEARCH PROCESS

Her Own Business is thus based on detailed responses to a four-page questionnaire returned by 117 women entrepreneurs and on information collected during structured, in-depth interviews with 70 of these respondents. Each interview lasted at least two hours; some sessions extended to three and even four hours in length. With only four exceptions, I visited each woman at her place of business, met her staff people, occasionally met her family, and in several instances accompanied her while she visited clients or attended necessary meetings that arose during my visit. Only 14.3 percent of the firms studied were home-based businesses; the remaining 85.7 percent were established in an outside location.

The interviews were done in three stages: those in California during the spring and summer of 1981; those on the eastern seaboard the following June; and Seattle and the Midwest during June of 1983. This process gave me time to transcribe the interviews in groups and to digest the massive amounts of material I had collected in both transcripts and questionnaires.

Another component of my research was the written impression I completed at the end of each interview. Although individual faces and personalities are indelibly imprinted in my mind, time tends to blur a once-accurate picture. Consequently, I decided at the outset to write a description of both the physical and the personal characteristics of the women I talked to so that their image would remain fresh and undistorted. Body language, tone of voice, eye contact, gestures, and other unspoken qualities often contributed as much to a woman's portrait as did her words.

Because some questionnaires were incomplete, all statistics in this book are based on the information collected from the 70 interviewees. The other questionnaires, however, contained valuable information which added depth and breadth to the study.

DESCRIPTION OF SAMPLE

Almost eighty percent of the businesses I studied were 100 percent women-owned. Slightly less than 6 percent of the interviewees had a fifty-fifty ownership with husband or mate, and the rest, or slightly more than 14 percent, owned majority interest ranging from 51 percent to 90 percent. In these cases, a husband, brother, father or son owned a share of the business but usually declined an active role in its management. In only five cases did the male partners actually work at the business, and in all five the women were clearly the managers and leaders of the enterprise.

The two smallest firms in my study were one-woman operations that employ occasional part-time help; the largest had over 600 employees. Gross income for the smallest business was under $10,000 and for the largest, over $10,000,000. The median number of people working for the new entrepreneurs was seven.

The median age of the firms studied was eight years, and more than half were structured as corporations:

Business Structure	Percent
Sole proprietorship	30.0
Corporation	57.1
Parternship	8.7
Other	4.2

Slightly more than 50 percent of the new entrepreneurs own service-related businesses; the rest are spread throughout the variety of industries listed in the following table.

Industrial Category	Percent *
General services †	55.7
Retail	15.7
Wholesale	11.4
Construction	8.6
Professional services	8.5
Manufacturing	5.7
Real estate	5.7
Education	4.3
Publishing	4.3
Insurance	2.9

* Figures add up to more than 100 because some businesses fall into more than one category.

† Service firms include business, personal, legal, computer, food, financial, transportation, construction, and training services.

THE QUESTIONNAIRE

1. How did you start your business: alone, with spouse, with family, with friend?

2. What year was it established?

3. How many employees?

4. Your business is a sole proprietorship, corporation, partnership, other?

5. Your business is 100 percent women-owned, 51 percent women-owned, 50 percent women-owned, less than 50 percent women-owned?

6. Your business is retail, wholesale, service, manufacturing, health, construction, agricultural, publishing, other?

7. What product or service do you provide?

8. How many brothers and sisters do you have?

9. What number are you in birth order (oldest, second, etc.)?

10. How many children do you have?

11. Please answer the following for when you started your business: age, marital status, years of school, degrees received, years of math studied in high school, field of study after high school.

12. How did you obtain financing to start your business: personal savings, family, friends, bank loan, government loan, other?

13. Do you take part in the active management of your business?
14. What is your position or role?
15. How well did your work experience prepare you to run a business?
16. Did/does anyone else in your family own a business? Please explain.
17. Why did you go into business for yourself?
18. What were the major problems in starting your business?
19. Who, if anyone, encouraged you to open your business?
20. Comment on the effect of any role models or mentors on your decision to open a business.
21. What resources were useful to you in gaining the knowledge and skills necessary to operate your business?
22. How long did it take you to gain the skills and knowledge necessary to control your business?
23. What areas of small-business management were problematic to you when you first began your business?
24. What are the advantages and disadvantages of being an entrepreneur?
25. Describe any major gender-related problems which you have encountered.
26. What does it take to succeed in running your own business?
27. What are the benefits of running your own business?
28. What are the drawbacks? Had you anticipated these?
29. If you have a family, how do you manage a dual career?
30. Your ethnic origin is black, Hispanic, Asian, white, other (please specify).
31. Your gross receipts for the past year were $10,000 to $99,999; $100,000 to $499,999; $500,000 to $999,999; $1,000,000 to $4,999,999; above $5,000,000.
32. Your contribution to total family income is 0–10 percent; 11–20 percent; 21–30 percent; 31–40 percent; 41–50 percent; 51–60 percent; 61–70 percent; 71–80 percent; 81–90 percent; 91–100 percent?

SUPPLEMENTAL QUESTIONNAIRE

Parents

1. Educational level of mother? of father?
2. Were either of your parents born outside the United States?

Education

1. If you attended college or vocational school, did you go there directly from high school?
2. If not, how many years elapsed between high school and beginning college or vocational school?
3. Did you complete college or vocational school without interruption, i.e., in two or four consecutive years?
4. If not, how many years did it take you to complete your schooling?

Marital Status

1. Age at marriage? Age at second marriage, if divorced? Age at divorce, if applicable?
2. Since you opened your business, has your marital status changed?
3. If yes, are you married? separated? divorced? widowed?

Children

1. Your age at birth of children: first child? second? third? fourth? fifth?
2. Age of children when you started your business: first child? second? third? fourth? fifth?
3. Were any of your children born after you opened your business?
4. If so, how long after?
5. After your children were born, did you leave the labor force for any period of time?
6. If so, how many years were you at home?
7. If you don't have children at present, do you plan on having any in the future?

THE INTERVIEW

The interview followed the general order of the questionnaires. As the interviewee reviewed her answers to the written questions, I asked her to discuss each issue in more depth. For example, the question, ''Why did you go into business for yourself?'' served as a springboard for a discussion on the risks involved and how each woman felt about risk taking in general. The question ''How did you obtain financing to open your business?'' included a discussion about obtaining loans and dealing with the banks. Thus the interviewee was asked to expand on her answers to each question.

In addition, I asked each woman to describe herself and her interests as a child and as an adolescent; her life goals when she was in high school; her parents' expectations for her future; and her experiences during her college years. If she had not already done so by the end of the questionnaires, I then asked her to describe each of her parents and her relationship to them. Toward the end of the interview, I inquired whether she belonged to any networks or professional associations and asked her to comment on her experiences with such groups.

APPENDIX B

Statistical Summary of Findings

BECOMING AN ENTREPRENEUR

How Started Business	Percent
Alone	55.7
With friend	24.3
With spouse	8.5
With other family member	2.9
Purchased alone	4.3
Inherited	4.3

Age at Start of Business	Percent
19–25	4.3
26–30	28.6
31–35	22.85
36–40	22.85
41–45	10.0
46–50	8.5
51–55	2.9

Years of Work Experience	Percent
1–5	17.2
6–10	14.3
11–15	32.8
16–20	20.0
over 20	15.7

Marital Status at Start of Business	Percent
Married	42.8
Single	24.3
Divorced or separated	30.0
Widowed	2.9

Number of Children at Start of Business	Percent		Financing	Percent*
None	52.8		Personal savings	75.7
One	8.6		Loan from family	14.2
Two	24.3		Loan from bank	12.9
Three	10.0		Loan from friend	5.7
Four or more	4.3		Government loan	2.9

*Figures add up to more than 100 percent because some women had more than one source of financing. The median age of the women in this sample was forty-one.

ENTREPRENEURIAL ROOTS

Economic Status of Parents	Percent		Economic Status of Parents	Percent
Upper middle class (professionals and owners of large businesses)	24.3		Working class (factory workers, waiters, phone operators, domestics)	14.3
Middle class (middle managers, civil servants, educators, owners of small businesses)	45.7		Economically oppressed	2.9
			Remember some period of economic hardship (includes women from all classes)	12.8

Position of Woman in Family	Percent		Tradition of Business Ownership in Family	Percent
Only or oldest child	55.7		One parent owned a business	57.2
Only daughter with one or more brothers	15.7		Other close relative owned a business	18.6
One of several daughters but identified self as "father's son"	5.7		No tradition of business in family	24.2
Second, third, fourth, fifth child	22.9			

Perception of Mothers	Percent		Perception of Fathers	Percent
Mother positive and dominant	55.7		Father positive and dominant	20
Mother negative and weak	22.9		Father negative and weak	58.6
Mother neutral	12.9		Father neutral	12.9
Mother strong but viewed as equal to father	8.5		Father strong but viewed as equal to mother	8.5

Median Level of Parents' Education	*Years*
Father	14
Mother	13

One or Both Parents Born Outside United States	*Percent*
Yes	18.5
No	81.5

Women's Level of Education	*Percent*
High school	5.75
Some college	22.8
Bachelor's degree	45.7
Master's degree	20.0
Doctorate	5.75

Women's Goals in High School	*Percent*
Teaching or other traditional career	25.7
Nontraditional career	10.0
College and/or marriage	64.3

Field of Study After High School	*Percent*
Liberal arts (includes teaching and journalism)	32.8
Business and economics	17.1
Social science	15.7
Math and science	14.3
Design	7.0
Architecture	2.9
Law	1.5
Other	2.9
No further study	5.8

MARRIAGE AND FAMILY

The typical interviewee married at a median age of 23 years. Whereas the average woman of her generation married at 20.3 years, this woman waited nearly 3 years longer. (For average age at marriage see *Current Population Reports*, Series P_{20}, Number 389, March, 1983. Yet just because she was older, her first marriage was not any more successful than the norm. Of the 90 percent who married, about half divorced, and of these 36 percent chose to marry again.

A minority (17 percent) divorced after starting their businesses, and an almost equal number (20 percent) married for the first or second time. In addition, one woman became a widow. The remaining women experienced no marital change. In fact, once they decided to become entrepreneurs, their personal life seemed to stabilize.

Perhaps the most significant finding is that 42.8 percent of the women interviewed are presently childless. Although 17 percent of these women hope to have children some day, their median age is now thirty-eight, and their childbearing years are drawing to a close. By contrast, among all women between thirty-five and forty-four, only 11 percent do not have children (see *Current Population Reports: The Fertility of American Women*, June 1980). Furthermore, those interviewees who became mothers did so at an older age than the national norm. The typical mother in this study had her first child at twenty-five, nearly three years later than other women in her age group, and she had an average of two children. (For U.S. women's average age at birth of first child, see *Vital Statistics of the United States, 1978*, vol. 1.)

The typical interviewee with children gave birth to her children before giving birth to her business. Just under half the new entrepreneurs were mothers at the moment of decision. Only 14.3 percent had a baby after starting the business, and for 70 percent of this small group that baby was their first child.

In general, as adolescents the new entrepreneurs did not expect to have a career. Nevertheless, almost all of them remained in the labor force from the time they left school until they opened their businesses. Only 12.9 percent of the entire group followed the more traditional path of withdrawing from the labor force soon after marriage for a substantial period of time to raise their families. Among the remaining mothers, not one became a full-time homemaker.

APPENDIX C

Resources

EDUCATION FOR ENTREPRENEURSHIP

American Women's Economic Development Corporation
  (AWED)
60 East 42d Street
New York, NY 10165
212-692-9100

Well-known for its dedication to women entrepreneurs and their success, AWED provides woman business owners with management training, technical assistance programs, a new publication called *The Woman Entrepreneur*, peer-group counseling; both long-term assistance and short training sessions are available.

Bank of America, Department 3120
P.O. Box 37000
San Francisco, CA 94137
415-622-2491

Write the Bank of America for information about its excellent series of publications, how to *The Small Business Reporter*, including issues on how to start a business, how to finance a business, retail business, franchising.

Best Employers Association
4201 Birch Street
Newport Beach, CA 92660
213-756-1000

Provides independent entrepreneurs with managerial, economic, financial, and sales information to help business growth and development.

Catalyst
250 Park Avenue South
New York, NY 10003
212-777-8900

Provides a career information service, a national network of career resource centers, and over sixty publications on careers for women, including entrepreneurship.

Center for Entrepreneurial Management
83 Spring Street
New York, NY 10012
212-925-7304

Through courses and seminars, provides assistance with developing a business plan; obtaining venture capital; organizing an entrepreneurial team; getting patents, trademarks, and copyrights: Maintains an extensive library of information of interest to the entrepreneur.

Center for Family Business
P.O. Box 24268
5862 Mayfield Road
Cleveland, OH 44124
216-442-0800

Offers educational programs directed at the family-owned business; topics include small-business management, business succession, and maintaining business continuity.

International Council for Small Business
c/o Virginia Wojtkowski
3642 Lindell Boulevard
St. Louis University
St. Louis, MO 63108
314-534-7232

Working with universities and local school systems, sponsors small-business management seminars throughout the world; members engage in research on issues related to entrepreneurship and the entrepreneur.

National Business League
4324 Georgia Avenue NW
Washington, DC 20011
202-829-5900

Promotes the economic development of minorities and encourages minority ownership and management of small businesses; has a special committee, Council of Women in Business, that focuses on issues of concern to women.

National Family Business Council
60 Revere Drive, Suite 500
Northbrook, IL 60062

Sponsors seminars on unique problems inherent in running a family business.

Office of Women's Business Ownership
Small Business Administration (SBA)
1441 L Street NW
Washington, DC 20416
202-653-8000

Sponsors University Business Development Centers at colleges and universities around the country (write them for local addresses); offers many fine publications about start-up, marketing, planning, financing, and general management practices.

SCORE (Service Corps of Retired Executives)
1129 20th Street NW
Washington, DC 20416
202-653-6279

Organization composed of retired business men and women that provides actual or potential entrepreneurs with free advice.

The Small Business Foundation of America
20 Park Plaza
Boston, MA 02116
617-350-5096

Nonprofit organization raises funds for education and research in small business and sponsors seminars and conferences for entrepreneurs.

The following three organizations offer special seminars for entrepreneurs:

The Country Business Brokers
225 Main Street
Brattleboro, VT 05301
802-254-4504

The Entrepreneurship Institute
90 East Wilson Bridge Road, #247
Worthington, OH 43085
614-855-0585

The School for Entrepreneurs
Tarrytown House
East Sunnyside Land
Tarrytown, NY 10591
212-933-1232
914-591-8200

SOURCES OF INFORMATION

Clearinghouse on Women's Issues
P.O. Box 70603
Friendship Heights, MD 20813
301-871-6106

Offers a regular newsletter that details government actions of national or local impact affecting women and minorities—reports on economic and labor issues of particular interest to entrepreneurs.

Jayne Townsend and Associates
250 27th Avenue
San Francisco, CA 94121
415-986-3105

Jayne Townsend has compiled a comprehensive directory of women's groups in the western states: $9.00 for one issue, $12 for updated yearly subscription of two issues.

National Council for Research on Women
Sara Delano Roosevelt Memorial House
47 East 65th Street
New York, NY 10021
212-570-5001

Conducts and promotes collaborative research on topics of concern to women; acts as clearinghouse for information of interest to women; offers seminars and conferences.

National Women's Mailing List
1195 Valencia Street
San Francisco, CA 94110
415-824-6800

Uses computer technology to promote networking between women and women's organizations; maintains databank on women's groups and services.

Small Business Legislative Council
1025 Vermont Avenue NW, Suite 1201
Washington, DC 20006
202-293-8830

Provides testimony before Congress on issues of concern to entrepreneurs and works on behalf of small-business interests.

Wider Opportunities for Women (WOW)
1325 G Street NW, Lower Level
Washington, DC 20005
202-638-3143

Monitors current policies and legislation on issues of concern to women, including entrepreneurs; offers training and education to prepare women for nontraditional careers.

CHAMBERS OF COMMERCE

Association of Asian-American Chambers
of Commerce
P.O. Box 1933
Washington, DC 20013
202-638-5595

Chambers of Commerce of the United
States
1615 H Street NW
Washington, DC 20062
202-659-6000

Council of State Chambers of Commerce
122 C Street NW, Suite 200
Washington, DC 20001
202-484-8103

National Association of Black and
Minority Chambers of Commerce
7700 Edgewater Drive, Suite 742
Oakland, CA 94621
415-639-7915

Northern California Black Chamber of
Commerce
7700 Edgewater Drive, Suite 725
Oakland, CA 94621
415-569-2705

U.S. Hispanic Chamber of Commerce
4900 Main Street, 7th Floor
Kansas City, MO 64112
816-842-2228

APPENDIX D

Networks and Professional Associations

Alliance of Female Owned Businesses
Involved in Construction
12864 Farmington Road
Livonia, MI 48150
313-427-8731

Alliance of Women in Architecture
P.O. Box 5136, FDR Station
New York, NY 10020
212-744-5200

American Association of Black Women
Entrepreneurs
814 Thayer Avenue, Suite 202
Silver Spring, MD 20910
301-231-3751

American AgriWomen
c/o Jeanne Mertz
Route 3, Box 260
Manhattan, KS 66502
913-456-9605

American Business Women's Association
P.O. Box 8727
9100 Ward Parkway
Kansas City, MO 64114
816-361-6621

American Council of Women
Chiropractors
c/o Herbie McMeunamy, DC
4002 Washington Street
Amarillo, TX 79110
806-355-7217

American Entrepreneurs Association
2311 Pontius Avenue
Los Angeles, CA 90064
213-478-0437

American Federation of Small Business
407 South Dearborn
Chicago, IL 60605
312-427-0270

American Society of Inventors
P.O. Box 58426
Philadelphia, PA 19102
215-799-8208

American Society of Professional and
Executive Women
1511 Walnut Street
Philadelphia, PA 19102
215-563-4415

American Society of Women Accountants
35 East Wacker Drive
Chicago, IL 60601
312-726-3030

Association for Small Business
  Advancement
7507 Standish Place
Rockville, MD 20855
301-770-6610

Association for Women Veterinarians
c/o Judith H. Spurling, DVM
P.O. Box 1051
Littleton, CO 80160
303-794-8145

Association of Collegiate Entrepreneurs
Center for Entrepreneurship, Box 147
Wichita State University
Wichita, KS 67208
316-689-3000

Coalition of Women in National and
  International Business
P.O. Box 950
Boston, MA 02119
617-265-5268

Committee on Women in Horticulture
c/o American Society for Horticultural
  Sciences
701 North St. Asaph Street
Alexandria, VA 22341
703-836-4606

Electrical Women's Roundtable
6130 Sunbury Road, Suite C
Westerville, OH 43081
614-895-1241

Entrepreneurs Center
1333 Lawrence Expressway, Number 150
Santa Clara, CA 95051
408-243-1200

Future Business Leaders of America
  (FBLA), Phi Beta Lambda
P.O. Box 17417
Washington, DC 20041
703-860-3334

Homeworkers Organized for More
  Employment
P.O. Box 10
Orland, ME 04472
207-469-7961

Junior Achievement
550 Summer Street
Stamford, CT 06901
203-359-2970

Latin American Manufacturers
  Association
419 New Jersey Avenue SE
Washington, DC 20003
202-546-3803

National Alliance of Home Based
  Business Women
P.O. Box 306
Midland Park, NJ 07432

National Alliance of Professional and
  Executive Women's Networks
113 West Franklin Street
Baltimore, MD 21201
301-752-1559

National Association for the Self-
  Employed
2121 Precinct Lane
Hurst, TX 6053
817-656-6313

National Association of Black Women
  Entrepreneurs
P.O. Box 1375
Detroit, MI 48231
313-961-7714

National Association for Women in
  Careers
7900 Cass Avenue, Suite 115
Darcia, IL 60559
312-870-8991

National Assoc. of Insurance Women
P.O. Box 4410
1847 East 15th Street
Tulsa, OK 74159
918-744-5195

National Association of Minority Women
in Business
906 Grand Avenue, Suite 500
Kansas City, MO 64116
816-421-3335

National Association of Secretarial
Services
240 Driftwood Road SE
St. Petersburg, FL 33705
813-823-3646

National Association of Small Business
Investment Companies
1156 15th Street NW, Number 1101
Washington, DC 20005
202-833-8230

National Association of Women Business
Owners
600 South Federal Street, Suite 400
Chicago, IL 60605
312-346-2330

National Association of Women in
Construction
327 South Adams
Fort Worth, TX 76104
817-877-5551

National Association of Women Lawyers
750 North Lake Shore Drive
Chicago, IL 60611
312-988-6186

National Business League
4324 Georgia Avenue NW
Washington, DC 20011
202-829-5900

National Council of Negro Women
1819 H Street NW, Suite 900
Washington, DC 20006
202-293-3902

National Federation of Business and
Professional Women's Clubs
2012 Massachusetts Avenue NW
Washington, DC 20036
202-293-1100

National Federation of Independent
Businesses
150 West 20th Avenue
San Mateo, CA 94403
415-341-7441

National Federation of Paralegal
Associations
Ben Franklin Station
P.O. Box 14103
Washington, DC 20044

National Forum for Executive Women
(Banking)
1101 15th Street NW
Washington, DC 20005
202-331-0270

National Network of Asian and Pacific
Women
P.O. Box 39180
Washington, DC 20016
800-638-8087

National Small Business Association
1155 15th Street NW, 7th Floor
Washington, DC 20005
202-293-8830

National Women's Forum
1731 Connecticut Avenue NW,
Suite 200
Washington, DC 20009
202-462-0430

Network for Professional Women
c/o Career Source
15 Lewis Street
Hartford, CT 06103
203-247-2011

Network of Women Entrepreneurs
108 East Fremont
Suite 5194
Sunnyvale, CA 94087
408-720-9520

Networks Unlimited
316 Fifth Avenue, Number 301
New York, NY 10001
212-868-3370

New England Women Business Owners
1357 Washington Street, Suite 5
West Newton, MA 02165
617-566-3013

Organization of Chinese American
  Women
1525 O Street NW
Washington, DC 20005
202-328-3185

Professional Association of Secretarial
  Services
11990 Grant Avenue, Number 201
Denver, CO 80233
303-451-5766

Professional and Technical Consultants
  Association
1330 South Bascom Avenue
Suite D
San Jose, CA 95128
408-287-8703

Professional Dimensions
231 West Wisconsin Avenue
Suite 1002
Milwaukee, WI 53203
414-273-1411

Professional Women in Construction
28 Easton Avenue
White Plains, NY 10605
914-328-9059

Roundtable for Women in Food Service
325 East 57th Street
New York, NY 10022
212-593-2791

Small Business Association of
  New England
69 Hickory Drive
Waltham, MA 02154
617-890-9070

Wilmington Women in Business
P.O. Box 2310
Wilmington, DE 10899
302-656-4411

Women Business Owners of Atlanta
175 West Wieuca Road NE, Suite 112
Atlanta, GA 30342
404-255-1327

Women's Council of Realtors
430 North Michigan Avenue
Chicago, IL 60611
312-329-8483

Women Entrepreneurs
1390 Market Street
Fox Plaza, Suite 908
San Francisco, CA 94102
415-626-8142

Women in Advertising and Marketing
4200 Wisconsin Ave. NW, Suite 106-238
Washington, DC 20016
301-279-9093

Women in Communications
P.O. Box 9561
Austin, TX 78766
512-346-9875

Women in Data Processing
P.O. Box 880866
San Diego, CA 92108
619-569-5615

Women in Information Processing
Lock Box 39173
Washington, DC 20016
202-328-6161

Women Involved in Farm Economics
Box 70
Animas, NM 88020
505-548-2420

Women's International Network
187 Grant Street
Lexington, MA 02173
617-862-9431

Women's Professional and Managerial
  Network
1107 East Olive Street
Seattle, WA 98122
206-328-1107

WOMEN'S SERVICE ORGANIZATIONS

National Association of Colored
Women's Clubs
5808 16th Street NW
Washington, DC 20011
202-726-2044

National Association of Negro Business
and Professional Women's Clubs
1806 New Hampshire Avenue NW
Washington, DC 20009
202-483-4206

Quota International
1828 L Street NW
Washington, DC 20036
202-331-9694

Venture Clubs of America
1616 Walnut Street
Philadelphia, PA 19103
215-732-0512

Zonta International
35 East Wacker Street
Chicago, IL 60601
312-346-1445

Notes

INTRODUCTION

1. *The State of Small Business: A Report to the President*, U.S. Government Printing Office, Washington, D.C., 1984, p. 351.
2. "Employment in Perspective: Women in the Labor Force, 3rd Quarter, 1985." Washington, D.C., U.S. Department of Labor, Bureau of Labor Statistics, Report 725, p. 1.
3. *The State of Small Business: A Report to the President*, p. 349.
4. "Versatile, Flexible Describes Businesswomen," *San Francisco Business Journal*, November 2, 1981, p. 6.

CHAPTER 2

1. David McClelland, "Business Drive and National Achievement," *Harvard Business Review*, vol. 40, July–August 1962, pp. 104–106.
2. Nathan Kogan and Karen Dorros, "Sex Differences in Risk-Taking and Its Attribution," *Sex Roles*, 1978, vol. 4, no. 5, p. 763.
3. Michael A. Wallach and Nathan Kogan, "Sex Differences and Judgment Processes," *Journal of Personality and Social Psychology*, 1959, vol. 27, no. 4, p. 561.
4. For discussions of the entrepreneurial personality, see Manfred F. R. Kets de Vries, "The Entrepreneurial Personality: A Person at the Crossroads," *Journal of Management Studies*, 1977, vol. 14, no. 1, pp. 53, 57; Orvis Collins, David Moore, and Darab Unwalla, *The Enterprising Man*, East Lansing, Mich., Michigan State University Business Studies, 1964; John Hornaday and Charles Bunker, "The Nature of the Entrepreneur," *Personnel Psychology*, 1970, vol. 23, no. 1, pp. 47–54; Robert

Brockhaus, Sr., "The Psychology of the Entrepreneur," in *Encyclopedia of Entrepreneurship*, Calvin Kent, Donald Sexton, and Karl Vesper, eds., Englewood Cliffs, N.J., Prentice Hall, 1983.

CHAPTER 3

1. Inge Broverman et al., "Sex Role Stereotypes and Clinical Judgments of Mental Health," *Journal of Consulting and Clinical Psychology*, February 1970, vol. 34, no. 1, p. 3.

2. William Wordsworth, "She Dwelt among the Untrodden Ways," in *Wordsworth: Representative Poems*, Arthur Beatty, ed., New York, Odyssey, 1937.

3. For discussions on the differential treatment and expectations parents hold for sons and daughters, see David F. Aberle and Kaspar D. Naegele, "Middle-Class Fathers' Occupational Attitudes towards Children," in *A Modern Introduction to the Family*, Norman Bell and Ezra Vogel, eds., Glencoe, Ill., Free Press, 1960, p. 132; Michael Lamb, Margaret Tresch Owen, and Lindsay Chase Tinsdale, "The Father-Daughter Relationship: Past, Present, and Future," in *Becoming Female*, Claire Kopp, ed., New York, Plenum, 1979, p. 101; David Lynn, *The Father: His Role in Child Development*, Monterey, Calif., Brooks Cole, 1976.

4. Rosalind C. Barnett and Grace K. Baruch, *The Competent Woman*, New York, Irvington, 1978, p. 81. See also Ruth E. Goldberg, "Sex Role Stereotypes and Career versus Homemaking Orientation," in *Emerging Woman: Career Analysis and Outlooks*, Samual Osipow, ed., Columbus, Ohio, Charles E. Merrill, 1975, pp. 97–98; Dale Spender, *Invisible Women*, London, Writers and Readers, 1982.

5. Benson Rosen and Thomas Jerdee, "Managerially Relevant Perceived Sex Differences," *Sex Roles*, December 1978, vol. 4, no. 6, p. 842. For further discussion regarding how slowly sex stereotypes have changed, see Thomas Cash and Louis Janda, "The Eye of the Beholder," *Psychology Today*, December 1984, pp. 46–52, and Spender, *Invisible Women*.

6. William Blackstone, *Selections from the Commentaries on the Laws of England*, vol. 1, San Francisco, Bancroft-Whitney, 1916, pp. 625–626.

7. John Johnston and Charles Knapp, "Sex Discrimination by Law: A Study in Judicial Perspective," *New York University Law Review*, 1971, vol. 46, p. 737.

8. William Kanowitz, *Women and the Law*, Albuquerque, New Mexico, University of New Mexico Press, 1969, p. 55.

9. Lenore J. Weitzman, "Legal Restrictions of Marriage: Tradition and Change," *California Law Review*, 1974, vol. 62, no. 2, p. 1182. For a detailed discussion of all laws that restrict a woman's capacity to engage in business activity, see Babcock, Barbara A., Freedman, Ann E., Norton, Eleanor H., and Ross, Susan C., *Sex Discrimination and the Law*, Boston, Little, Brown, 1976, ch. 3, especially pp. 600–602.

10. Johnston and Knapp, "Sex Discrimination by Law," p. 689.

11. Lyrics from the song, "A Hymn to Him," from the musical *My Fair Lady*, by Alan Jay Lerner and Frederick Loewe. Used by permission.

12. Broverman, "Sex Role Stereotypes," pp. 4–6.

13. Jean Baker Miller, *Toward a New Psychology of Women*, Boston, Beacon, 1976, pp. 35–36.

CHAPTER 4

1. Henry Biller, "The Father and Sex Role Development," in *The Role of the Father in Child Development*, Michael Lamb, ed., New York, John Wiley, 1981, p. 341.

2. Norma Radin, "The Role of the Father in Cognitive, Academic, and Intellectual Development," in Lamb, *Role of the Father*, p. 399. See also David Lynn, *The Father: His Role in Child Development*, Monterey, Calif., Brooks Cole, 1974; Miriam M. Johnson, "Sex Role Learning in the Nuclear Family," *Child Development*, 1963, vol. 34, no. 2, pp. 319–333.

3. Candace Borlund, *Locus of Control, Need for Achievement, and Entrepreneurship*, cited by David Hull, John Bosley, and Gerald Udell, "Renewing the Hunt for the Heffalump: Identifying Potential Entrepreneurs by Personality Characteristics," *Journal of Small Business Management*, January 1980, vol. 18, no. 1, p. 14.

4. Several other studies have found that in general male entrepreneurs remember their fathers as critical, cold, distant, or absent or as failures. My research suggests this may be a common theme in the life stories of both men and women entrepreneurs. For comparative discussions of this topic, see Orvis Collins, David Moore, and Darab Unwalla, *The Enterprising Man*, East Lansing, Mich., Michigan State University Business Studies, 1964; John Hornaday and Charles Bunker, "The Nature of the Entrepreneur," *Personnel Psychology*, Spring 1970, vol. 23, no. 1, pp. 47–54; Manfred F. R. Kets deVries, "The Entrepreneurial Personality: A Person at the Crossroads," *Journal of Management Studies*, 1977, vol. 14, no. 1, pp. 34–57.

5. The new entrepreneurs were hardly unique in their reaction to the hall of mirrors. Anne Petersen, a professor at Pennsylvania State University, just completed a study of 355 Chicago area students. She found that "girls whose achievement drops between 6th and 8th grade show *increases* in self-image." This finding suggests how little sex-role stereotypes have changed in recent years. Anne Petersen, "Early Adolescence: A Critical Developmental Transition?" Paper presented at the Annual Meeting of the American Educational Research Association, San Francisco, April 1986. See also Elizabeth Douvan and Judith Bardwick, "Ambivalence: The Socialization of Women," in *Readings in the Psychology of Women*, J. Bardwick, ed., New York, Harper and Row, 1972; Matina Horner, "Achievement-Related Conflicts in Women," *Journal of Social Issues*, 1972, vol. 28, no. 2, pp. 151–176.

6. For illumination on these points, see Jean Baker Miller, *Toward a New Psychology of Women*, Boston, Beacon, 1976, and Carol Gilligan, *In a Different Voice: Psychological Theory and Women's Development*, Cambridge, Mass., Harvard University Press, 1983.

CHAPTER 5

1. At least one other study has found results more consistent with the popular view. See Orvis Collins, David Moore, and Darab Unwalla, *The Enterprising Man*, East Lansing, Mich., Michigan State University Business Studies, 1964.

CHAPTER 8

1. Phyllis Chesler and Emily Jane Goodman, *Women, Money, and Power*, New York, William Morrow, 1976, pp. 18, 19.
2. Nancy Rytina, "Earnings of Men and Women: A Look at Specific Occupations," *Monthly Labor Review*, April 1982, p. 31.
3. Sandra Bem, "Androgyny vs. the Tight Little Lives of Fluffy Women and Chesty Men," *Psychology Today*, September 1975, pp. 61–62.
4. Ibid.

CHAPTER 9

1. Donald J. Treiman and Heidi I. Hartman, eds., *Women, Work, Wages: Equal Pay for Jobs of Equal Value*, Washington, D.C., National Academy Press, 1981, p. 93.
2. Phyllis Chesler and Emily Jane Goodman, *Women, Money, and Power*, New York, William Morrow, 1976, p. 21.
3. Ibid., p. 18.
4. John Galvin and Ethel Mendelsohn, "The Legal Status of Women," in *The Book of the States, 1980–1981*, Lexington, Ky.: Council of State Governments, p. 38.
5. Lily Pilgrim, "Credit Discrimination against Women," *Banking Law Journal*, April 1977, p. 349.
6. Ibid.

CHAPTER 10

1. Carol Gilligan, *In a Different Voice: Psychological Theory and Women's Development*, Cambridge, Mass., Harvard University Press, 1983, pp. 49, 62.

CHAPTER 12

1. Jessie Bernard, "The Paradox of the Happy Marriage," in *Women and Sexist Society*, Vivian Gornick and Barbara Moran, eds., New York, Basic Books, 1971, pp. 153–158.

2. Philip Blumstein and Pepper Schwartz, *American Couples*, New York, Pocket Books, 1983, p. 309.

3. According to the 1983 *Handbook on Women Workers*, 60 percent of all women between the ages of twenty and fifty-four are in the labor force. This includes 58 percent of all mothers. See U.S. Department of Labor, *Time of Change: 1983 Handbook on Women Workers*, Washington, D.C., pub. 298, pp. 11, 17.

4. Blumstein and Schwartz, *American Couples*, p. 311.

5. Lillian Rubin, *Intimate Strangers: Men and Women Together*, New York, Harper and Row, 1983, p. 155.

CHAPTER 13

1. Cynthia Epstein, *A Woman's Place*, Berkeley, Calif., University of California Press, 1970, p. 108.

2. Sara Yogev, "Do Professional Women Have Egalitarian Marital Relationships?" *Journal of Marriage and the Family*, November 1981, p. 868.

3. Epstein, *A Woman's Place*, p. 32.

4. Jean E. Collins, "If It's Thursday, It Must Be Asparagus," *Savvy*, August 1980, p. 67.

5. Ibid.

CHAPTER 14

1. Ann Ulanov, *Receiving Woman*, Philadelphia, Westminster, 1981, p. 133.

2. *The State of Small Business: A Report to the President*, U.S. Government Printing Office, Washington, D.C., 1984, p. xvi.

3. See Robert Reich, *The Next American Frontier*, New York, Penguin Books, 1983; two works by Rosabeth Moss Kanter: *Men and Women of the Corporation*, New York, Basic Books, 1977, and *The Change Masters*, New York, Simon and Schuster, 1983; William G. Ouchi, *Theory Z: How American Business Can Meet the Japanese Challenge*, Reading, Mass., Addison-Wesley, 1981; Lynn Rosener and Judy Rosener, "Alpha + Beta = A New Achievement," a working paper, August 1982; Thomas Peters and Charles Waterman, *In Search of Excellence*, New York, Harper and Row, 1983.

4. For an excellent discussion of feminine leadership in the U.S. corporation, see Marilyn Loden, *Feminine Leadership, or How To Succeed in Business Without Being One of the Boys*, New York, Times Books, 1985.

Bibliography

ENTREPRENEURS, ENTREPRENEURSHIP, GENERAL BUSINESS STUDIES

Aitkin, Hugh, ed. *Explorations in Enterprise*. Cambridge, Mass.: Harvard University Press, 1965.

Ash, Mary Kay. *Mary Kay on People Management*. New York: Warner Books, 1984.

Bafaro, Johanna, and Melvin H. Freedman. *The Entrepreneur's Information Sourcebook*. New York: Entrepreneurs Productions, 1985.

Bekey, Michelle. "Born and Bred Entrepreneurs." *Venture*, March 1981, pp. 36–41.

Berkley, Frances. "Owning One's Own Business." *Journal of Home Economics*, vol. 55, no. 10, December 1963, pp. 767–769.

Bird, Caroline. *Enterprising Women*. New York: W. W. Norton, 1976.

Borland, Candace. *Locus of Control, Need for Achievement, and Entrepreneurship*. Ph.D. diss., University of Texas at Austin, 1974.

Brockhaus, Robert A. "An Exploration of Factors Affecting the Entrepreneurial Decision: Personal Characteristics vs. Environmental Calculations." *Academy of Management Proceedings*, 1979, pp. 364–368.

————. "Internal/External Locus of Control Scores as Predictors of Entrepreneurial Intentions." *Academy of Management Proceedings*, 1975, pp. 433–435.

————. "Psychological and Environmental Factors Which Distinguish Successful and Unsuccessful Entrepreneurs." *Academy of Management Proceedings*, 1980, pp. 368–372.

————. "Risk-Taking Propensity of Entrepreneurs." *Academy of Management Journal*, vol. 23, no. 3, 1980, pp. 509–520.

————. "The Effect of Job Dissatisfaction on the Decision to Start a Business." *Journal of Small Business Management*, vol. 18, no. 1, January 1980, pp. 37–43.

Broehl, Wayne. "A Less Developed Entrepreneur?" *Columbia Journal of World Business*, vol. 5, March–April 1970, pp. 25–34.

Charan, Ram, Charles Hofer, and John Mahon. "From Entrepreneurial to Professional Management: A Set of Guidelines." *Journal of Small Business Management*, vol. 18, no. 1, January 1980, pp. 1–10.

Cochran, Thomas. *Basic History of American Business*. Princeton, N.J.: Van Nostrand, 1959.

Cole, Arthur H. *Business Enterprise in Its Social Setting*. Cambridge, Mass.: Harvard University Press, 1959.

Collins, Orvis, and David Moore, and Darab Unwalla. *The Enterprising Man*. East Lansing, Mich.: Michigan State University Business Studies, 1964.

Cooper, Arnold C., and William C. Dunkelberg. "Influences upon Entrepreneurship—A Large Scale Study." Paper presented at the Annual Meeting of the Academy of Management, San Diego, Calif., August 1981.

————, and ————. "A New Look at Business Entry—The Experiences of 1805 Entrepreneurs." Paper presented at the Conference on Frontiers of Entrepreneurship, Babson College, Boston, April 1981.

————, and John L. Komives, eds. *Technical Entrepreneurship: A Symposium*. Milwaukee: Center for Venture Management, 1972.

DeCarlo, James, and Paul Lyons. "A Comparison of Selected Personal Characteristics of Minority and Non-Minority Female Entrepreneurs." *Journal of Small Business Management*, vol. 17, no. 4, October 1979, pp. 22–29.

————, and ————. "Toward a Contingency Theory of Entrepreneurship." *Journal of Small Business Management*, vol. 18, July 1980, pp. 37–42.

Deeks, John. *The Small Firm Owner-Manager: Entrepreneurial Behavior and Management Practice*. New York: Praeger, 1976.

Depner, Charlene, and Joseph Veroff. "Varieties of Achievement Motivation." *American Journal of Social Psychology*, vol. 107, April 1979, p. 83.

Douglass, Merrill E. and Eric Ericksen. "Limits to Growth—Entrepreneurial Characteristics of Small Business Owners," *Academy of Management Proceedings*, 1980, p. 438.

Douglass, Merrill E. "Entrepreneurial Educational Level Related to Business Performance." *Academy of Management Proceedings*, 1976, pp. 461–464.

Drucker, Peter. *Innovation and Entrepreneurship: Practice and Principles*. New York: Harper and Row, 1985.

Filley, Alan C., Robert J. House, and Stephen Kerr. *Managerial Process and Organizational Behavior*. Glenview, Ill.: Scott, Foresman, 1976.

Finney, Ruth. *Towards a Typology of Women Entrepreneurs*. Honolulu: East-West Center, 1977.

Gasse, Yvon. "The Processing of Information in Small Business and the Entrepreneur as Small Business Processor." *Academy of Management Proceedings*, 1980, p. 438.

Goleman, Daniel. "The Psyche of the Entrepreneur." *New York Times Magazine*, February 2, 1986, pp. 30–32.

Goodwin, Susan. "Commentary: Opportunities for Women in Small Business." *Business and Economic Review*, vol. 22, March 1976, pp. 17–22.

Greenfield, S. M., and A. Stricton. "New Paradigms for the Study of Entrepreneurship and Social Change." *Economic Development and Cultural Change*, vol. 29, April 1981, pp. 467–499.

Hartman, Heinz. "Managers and Entrepreneurs: A Useful Distinction." *Administration Science Quarterly*, vol. 3, no. 4, March 1959, 429–451.

———. "The Enterprising Woman: A German Model." *Columbia Journal of World Business*, vol. 5, no. 2, March-April 1970, pp. 61–66.

Hebert, Robert F., and Albert N. Link. *Entrepreneur*. New York: Praeger, 1982.

Heller, Robert. "Lessons of the Entrepreneur." *Management Today*, April 1981, pp. 54–59.

Higgins, Benjamin. *Economic Development*. New York: W. W. Norton, 1968.

Hornaday, John et al., eds. *Frontiers of Entrepreneurship Research*. Wellesley, Mass., Babson College, 1983.

———, and John Aboud. "Characteristics of Successful Entrepreneurs." *Personnel Psychology*, vol. 24, Summer 1971, pp. 141–153.

———, and Charles Bunker. "The Nature of the Entrepreneur." *Personnel Psychology*, vol. 23, no. 1, Spring 1970, pp. 47–54.

Hull, David, John Bosley, and Charles Bunker. "Renewing the Hunt for the Heffalump: Identifying Potential Entrepreneurs by Personality Characteristics." *Journal of Small Business Management*, vol. 18, no. 1, January 1980, pp. 11–18.

Hurwitt, Anne. "Women Business Owners: Small but Growing Minority." *New Directions for Women*, vol. 7, Winter 1978–1979, p. 11.

Jeffries, Georgia. "Women's Work: Small Business." *National Business Woman*, May 1974, pp. 4–5, 13.

Kanter, Rosabeth Moss. *The Change Masters: Innovation for Productivity in the American Corporation*. New York: Simon and Schuster, 1983.

———. *Men and Women of the Corporation*. New York: Basic Books, 1977.

Kent, Calvin. *The Environment for Entrepreneurship*. Lexington, Mass: Lexington Books, 1984.

———, Donald Sexton, and Karl Vesper, eds. *Encyclopedia of Entrepreneurship*. Englewood Cliffs, N.J.: Prentice-Hall, 1983.

Kets deVries, Manfred F. R. "The Entrepreneurial Personality: A Person at the Crossroads." *Journal of Management Studies*, vol. 14, no. 1, 1977, pp. 34–37.

Kierulff, Herbert. "Can Entrepreneurs Be Developed?" *Michigan State University Business Topics*, vol. 23, no. 1, Winter 1975, pp. 39–44.

Kilby, Peter, ed. *Entrepreneurship and Economic Development*. New York: Free Press, 1971.

Kimberly, John R., and Robert Miles H., eds. *The Organizational Life Cycle*. San Francisco: Jossey-Bass, 1980.

Lawler, E. E., and J. A. Drexler. "Entrepreneurs in the Large Corporation." *Management Review*, vol. 70, Fall 1981, pp. 8–11.

Levitt, Theodore. "Innovative Imitation." *Harvard Business Review*, vol. 44, September–October 1966, pp. 63–70.

Liles, Patrick. "Who Are the Entrepreneurs?" *Michigan State University Business Topics*, Winter 1974, pp. 5–14.

McClelland, David. "Business Drive and National Achievement." *Harvard Business Review*, vol. 40, July–August 1962, pp. 99–112.

————. "Need Achievement and Entrepreneurship: A Longitudinal Study." *Journal of Personality and Social Psychology*, vol. 1, no. 4, 1965, pp. 389–392.

————, et al. *The Achievement Motive*. New York: Irvington, 1976.

McCoy-Rich, Lois. *Millionairess: Self-Made Women of America*. New York: Harper and Row, 1978.

"More Women Going to Work for Themselves." *Christian Science Monitor*, September 13, 1982.

Murphy, Thomas. "Making It as an Entrepreneur." *Forbes*, July 15, 1977, pp. 92–93.

Obrero, Dolores, and Cheryl Steward. "A Business Plan for Women Entrepreneurs." Master's thesis, University of California Graduate School of Business Administration, June 1979.

On Their Own. Santa Cruz, Calif.: Resources for Women, 1979.

Organ, Dennis W., and Charles N. Greene. "Role Ambiguity, Locus of Control, and Work Satisfaction." *Journal of Applied Psychology*, vol. 59, no. 1, 1974, pp. 101–102.

Ouchi, William. *Theory Z: How American Business Can Meet the Japanese Challenge*. Reading, Mass.: Addison Wesley, 1981.

Palmer, Michael. "The Application of Psychological Testing to Entrepreneurial Potential." *California Management Review*, vol. 13, no. 3, Spring 1971, pp. 32–38.

Pandey, Janak, and N. B. Teway. "Locus of Control and Achievement Values of Entrepreneurs." *Journal of Occupational Psychology*, vol. 52, no. 2, June 1979, pp. 107–111.

Papanek, Gustav. "The Development of Entrepreneurship." *American Economic Review*, vol. 52, May 1962, pp. 46–58.

Peters, Thomas J., and Charles W. Waterman. *In Search of Excellence*. New York: Harper and Row, 1982.

Pickle, Hal. *Personality and Success: An Evaluation of the Personal Characteristics of Successful Small Business Managers*. Washington, D.C.: Small Business Administration, 1964.

Poindexter, S. F. "Reestablishing the Spirit of Entrepreneurship in the Workforce." *Management World*, vol. 9, October 1980, p. 1.

Powell, James, and Charles Bimmerle. "A Model of Entrepreneurship: Moving toward Precision and Complexity." *Journal of Small Business Management*, vol. 18, no. 1, January 1980, pp. 33–36.

Reich, Robert. *The Next American Frontier*. New York: Penguin Books, 1983.

Rondstadt, Robert. *Entrepreneurship: Essential Readings and Bibliography*. Dover, Mass.: Lord Publications, 1985.

Rosener, Lynn, and Judy B. Rosener. "Alpha + Beta = A New Effectiveness: Leaders and Followers in the 1980s." Working paper, August 1982.

––––––, and Peter Schwartz. "Women, Leadership and the 1980s: What Kind of Leaders Do We Need?" Project on New Leadership in the Public Interest, N.O.W. Legal Defense and Education Fund, December 1980, pp. 25–35.

Scholss, Henry. "The Concept of Entrepreneurship in Economic Development." *Journal of Economic Issues*, vol. 2, no. 2, June 1968, pp. 228–232.

Schon, Donald A. *Technology and Change: The Impact of Invention and Innovation on American Social and Economic Development*. New York: Delta, 1967.

Schrage, Harry. "The R and D Entrepreneur: Profile of Success." *Harvard Business Review*, November–December 1965, pp. 56–69.

Schreier, James W. "Is the Female Entrepreneur Different?" *MBA*, vol. 10, no. 3, March 1976, p. 42.

––––––. "The Career Decision of the Woman Entrepreneur." *Enterprising Women*, vol. 2, no. 4, December 1976, pp. 1–2.

Schreier, James W., and John L. Komives. *The Entrepreneur and New Enterprise Formation: A Resource Guide*. Milwaukee: Center for Venture Management, 1974.

Schumpeter, Joseph. *The Theory of Economic Development*. New York: Oxford University Press, 1961.

Schwartz, Eleanor Brantley. "Entrepreneurship: A New Female Frontier." *Journal of Contemporary Business*, vol. 5, Winter 1976, pp. 47–76.

Shapero, Albert. "Have You Got What It Takes to Start Your Own Business?" *Savvy*, April 1980, pp. 33–37.

––––––. "The Displaced, Uncomfortable Entrepreneur." *Psychology Today*, November 1975, pp. 83–86, 103.

Shepherd, N. "Women's Work." *Black Enterprise*, vol. 11, Fall 1981, pp. 57–58.

"Special Programs for Women Dying Away at Reagan's SBA." *Wall Street Journal*, November 16, 1981.

Stacey, N. A. H. "Sociology of the Entrepreneur." *Accountant*, November 29, 1980, p. 851.

Strauss, James H. "The Entrepreneur: The Firm." *Journal of Political Economics*, vol. 52, no. 2, 1944, pp. 112–127.

Swayne, Charles B., and William R. Tucker. *The Effective Entrepreneur*. Morristown, N.J.: General Learning Press, 1973.

Tepper, Teri, and Nona Tepper. *The New Entrepreneurs: Women Working at Home*. New York: Universe Books, 1980.

"Versatile, Flexible Describes Businesswomen." *San Francisco Business Journal*, November 2, 1981, p. 6.

Vesper, Karl, ed. *Frontiers of Entrepreneurship Research. Proceedings of the 1981 Conference on Entrepreneurship*. Wellesley, Mass.: Babson College, 1981.

Wainer, Herbert A., and Irwin M. Rubin. "Motive of Research and Development Entrepreneurs: Determinants of Company Success." *Journal of Applied Psychology*, vol. 53, no. 3, 1969, pp. 178–184.

Webster, Frederick. "The Independent Entrepreneur and the Firm: A Revisit." *Academy of Management Proceedings*, 1975, pp. 429–431.

Webb, Terry, Thelma Quince, and David Watkins, eds. *Small Business Research: The Development of Entrepreneurs*. Aldershot, Hampshire, England: Gower, 1982.

Weinrauch, J. Donald. "The Second Time Around: Entrepreneurship as a Mid-Career Alternative." *Journal of Small Business Management*, vol. 18, no. 1, January 1980, pp. 25–32.

Winston, Sandra. *The Entrepreneurial Woman*. New York: Newsweek Books, 1979.

"Women at Work: AMA Survey Shows How and Why Females Succeed as Businessowners." *Management Review*, vol. 67, no. 11 (November, 1978), p. 56.

"Women Business Owners List Causes of Their Worst Problems." *Wall Street Journal*, July 7, 1980.

"Women Entrepreneurs: The New Business Owners." Special issue, *Venture*, July, 1986.

Zaleznik, Abraham. "Managers and Leaders: Are They Different?" *Harvard Business Review*, vol. 55, May–June 1977, pp. 67–78.

PRACTICAL GUIDES

Broom, Halsey N., and Justin C. Longenecker. *Small Business Management*. Cincinnati, Ohio: Southwestern Publishing, 1975.

Butler, Pamela. *Self-Assertion for Women*. San Francisco: Canfield Press, Harper and Row, 1976.

Dominguez, John R. *Venture Capital*. Lexington, Mass.: Lexington Books, D. C. Heath, 1974.

Gillis, Phyllis. *Entrepreneurial Mothers*. New York: Rawson Associates, 1984.

Jessup, Claudia, and Genie Chipps. *The Woman's Guide to Starting a Business*, rev. ed. New York: Holt, Rinehart, and Winston, 1979.

Klug, John R. *The Basic Book of Business*. Boston: Cahners Books, 1977.

McCaslin, Barbara, and Patricia McNamara. *Be Your Own Boss: A Woman's Guide to Planning and Running Her Business*. Englewood Cliffs, N.J.: Prentice-Hall, 1980.

McVicar, Mary, and Julia Craig. *Minding My Own Business*. New York: Richard Marek, 1981.

Mancuso, Joseph. *The Entrepreneur's Handbook*, 2 vols. Dedham, Mass.: Artech House, 1974.

————. *How to Start, Finance, and Manage Your Own Small Business*. Englewood Cliffs, N.J.: Prentice Hall, 1978.

————. *Small Business Survival Guide*. Englewood Cliffs, N.J.: Prentice-Hall, 1980.

Moran, Peg. *Invest in Yourself: A Woman's Guide to Starting Her Own Business*. Garden City, N.Y.: Doubleday, 1983.

Ross, Ruth. *Prospering Woman*. Mill Valley, Calif.: Whatever Publishing, 1982.

Siegelman, Ellen Y. *Personal Risk*. New York: Harper and Row, 1983.

Siropolis, Nicholas C. *Small Business Management: A Guide to Entrepreneurship*. Boston: Houghton Mifflin, 1977.

Taylor, Charlotte. *Women and the Business Game*. New York: Simon and Schuster, 1980.

Winter, Meridee Allen. *Mind Your Own Business, Be Your Own Boss*. Englewood Cliffs, N.J.: Prentice-Hall, 1980.

GOVERNMENT STUDIES

Annual Report to the President, 1980. Interagency Committee on Women's Business Enterprise. Washington, D.C.: Small Business Administration, June 1980.

The Bottom Line: Unequal Enterprise in America. Washington, D.C.: U.S. Government Printing Office, June 1978.

Directory of Federal Government Business Assistance Programs for Women Business Owners. Washington, D.C.: Small Business Administration, 1980.

Minorities and Women as Government Contractors: A Report of the United States Commission on Civil Rights. Washington, D.C., May 1975.

Time of Change: 1983 Handbook on Women Workers. Washington, D.C.: U.S. Department of Labor, Women's Bureau, Bulletin 298.

Report to the Administrator, Small Business Administration: A Need to Determine Whether Existing Federal Programs Can Meet the Needs of Women Entrepreneurs. Washington, D.C.: U.S. Government Printing Office, April 1981.

Selected Characteristics of Women-Owned Businesses. Washington, D.C.: U.S. Department of Commerce, Bureau of the Census, 1977.

Sole Proprietorship Returns, 1979–1980. Washington, D.C.: Internal Revenue Service, 1981.

The State of Small Business: A Report of the President. Washington, D.C.: U.S. Government Printing Office, 1984.

WOMEN: EARNINGS, MONEY, AND CREDIT

Blau, Francine, and Wallace Hendricks. "Occupational Segregation by Sex." *The Journal of Human Resources* vol. 14, no. 2, Spring 1979, pp. 197–211.

Chapman, Jane, ed. *Economic Independence for Women*. Beverly Hills, Calif.: Sage, 1976.

——— and Margaret Gates, eds. *Women into Wives: The Legal and Economic Impact of Marriage*. Beverly Hills, Calif.: Sage, 1977.

Chesler, Phyllis, and Emily Jane Goodman. *Women, Money, and Power*. New York: William Morrow, 1976.

Title V: Equal Credit Opportunity Act, Pub. L. 93-495, 1974.

Geck, Donna. "Note: Equal Credit—You Can Get There from Here—The Equal Credit Opportunity Act." *North Dakota Law Review*, vol. 52, 1976, pp. 381–409.

Hahne, Hilda, and Andrew Kohen. "Economic Perspectives on the Role of Women in the American Economy." *Journal of Economic Literature*, vol. 13, 1975, pp. 1249–1292.

Henle, Peter, and Paul Rejscavage. "The Distribution of Earned Income among Men and Women, 1958–1977." *Monthly Labor Review*, April 1980, pp. 3–10.

Klein, Barbara. "The Equal Credit Opportunity Act Amendments of 1976." *Catholic University Law Review*, vol. 26, Fall 1976, pp. 149–167.

Kreps, Juanita, ed. *Women and the American Economy*. Englewood Cliffs, N.J.: Prentice-Hall, 1976.

Lally, Maureen. "Comments: Women and Credit." *Duquesne Law Review*, vol. 12, Summer 1974, pp. 863–890.

Littlefield, Neil. "Sex-Based Discrimination and Credit Granting Practices." *Connecticut Law Review*, vol. 5, Spring 1973, pp. 575–597.

Matthaei, Julie A. *An Economic History of Women in America*. New York: Schocken, 1982.

O'Connor, T. H. "Sex Discrimination in Acquiring Credit." *Journal of Social Psychology*, vol. 6, October 1978, pp. 106–135.

Perkins, Charlotte Gilman. *Women and Economics*. New York: Harper and Row, rev. ed. edited by Peter Degler, 1966.

Perspectives on Working Women: A Databook. U.S. Department of Labor, Bureau of Labor Statistics, October 1980.

Pilgrim, Lily. "Credit Discrimination against Women." *Banking Law Journal*, vol. 94, April 1977, pp. 348–351.

Rytina, Nancy. "Earnings of Men and Women: A Look at Specific Occupations." *Monthly Labor Review*, April 1982, pp. 25–31.

Treiman, Donald, and Heidi Hartmann, eds. *Women, Work, and Wages*. Washington, D.C.: National Academy Press, 1981.

SEX ROLES, CAREER CHOICES, AND FEMALE IDENTITY DEVELOPMENT

Adams, John, Fred Lawrence, and Sharla Cook. "Analyzing Stereotypes of Women in the Work Force." *Sex Roles*, vol. 5, no. 5, October 1979, pp. 581–594.

Adams, Russell, and Beeman N. Phillips. "Motivational and Achievement Differences among Children of Various Ordinal Birth Positions." *Child Development*, vol. 43, no. 3, 1972, pp. 155–164.

Almquist, Elizabeth M., and Shirley S. Angrist. "Role Model Influences on College Women's Career Aspirations." *Merrill-Palmer Quarterly*, vol. 17, no. 1, 1971, pp. 263–277.

Appleton, William. *Daughters and Fathers*. Garden City, New York: Doubleday, 1981.

Astin, Helen, and Thelma Myint. "Career Development of Young Women during the Post High School Years." *Journal of Counseling Psychology*, vol. 18, no. 4, 1971, pp. 77–80.

Atkinson, John W. "Motivational Determinants of Risk-Taking Behavior." *Psychological Review*, vol. 64, no. 6, November 1957, pp. 359–372.

Barach, Rhoda. "The Achievement Motive in Women: Implications for Career Development." *Journal of Personality and Social Psychology*, vol. 5, no. 3, 1967, pp. 260–267.

Bardwick, Judith. *Psychology of Women*. New York: Harper and Row, 1971.

————, and Elizabeth Douvan, eds. *Readings in the Psychology of Women*. New York: Harper and Row, 1972.

Barnett, Rosalind, and Grace Baruch. *Determinants of Fathers' Participation in Family Work*. Wellesley, Mass.: Wellesley College Center for Research on Women, Working Paper no. 136, 1984.

————, and ————. *Fathers' Participation in Family Work: Effects on Children's Sex Role Attitudes*. Wellesley, Mass.: Wellesley College Center for Research on Women, Working Paper no. 126, 1984.

————, and ————. *The Competent Woman*. New York: Irvington, 1978.

Baruch, Grace. "Feminine Self-Esteem, Self Ratings of Competence, and Maternal Career Commitment." *Journal of Counseling Psychology*, vol. 20, no. 5, September 1973, pp. 487–488.

Bedeian, Arthur, and John Touliatos. "Work-Related Motives and Self-Esteem in American Women." *Journal of Psychology*, vol. 99, May 1978, pp. 63–70.

Bell, Norman, and Ezra Vogel. *A Modern Introduction to the Family*. Glencoe, Ill.: Free Press, 1960.

Bem, Sandra. "Androgyny vs. the Tight Little Lives of Fluffy Women and Chesty Men." *Psychology Today*, September 1975, pp. 58–62.

Bernard, Jessie. *The Future of Marriage*. New York: Bantam, 1973.

———. "The Paradox of the Happy Marriage." In *Women in Sexist Society*, Vivian Gornick and Barbara K. Moran, eds. New York: Basic Books, 1971, pp. 145–162.

———. *Women and the Public Interest*. Chicago: Aldine, Atherton, 1971.

Biller, Henry. *Father, Child, and Sex Roles*. Lexington, Mass.: Lexington Books, D. C. Heath, 1971.

———. *Paternal Deprivation*. Lexington, Mass.: Lexington Books, D. C. Heath, 1974.

Bird, Caroline. *The Two Paycheck Marriage*. New York: Rawson, Wade, 1979.

Blachman, Linda. *Dancing in the Dark: Motherhood and the Search for Self*. New York: Simon and Schuster, forthcoming.

Blaxhall, Martha, and Barbara Reagan. *Women and the Workplace*. Chicago: University of Chicago Press, 1976.

Bleier, Ruth. *Science and Gender: A Critique of Biology and Its Theories on Women*. New York: Pergamon, 1984.

Blumstein, Philip, and Pepper Schwartz. *American Couples*. New York: Pocket Books, 1983.

Broverman, D. M. "Sex Role Stereotypes: Their Development and Relationship to Life Styles of Women." In *Women Today! Tomorrow?*, Eileen T. Nickerson and Elizabeth S. Williams, eds. Dubuque, Iowa: Kendall, Hunt, 1975.

Broverman, Inge, et al. "Sex Role Stereotypes and Clinical Judgments of Mental Health." *Journal of Consulting and Clinical Psychology*, vol. 34, no. 1, February 1970, pp. 1–7.

Caballero, Carmen, Philip Shaver, and Pat Giles. "Sex Role Traditionalism and Fear of Success." *Sex Roles*, vol. 1, no. 4, December 1975, pp. 319–326.

Cash, Thomas F., and Louis H. Janda. "The Eye of the Beholder." *Psychology Today*, vol. 18, no. 12, December 1984, pp. 46–52.

Casserly, Patricia Lund. "Helping Able Young Women Take Math and Science Seriously in School." In *New Voices in Counseling the Gifted*. Nicholas Colangelo and Ronald T. Zaffrann, eds. Dubuque, Iowa: Kendall, Hunt, 1979.

Chodorow, Nancy. "Family Structure and Feminine Personality." In *Women, Culture, and Society*, Michelle Zimbalist Rosaldo and Louise Lamphere, eds., Stanford, Calif.: Stanford University Press, 1974.

Chodorow, Nancy. *The Reproduction of Mothering: Psychoanalysis and the Sociology of Gender*. Berkeley, Calif.: University of California Press, 1978.

Costrich, Norma, et al. "When Stereotypes Hurt: Three Studies of Penalties for Sex Role Reversals." *Journal of Experimental Social Psychology*, vol. 11, no. 6, November 1975, pp. 520–530.

Crowly, Joan, et al. "Seven Deadly Half-Truths about Women." *Psychology Today*, March 1973, pp. 94–96.

Darley, Susan. "Big Time Careers for the Little Woman." *Journal of Social Issues*, vol. 32, no. 3, 1976, pp. 85–98.

Darmofall, Sharon, and Richard McCarbery. "Achievement Motivation in Females: A Social Psychological Perspective." *The Psychological Record*, vol. 29, no. 1, 1979, pp. 15–41.

Deaux, Kay. "Self-Evaluations of Male and Female Managers." *Sex Roles*, vol. 5, no. 5, October 1979, pp. 571–580.

———, and Tim Emswiller. "Explanations of Successful Performance on Sex-Linked Tasks: What Is Skill for the Male Is Luck for the Female." *Journal of Personality and Social Psychology*, vol. 29, no. 1, 1974, pp. 80–85.

Della Cava, Frances, and Madeline Engel. "Resistance to Sisterhood: The Case of the Professional Woman." *International Journal of Women's Studies*, vol. 2, no. 6, November–December 1979, pp. 505–512.

Depner, Charlene, and Virginia O'Leary. "Understanding Female Careerism: Fear of Success and New Directions." *Sex Roles*, vol. 2, no. 3, September 1976, pp. 259–268.

Diener, Carol I., and Carol S. Dweck. "An Analysis of Learned Helplessness: II, The Processing of Success." *Journal of Personality and Social Psychology*, vol. 38, 1980, pp. 940–952.

Douvan, Elizabeth, and Joseph Adelson. *The Adolescent Experience*. New York: John Wiley, 1966.

Dweck, Carol S. "The Role of Expectations and Attributions in the Alleviation of Learned Helplessness." *Journal of Personality and Social Psychology*, vol. 31, no. 4, 1975, pp. 674–685.

———, and Ellen S. Bush. "Sex Differences in Learned Helplessness." *Developmental Psychology*, vol. 12, no. 2, 1976, pp. 147–156.

———, et al. "Sex Differences in Learned Helplessness." *Developmental Psychology*, vol. 14, no. 3, 1978, pp. 268–276.

Epstein, Cynthia. *Woman's Place*. Berkeley, Calif.: University of California Press, 1970.

Farmer, Helen. "What Inhibits Career Development in Women?" *The Counseling Psychologist*, vol. 6, no. 2, 1976, pp. 12–14.

Fitzgerald, Louise, and John O. Crites. "Toward a Career Psychology of Women: What Do We Know? What Do We Need to Know?" *Journal of Counseling Psychology*, vol. 27, January 1980, pp. 44–62.

Fox, Lynn, Linda Brody, and Dianne Tobin, eds. *Women and the Mathematical Mystique*. Baltimore: Johns Hopkins, 1980.

Fraker, Susan. "Why Women Aren't Getting to the Top." *Fortune*, April 16, 1984, pp. 40–45.

Gilbert, Lucia A., Connie J. Deutsch, and Robert J. Straham. "Feminine and Masculine Dimensions of the Typical, Desirable, and Ideal Woman and Man." *Sex Roles*, vol. 4, no. 5, October 1978, pp. 767–778.

Gilligan, Carol. *In a Different Voice: Psychological Theory and Women's Development.* Cambridge, Mass.: Harvard University Press, 1982.

Gold, Alice Ross. "Reexamining Barriers to Women's Career Development." *American Journal of Orthopsychiatry*, vol. 48, no. 4, October 1978, pp. 690–702.

Goldberg, Ruth. "Sex Role Stereotypes and Career versus Homemaking Orientations in Women." In *Emerging Women: Career Analysis and Outlooks*, Samual Osipow, ed. Columbus, Ohio: Charles E. Merrill, 1975.

Gove, Walter R. "The Relationship between Sex Roles, Marital Status, and Mental Illness." *Social Forces*, vol. 51, September 1972, pp. 34–44.

———, and J. F. Tudor. "Adult Sex Roles and Mental Illness." *American Journal of Sociology*, vol. 98, 1973, pp. 821–835.

Green, Laurence, and Harry Parker. "Parental Influences on Adolescent's Occupational Choice." *Journal of Counseling Psychology*, vol. 4, Winter 1965, pp. 379–383.

Haas, Violet B., and Carolyn C. Perrucci, eds. *Women in Scientific and Engineering Professions.* Ann Arbor, Mich.: University of Michigan Press, 1984.

Harlan, Anne, and Carol Weiss. *Moving Up: Women in Managerial Careers.* Wellesley, Mass.: Wellesley College Center for Research on Women, Working Paper no. 86, 1981.

Harmon, Lenore W. "Anatomy of Career Commitment in Women." *Journal of Counseling Psychology*, vol. 17, no. 1, 1970, pp. 77–80.

Heilbrun, Alfred B. "An Empirical Test of the Modeling Theory of Sex Role Learning." *Child Development*, vol. 36, no. 3, September 1965, pp. 789–799.

Helsen, Ravenna. "The Changing Image of the Career Woman." *Journal of Social Issues*, vol. 28, no. 2, 1972, pp. 33–46.

Hennig, Margaret, and Anne Jardim. *The Managerial Woman.* New York: Pocket Books, 1978.

Hetherington, E. Mavis. "A Developmental Study of the Effect of Sex of the Dominant Parent on Sex Role Preference, Identification, and Imitation in Children." *Journal of Personality and Social Psychology*, vol. 2, no. 2, 1965, pp. 188–194.

———. "Effects of Father-Absence on Personality Development in Adolescent Daughters." *Developmental Psychology*, vol. 7, 1972, pp. 313–326.

Hiller, Dana V., and William W. Philliber. "Predicting Marital and Career Success among Dual Worker Couples." *Journal of Marriage and the Family*, vol. 74, February 1982, pp. 53–62.

Hoffman, Lois. "Early Childhood Experiences and Women's Achievement Motives." *Journal of Social Issues*, vol. 28, no. 2, 1972, pp. 29–55.

Horner, Matina. "Achievement-Related Conflicts in Women." *Journal of Social Issues*, vol. 28, no. 2, 1972, pp. 157–175.

Huber, Joan. *Changing Women in a Changing Society*. Chicago: University of Chicago Press, 1973.

Johnson, Miriam. "Sex Role Learning in the Nuclear Family." *Child Development*, vol. 34, no. 2, June 1963, pp. 319–333.

Katz, Phyllis. "The Development of Female Identity." *Sex Roles*, vol. 5, no. 2, April 1979, pp. 155–178.

Kessler, Ronald, and James McRae, Jr. "The Effect of Wives' Employment on the Mental Health of Married Men and Women." *American Sociological Review*, vol. 47, April 1982, pp. 216–226.

Kogan, Nathan, and Karen Dorros. "Sex Differences in Risk-Taking and Its Attribution." *Sex Roles*, vol. 4, no. 5, October 1978, pp. 755–765.

Kolbenschlag, Madonna. *Kiss Sleeping Beauty Good-Bye*. New York: Bantam New Age Books, 1981.

Kopp, Claire, ed. *Becoming Female*. New York: Plenum, 1979.

Kratz, Marilyn. "Socializing Females for Reality." *Social Studies*, vol. 69, no. 3, May–June 1978, pp. 122–125.

Kriger, Sara F. "N Ach and Perceived Parental Child-Rearing Attitudes of Career Women and Homemakers." *Journal of Vocational Behavior*, vol. 2, no. 4, 1972, pp. 419–432.

Kundsin, Ruth B., ed. *Women and Success: The Anatomy of Achievement*. New York: William Morrow, 1974.

Lamb, Michael, ed. *The Role of the Father in Child Development*. New York: John Wiley, 1976.

Lawlis, G. Frank, and Jim D. Crawford. "Cognitive Differentiation in Women and Pioneer-Traditional Career Choices." *Journal of Vocational Behavior*, vol. 6, no. 2, 1975, pp. 263–267.

Lefcourt, H. M. "Internal vs. External Control of Reinforcement: A Review." *Psychological Bulletin*, vol. 65, 1966, pp. 206–220.

Lemkau, Jeanne Parr. "Personality and Background Characteristics of Women in Male-Dominated Occupations: A Review." *Psychology of Women Quarterly*, vol. 5, Winter 1979, pp. 221–240.

Lenz, Elinor, and Barbara Myerhoff. *The Feminization of America*. Los Angeles: Jeremy Tarcher, 1985.

Leonard, Linda. *The Wounded Woman*. Boulder, Colo.: Shambala Press, 1983.

Lips, Hilary. *Women, Men, and the Psychology of Power*. Englewood Cliffs, N.J.: Prentice-Hall, 1981.

Loden, Marilyn. *Feminine Leadership, or How to Succeed in Business without Being One of the Boys*. New York: Times Books, 1985.

Lynn, David. *The Father: His Role in Child Development*. Monterey, Calif.: Brooks-Cole, 1974.

Maccoby, Eleanor, and Carol Jacklin. *The Psychology of Sex Differences*. Stanford, Calif.: Stanford University Press, 1974.

McGhee, Paul E., and Virginia C. Crandall. "Beliefs in Internal-External Control of Reinforcement and Academic Performance." *Child Development*, vol. 39, no. 1, 1968, pp. 91–102.

Major, Brenda. "Sex Role Orientation and Fear of Success." *Sex Roles*, vol. 5, no. 1, February 1979, pp. 63–70.

Makosky, Vivian Parker. "Sex Role Compatibility of Task and of Competition and Fear of Success as Variables Affecting a Woman's Performance." *Sex Roles*, vol. 2, no. 3, September 1976, pp. 237–248.

Malmaud, Roslyn K., *Work and Marriage: The Two-Profession Couple*. Ann Arbor, Mich.: University of Michigan Press, 1984.

Mausner, Bernard, and Barbara Coles. "Avoidance of Success among Women." *International Journal of Women's Studies*, vol. 1, no. 1, January–February 1978, p. 46.

Messingill, Douglas, and Nicholas DiMarco. "Sex Role Stereotypes and Requisite Management Characteristics: A Current Replication." *Sex Roles*, vol. 5, no. 5, October 1979, pp. 561–570.

Miller, Dale, and Carol Porter. "Self-Blame in Victims of Violence." *Journal of Social Issues*, vol. 39, no. 2, 1983, pp. 139–152.

Miller, Jean Baker. *Toward a New Psychology of Women*. Boston: Beacon, 1976.

Millman, Marcia, and Rosabeth Moss Kanter, eds. *Another Voice*. Garden City, New York: Doubleday, Anchor Press, 1975.

Minnigrode, Fred A. "Attitudes toward Women, Sex Role Stereotyping, and Locus of Control." *Psychological Reports*, vol. 38, 1976, pp. 1301–1302.

Missirian, Agnes. "The Female Manager as Shelf Sitter." *Human Resources Management*, vol. 17, Winter 1978, pp. 29–32.

Mulvey, Mary. "Psychological and Social Factors in the Prediction of Career Patterns for Women." *Genetic Psychology Monographs*, vol. 68, no. 2, 1963, pp. 309–386.

Nicholls, John G. "Causal Attributions and Other Achievement-Related Cognitions: Effects of Task Outcome, Attainment Value, and Sex." *Journal of Personality and Social Psychology*, vol. 31, no. 3, 1975, pp. 379–389.

O'Donnell, Jo Anne and Dale Andersen. "Factors Influencing Choice of Major and Career of Capable Women." *Vocational Guidance Quarterly*, vol. 26, March 1978, pp. 214–221.

O'Leary, Virginia. "Some Attitudinal Barriers to Occupational Aspirations in Women." *Psychological Bulletin*, vol. 81, no. 11, 1974, pp. 809–826.

Osipow, Samuel, ed. *Emerging Woman: Career Analysis and Outlooks*. Columbus, Ohio: Charles E. Merrill, 1975.

Parsons, Talcott. "Age and Sex in the Social Structure of the United States." *American Sociological Review*, vol. 7, 1942, pp. 604–616.

Petersen, Anne. "Early Adolescence: A Critical Developmental Transition?" Paper presented at the Annual Meeting of the American Educational Research Association, San Francisco, April, 1986.

Price, Margaret. "Women Reaching for the Top." *Industry Week*, May 16, 1983, pp. 38–42.

Rice, David G. *Dual Career Marriage: Conflict and Treatment*. New York: Free Press, 1979.

Rosen, Benson, and Thomas Jerdee. "Sex Stereotyping in the Executive Suite." *Harvard Business Review*, March–April, 1974, pp. 45–58.

———, and ———. "Managerially Relevant Perceived Sex Differences." *Sex Roles*, vol. 4, no. 6, December 1978, pp. 837–843.

Rosenberg, Flor, and Roberta Simmons. "Sex Differences in Self-Concepts in Adolescence." *Sex Roles*, vol. 1, no. 2, June 1975, pp. 147–159.

Rosenkrantz, Paul, et al. "Sex Role Stereotypes and Self-Concepts among College Students." *Journal of Consulting and Clinical Psychology*, vol. 32, 1968, pp. 287–295.

Rubin, Lillian. *Intimate Strangers: Men and Women Together*. New York: Harper and Row, 1983.

Sears, Robert R. "The Relation of Early Socialization Experiences to Self-Concepts and Gender Role in Middle Childhood," *Child Development*, vol. 54, no. 2, 1970, pp. 267–290.

Sells, Lucy W. "Mathematics: The Invisible Filter." *Engineering Education*, vol. 70, no. 4, January 1980, pp. 340–341.

Sheehy, Gail. *Passages: Predictable Crises of Adult Life*. New York: Bantam, 1977.

Siegel, Alberta E., and Elizabeth A. Curtis. "Familial Correlates of Orientation toward Future Employment among College Women." *Journal of Educational Psychology*, vol. 54, no. 1, 1963, pp. 33–37.

Spender, Dale. *Invisible Women*. London: Writers and Readers, 1982.

Staines, Graham, Carol Tavris, and Toby Jayaratne. "The Queen Bee Syndrome." *Psychology Today*, vol. 17, no. 8, January 1974, pp. 55–60.

Standley, Kay, and Bradley Soule. "Women in Male-Dominated Professions: Contrasts in Their Personal and Vocational Histories." *Journal of Vocational Behavior*, vol. 4, no. 2, 1974, pp. 245–258.

Steinmann, Anne, Joseph Levi, and David Fox. "Self-Concept of College Women Compared with Their Concept of Ideal Woman and Men's Ideal Woman." *Journal of Counseling Psychology*, vol. 11, no. 4, 1964, pp. 370–374.

Tangri, Sandra Schwartz. "Occupational Role Innovation among Women." *Journal of Social Issues*, vol. 28, no. 2, 1972, pp. 177–200.

Tolor, Alex, Bryan Kelly, and Charles Stebbins. "Assertiveness, Sex Role Stereotyping and Self Concept." *The Journal of Psychology*, vol. 93, 1976, pp. 157–164.

Trigg, Linda J., and Daniel Perlman. "Social Influences on a Woman's Pursuit of a

Nontraditional Career." *Psychology of Women Quarterly*, vol. 1, no. 2, 1976, pp. 138–150.

Ulanov, Ann B. *Receiving Woman*. Philadelphia: Westminster, 1981.

Unger, Rhoda. "Male Is Greater than Female: The Socialization of Status Inequality." *Counseling Psychologist*, vol. 6, no. 2, 1976, pp. 2–9.

Vogel, Susan, et al. "Maternal Employment and Perception of Sex Roles among College Students." *Developmental Psychology*, vol. 3, no. 3, 1970, pp. 384–391.

Wallach, Michael A., and Nathan Kogan. "Sex Differences and Judgment Processes." *Journal of Personality and Social Psychology*, vol. 27, no. 4, December 1959, pp. 555–564.

Walshok, Mary Lindenstein. *Blue Collar Women*. Garden City, New York: Doubleday, Anchor Books, 1981.

Weingarten, K. "The Employment Pattern of Professional Couples and Their Distribution of Involvement in the Family." *Psychology of Women Quarterly*, vol. 3, 1978, pp. 43–53.

Weitzman, Lenore. *Sex Role Socialization*. Palo Alto, Calif.: Mayfield, 1979.

Wolfson, Karen P. "Career Development Patterns of College Women." *Journal of Counseling Psychology*, vol. 23, no. 2, 1976, pp. 119–125.

Yogev, Sara. "Do Professional Women Have Egalitarian Marital Relationships?" *Journal of Marriage and the Family*, November 1981, pp. 865–871.

SEXISM IN AMERICA

Abzug, Bella. *Gender Gap*. Boston: Houghton Mifflin, 1984.

Babcock, Barbara, et al. *Sex Discrimination and the Law: Causes and Remedies*. Boston: Little, Brown, 1975.

Bardwick, Judith. *In Transition*. New York: Holt, Rinehart, and Winston, 1979.

Bem, Sandra, and Daryl Bem. "Teaching the Woman to Know Her Place: The Power of a Non-Conscious Ideology." In Michele H. Garskof, ed., *Roles Women Play*, Belmont, Calif.: Brooks Cole, 1971.

Bird, Caroline with Sarah W. Briller. *Born Female*. New York: David McKay, 1968.

Davidson, Kenneth, Ruth Ginsberg, and Herma Hill Kay. *Sex-Based Discrimination: Text, Cases, and Materials*. St. Paul, Minn.: West, 1974.

DeCrow, Karen. *Sexist Justice*. New York: Vintage, 1975.

Farley, Lin. *Sexual Shakedown: The Sexual Harassment of Women on the Job*. New York: McGraw-Hill, 1978.

Flexner, Eleanor. *Century of Struggle*, rev. ed. Cambridge, Mass.: Belknap Press, 1975.

Friedan, Betty. *The Feminine Mystique*. New York: W. W. Norton, 1963.

————. *The Second Stage*. New York: Summit, 1981.

Galvin, John, and Ethel Mendelsohn. "The Legal Status of Women." In *The Book of the States*, 1980–1981, Lexington, KY: The Council of State Governments.

Gornick, Vivian, and Barbara Moran. *Women in Sexist Society*. New York: Basic Books, 1971.

Janeway, Elizabeth. *Man's World, Woman's Place: A Study in Social Mythology*. New York: William Morrow, 1971.

Jaquette, Jane S., ed. *Women and Politics*. New York: Wiley, 1974.

Johnston, John, and Charles Knapp. "Sex Discrimination by Law: A Study in Judicial Perspective." *New York Law Review*, vol. 46, 1971, pp. 687–739.

Kanowitz, Leo. *Women and the Law*. Albuquerque, N.M.: University of New Mexico Press, 1969.

Levitin, Teresa, Robert Quinn, and Graham Staines. "Sex Discrimination against the American Working Woman." *American Behavioral Scientists*, vol. 15, no. 2, November, December 1971, pp. 237–254.

Lifton, R. J. *The Woman in America*. Boston: Houghton Mifflin, 1965.

Mill, John Stuart. *The Subjection of Women*. London: Longmans, Green, Reader and Dyer, 1869. Unabridged replication, New York: Source Books, 1970.

Morgan, Robin, ed. *Sisterhood Is Powerful*. New York: Vintage Books, 1970.

Morris, Richard. *Studies in the History of American Law*. New York: Columbia University Press, 1930.

Rosen, Benson, and Thomas Jerdee. "Influences of Sex Role Stereotypes on Personnel Decisions." *Journal of Applied Psychology*, vol. 59, no. 1, 1974, pp. 9–14.

―――, and ―――. "Effects of Applicants' Sex and Difficulty of Job on Evaluation of Candidates for Managerial Positions." *Journal of Applied Psychology*, vol. 59, no. 4, 1974, pp. 511–512.

Sachs, Albie and Joan H. Wilson. *Sexism and the Law*. Oxford: Martin Robertson, 1978.

Safran, Claire. "Corporate Women: Just How Far Have We Come?" *Working Woman*, March 1984, pp. 99–104.

Schwartz, Eleanor. *The Sex Barrier in Business*. Atlanta: Georgia State University Press, 1971.

Weitzman, Lenore. "Legal Restrictions of Marriage: Tradition and Change." *California Law Review*, vol. 62, no. 2, 1974, pp. 1169–1288.

MENTORS AND NETWORKS

Collins, Elizabeth, and Patricia Scott, eds. "Everyone Who Makes It Has a Mentor." *Harvard Business Review*, vol. 56, no. 4, July-August 1978, pp. 89–101.

Collins, Nancy. *Professional Women and Their Mentors*. Englewood Cliffs, N.J.: Prentice-Hall, 1983.

Cook, Mary F. "Is the Mentor Relationship Primarily a Male Experience?" *The Personnel Administrator*, vol. 24, 1979, pp. 82–84.

Kleiman, Carol. *Women's Networks: The Complete Guide to Getting a Better Job, Advancing Your Career, and Feeling Great as a Woman through Networking.* New York: Ballantine Books, 1980.

Lipnack, Jessica, and Jeffrey Stamps. *Networking: The First Report and Directory.* Garden City, N.Y.: Doubleday, 1982.

"Mentors for Women: Like It or Not, It's a Two Way Street." *Management Review*, vol. 69, June 1980, p. 6.

Missirian, Agnes. *The Corporate Connection.* Englewood Cliffs, N.J.: Prentice-Hall, 1982.

Price, Margaret. "Networks: Businesswomen Expand Their Horizons." *Industry Week*, June 28, 1982, pp. 57–60.

Shapiro, Eileen, Florence Haseltine, and Mary Rowe. "Moving Up: Role Models, Mentors, and 'Patrons.' " *Sloan Management Review*, vol. 19, no. 3, 1978, pp. 51–58.

Stern, Barbara A. *Is Networking for You? A Working Women's Alternative to the Old Boy System.* Englewood Cliffs, N.J.: Prentice-Hall, 1981.

Speizer, Jeanne. "Role Models, Mentors, and Sponsors: The Elusive Concept." *Signs*, vol. 6, no. 4, Summer 1981, pp. 692–712.

Thompson, Jacqueline. "Patrons, Rabbis, Mentors—Whatever You Call Them, Women Need Them, Too." In Bette Anne Stead, *Women in Management.* Englewood Cliffs, N.J.: Prentice-Hall, 1978.

Welch, Mary-Scott. "How to Start A Women's Network." *Working Woman*, March 1980, pp. 82–83.

————. *Networking: The Great New Way for Women to Get Ahead.* New York: Harcourt Brace Jovanovich, 1980.

Wilson, Jane. "Networks." *Savvy*, January 1980, pp. 18–23.

Index